# HUMBLE
# HISTORY
# ON DRUGS

# HUMAN HISTORY ON DRUGS

### AN UTTERLY SCANDALOUS
### BUT ENTIRELY TRUTHFUL LOOK AT
### HISTORY UNDER THE INFLUENCE

## SAM KELLY

PLUME

**PLUME**

An imprint of Penguin Random House LLC
1745 Broadway, New York, NY 10019
penguinrandomhouse.com

A version of chapter 13 was previously published as "Queen Victoria and the
First Opium War" in *History Is Now Magazine* on March 9, 2021. A version
of chapter 14 was previously published as "The Pope Who Drank Cocaine
Wine" in *History Is Now Magazine* on April 7, 2021. A version of chapter 20
was originally published as "The Adventures of Jean-Paul Sartre" in
*Philosophy Now*, issue 145 (August/September 2021), 8–10.

 REGISTERED TRADEMARK—MARCA REGISTRADA

Illustrations by Paul Girard
Photograph on page 71: Wikimedia Commons
Photograph on page 113: Public Domain

Book design by Silverglass Studio

LIBRARY OF CONGRESS CATALOGING–IN–PUBLICATION DATA
has been applied for.

ISBN 9780593476048 (paperback)
ISBN 9780593476055 (ebook)

Printed in the United States of America

1st Printing

The authorized representative in the EU for product safety and compliance
is Penguin Random House Ireland, Morrison Chambers, 32 Nassau Street,
Dublin D02 YH68, Ireland, https://eu-contact.penguin.ie.

*To Chocolate, my small furry coworker*
*of many years, I miss you*

# CONTENTS

# HUMAN HISTORY ON DRUGS

# INTRODUCTION

**Y**ou learned about history in school—or you thought you did. You read in textbooks about famous men and women who accomplished extraordinary things. But those textbooks were whitewashed. Important facts were redacted, omitted, and censored to hide the truth. The historical figures you read about weren't one-dimensional stick figures who popped into existence for a single day to win a pivotal battle or make a technological breakthrough. They were multifaceted individuals who led complicated, messy, often bizarre lives—like we all do—and yet textbooks seldom tell you what inspired their successes or how they coped with their occasional failures.

The truth is, many historical figures were on drugs: George Washington, Queen Victoria, Sigmund Freud, Adolf Hitler, and countless others—they were real people, with real flaws and real vices. Teachers couldn't tell you this stuff when you were a child; there are certain truths that impressionable young minds aren't ready to hear. But you're older now, you deserve to know their real stories—the stuff you didn't learn in school.

So, what's the deal: Are drugs good or are they bad? Honestly, there is no one-size-fits-all answer to that question. Some of these individuals genuinely believed their drug use helped them to achieve their goals. But, for countless others, drug use was responsible for their downfall—and, in many cases, their death.

This book tells both sides.

Education is one of the key themes of the book. Drugs are tools: amphetamines, opioids, barbiturates—even psychedelics—have valid medical uses that can improve a person's well-being when administered in the proper manner and dosage by a trained professional. But people often suffer serious harm when they're not properly educated about the powerful effects and consequences of these drugs. The truth is, many of these historical figures could have made much smarter choices if only they had known the facts.

Whitewashing textbooks isn't the answer. Scrubbing away references to drug use and pretending it didn't happen won't make the underlying problems go away. If you want people to learn from history, *they need to know what actually happened.*

I've been obsessed with history since I was a little kid. In elementary school, I'd beg my history teacher to let me take home the teacher's edition of the textbook so I could read ahead and see the extra info they put in the margins to help teachers provide context. When my mom came to wake me in the morning, she'd find me sprawled on top of the bed with the history book still lying open on my chest.

History doesn't have to be dull and lifeless. It's not about memorizing names and dates, knowing who won what battle and when. I've always believed a history textbook should be the single most fascinating book of all time—as if someone took all the most dramatic things that ever happened and brought them together in one place. Who wouldn't want to read that?

That's why I decided to write this book, because the history text I've always envisioned hasn't been written yet. My goal is to create a book that gathers together the most amazing true stories from the past and serves them up in a fun, engaging way that makes people actually *want* to learn about history.

I'm on the autism spectrum. When I get interested in something, I really dig into it. I'm incapable of browsing casually; instead, I develop an almost physical compulsion to know everything there is to know on a subject. As a result, I spend hours every day looking stuff up, going on tangents, and uncovering every last stubborn detail.

I studied history at Stanford University, but that's putting it mildly—I gobbled up history courses like Pac-Man eats ghosts. By the time I graduated, I had lived in three foreign countries (England, Italy, and Germany) to better immerse myself in world history, and had studied under the tutelage of some of Stanford's most esteemed history scholars.

For a long time, I aspired to be a teacher. I dreamed of standing at the front of a classroom, regaling students with awesome historical anecdotes. I wanted to show my students that history doesn't have to be dry and boring. It can be as exciting as any Marvel superhero movie, but starring real-life heroes and villains. I was sure I could inspire my students to feel the same passion for history that I do.

Ultimately, though, I decided that I could reach far more people as a writer. As a teacher, I could reach maybe thirty students at a time. But as a writer, I can potentially impact tens of thousands.

Here's my promise to you: this book won't glamorize drug use, nor vilify it. I simply want to report the facts, fill in the blanks, and set the historical record straight—and hopefully have a little fun along the way. For better or worse, drug use has been around since the beginning of recorded time. Yet these stories have rarely, if ever, been told. Until now. Until this book.

I've included an appendix in which I list some of my sources.

Not all of them, of course, because then the appendix would be longer than the book itself. I have spent thousands upon thousands of hours researching drug use by historical figures. I have read dozens of books and tens of thousands of individual articles. I'm not exaggerating when I say there are more than a thousand bookmarks on my computer—or at least there were before the darn thing crashed.

I can't help it, I love this stuff. The bottom line is this: I have gone down every rabbit hole, pulled every thread, followed every lead, and gone off on every tangent—all so you don't have to.

I have swept away the chaff, picked out the stems and seeds, and boiled it down to its purest form. You only get the good stuff.

Enjoy the journey. I hope it's a good trip.

# PART 1

# ANCIENT POTIONS

# CHAPTER 1

# The Oracle of Delphi Was Huffing Fumes

ou've heard of the Oracle of Delphi, right? The all-knowing seer of the future who channeled the wisdom of the gods and advised Greek kings on their most momentous decisions? Yeah, she was on drugs.

When the ancient Greeks had important decisions to make, they wanted advice from the gods, so they'd travel all the way to the Oracle of Delphi. It was quite a schlep. The oracle was located a hundred miles away from Athens, on a high mountain surrounded by treacherous cliffs. Getting there required either a long trek over mountaintops or a perilous sea voyage. Either way, the trip would take days, or even weeks.

So why'd they go to all that muss and fuss? After all, the ancient Greeks had developed all sorts of highly scientific methods to determine what the gods were thinking, such as drawing lots, rolling dice, studying the cracks in chicken bones, and—this is my personal favorite—massaging the entrails of a dead animal, especially the liver, which was considered to be the ripest organ for purposes of prophetic prognostication.

Yet they chose to visit the oracle for one simple and compelling reason: the oracle was never wrong. Palpating a sheep's liver was fine for the mundane decisions of everyday life, such as which crops to plant that year, but when it came to making crucial decisions that would potentially determine whether an empire would rise or fall, you couldn't half-ass it. You had to seek out the oracle.

You see, the Oracle of Delphi was no ordinary priest. The oracle was the handpicked messenger of Apollo, a human conduit to the all-seeing gods. Apollo's words flowed through the oracle, transforming her into a perfect vessel of wisdom, insight, and knowledge of future events.

That's right, "her." The oracle was a woman—which is shocking when you consider that ancient Greece was an immensely patriarchal society in which girls were not allowed to go to school and were typically married off by the time they reached age fourteen. Yet when the alpha males who ruled over ancient Greece needed advice on their most vital matters of state, they sought the counsel of a woman—and not always the same woman. The Oracle of Delphi was an institution that lasted over a thousand years, from 1400 BCE to 400 BCE, so, obviously, no one woman was around the entire time. There was a high priestess known as the Pythia, and over the years, when one Pythia expired, the gods would "divinely" select another woman to become the new Pythia.

But here's the twist: all these women were on drugs. It wasn't an individual choice; it was a geographical imperative. You need to understand a bit about the topography of Delphi. People seeking the oracle's wisdom would line up at dawn and ascend a steep, winding path known as "the Sacred Way." From there, robed attendants would guide them, one at a time, into a sunken chamber hidden deep in the bowels of a remote cave, where the Pythia would be waiting for them. According to ancient scholars who actually witnessed the Pythia deliver a prophecy, there was a three-legged stool located directly above a fissure in the floor of the cave, and weird vapors rose from the fissure. The Pythia would sit down on the three-legged stool, inhale the mysterious fumes rising from the ground, and enter into a dreamlike trance. Her body would begin to quiver and writhe (thereby "confirming" she'd entered into a state of divine possession), her voice would change, she'd make a bunch of crazy noises, and then, finally, she'd deliver a cryptic prophecy that was often only a few words long.

If that description sounds to you like someone who's experiencing an intense drug trip, you are absolutely correct. Because it turns out those mysterious fumes she was inhaling were more than eerie set dressing; they were psychoactive vapors. Historians have long suspected the oracle was high as a kite, and now modern science has proven it. A team of scientists comprising a geologist, an archaeologist, and a chemist traveled to Delphi between 1995 and 2000 to study rock samples near the site. They discovered the oracle's chamber was built over a geological fault that released a naturally occurring substance called ethylene. It's a sweet-smelling petrochemical gas that produces disembodied euphoria, an altered mental state, and other intoxicating effects—or, as they described it, the feeling you get from huffing glue. Basically, the Oracle of Delphi was tripping balls.

But wait, it gets better: these psychoactive vapors weren't the only thing she was tripping on. Remember, her temple was located on a remote mountainside. This meant she was forced to subsist on a narrow range of foods that could be locally sourced. Plus, she was a religious ascetic who didn't necessarily feel it was appropriate to luxuriate in her food, so she was willing to eat things that were unappetizing or sometimes even dangerous. One of the staples of her diet was oleander leaves, which grew near the temple—and they are highly toxic. You heard me right: the oracle was munching on poison.

Fortunately, the human body is an amazing machine that can build up a tolerance to toxic substances by ingesting small amounts on a regular basis. Remember that line from *The Princess Bride*: "I spent the last few years developing an immunity to iocane pow-der"? It's the same basic principle behind vaccinations—injecting a small amount of a virus into your body to train your immune sys-tem to recognize and combat it. Johns Hopkins University Press published an article in 2014 suggesting the Oracle of Delphi de-liberately ingested oleander poison as a way to help inspire the di-vine frenzy that she exhibited when she bestowed her bizarre prophecies.

So, there wasn't just one geological feature of Delphi that in-spired the oracle's drugged-out behavior, there were two: (1) psy-choactive vapors that caused vivid hallucinations, and (2) a poisonous plant that provoked frenzied body tremors. The combination of these two substances caused the oracle to behave in ways so utterly bizarre and otherworldly that, to the ancient Greeks, divine inspi-ration was the only logical explanation.

But wait—if the oracle wasn't actually communicating with the gods, how is it possible that she was always right? After all, the ac-curacy of the oracle's prophecies is an indisputable part of Greek history, so doesn't that suggest she had some sort of supernatural ability?

No, not really. Much like Liam Neeson in *Taken*, the oracle had a very particular set of skills, but it wasn't supernatural. She was always right for the simple reason that she never gave a clear answer to the questions posed to her. She was notorious for delivering cryptic prophecies that were difficult to decipher and susceptible to multiple (often conflicting) interpretations.

One of the most famous examples is the advice she gave to King Croesus in 550 BCE. The king asked the oracle to tell him whether he should wage war against the Persian Empire. The oracle replied, "If Croesus goes to war, a great empire shall fall." Croesus was pumped! He was convinced this meant his victory was guaran-teed. He assembled his troops, formed the necessary alliances, and attacked the Persians with everything he had—only to be utterly defeated. The Persian emperor, Cyrus the Great, took King Croesus prisoner and ordered him to be burned alive. The story goes that Croesus cried out to the gods, pleading to know why the Oracle of Delphi had betrayed him, and the gods answered, telling him the oracle had spoken the truth. You did destroy a great empire—*but it was your own empire, not theirs.* Twist!

Amazingly, all the textbooks lay the blame on Croesus, not the oracle. Everywhere you look, the lesson of the story is that Croesus was a victim of his own ego for daring to believe he had properly interpreted the oracle's prophecy. You couldn't blame the gods for his hubris, nor could you blame their vapor-huffing priestess. It is historical canon that the oracle's prophecies were invariably accurate, so if something happened to go wrong (which it often did), it meant the person receiving the prophecy was not wise enough to decipher its true meaning. This was the ultimate secret of the oracle's success: it's impossible to be wrong if you never give a straight answer.

The real question is, did the oracle know she was lying to people? Maybe not. Between the hallucinogenic cave gases and the oleander poison, she was pretty much in a perpetual state of altered consciousness. Besides, she was a priestess, not a scientist, so maybe she genuinely believed that her interminable intoxication was due to a psychic link to the gods, not to taking drugs.

That's the charitable view. The more cynical view is she knew full well she couldn't see the future, and she was deliberately lying to people. Worse, she was gaslighting them—making them believe that if her prophecies worked out badly for them (as one of them did for King Croesus) it was their own fault, not hers.

Here's how I like to think about it: the Oracle of Delphi was straight-up trolling people, thousands of years before the internet was invented for the very same purpose.

# CHAPTER 2

# Pharaoh Ramesses II Wanted Ganja

ou're going to love what they found inside the mummy of Pharaoh Ramesses II, commonly known as Ramses the Great. As his nickname suggests, he was one of the greatest pharaohs of all time. He erected more statues and monuments than any other pharaoh, fathered more children than any other pharaoh (more than one hundred!), and nine subsequent pharaohs each chose to take his name when they ascended the throne, so it's safe to say he was a popular dude.

But for thousands of years, his mummy was missing. He was originally buried in the prestigious Valley of the Kings, where only the greatest pharaohs were interred—but when archaeologists excavated his tomb, it was empty. It seems his loyal priests were afraid thieves would raid the tomb, so they repeatedly moved the mummy from one place to another like it was a highborn hot potato. Scholars weren't able to track down his final resting place until 1881, when they discovered the pharaoh's body had been tucked away in a large burial site known as the Royal Cache, which housed the mummies of more than fifty kings, queens, and assorted family members—sort of a WeWork space for dead Egyptian royalty.

But the big reveal came more than a hundred years later, in

1985, when a French ethnobotanist named Arlette Leroi-Gourhan performed a full scientific examination of the mummy to see what she could learn about the pharaoh's lifestyle from the plant compounds buried deep within his royal body tissue. And can you guess what she found?

Cannabis!

That's right, seven grains of cannabis pollen were hiding inside the pharaoh's abdominal cavity. While seven grains might not seem like an impressive number, bear in mind these were the few grains of pollen to survive the passage of thousands of years. Just imagine how many grains of pollen there must have been when Ramses died way back in 1213 BCE. Cannabis pollen must have been sprinkled over his mummy like powdered sugar on a doughnut.

Some people theorize that a large stash of cannabis was probably stored in containers near the tomb, although it's impossible to know for sure because, over the centuries, that portion of the Valley of the Kings has flooded no fewer than seven times. But we know it was customary to bury a pharaoh with all the goodies and trinkets he wanted to bring with him into the afterlife—everything from food and drink to jewelry and pets—and judging from the evidence in Ramses's belly, his most precious cargo might have been cannabis.

To understand why Ramses loved cannabis so much, you need to know something about the meaning of the word "pharaoh." While it is often translated as "king" or "ruler," that's a colossal understatement. "God in human form" is more accurate. The pharaoh was the ancient world's equivalent of a superhero, and he was expected to function as both the king and the most fearless warrior—sort of like King T'Challa in *Black Panther*. Ramses would never have earned the respect of his people if he had supervised military campaigns from the safety of the palace. No way; his subjects wanted him to be front and center on the battlefield, personally leading the charge against the enemy troops, with thousands of bloodthirsty soldiers lined up behind him.

But guess what happens to pharaohs who go into battle. They get injured—and unlike their troops, they can't afford to let people know they've been injured because bleeding on the royal carpet tends to detract from the whole "god-king" image.[1] This is probably why Ramses wanted access to plenty of cannabis, because even back then, cannabis was recognized as having important medicinal uses. Scholars have discovered an ancient papyrus medical textbook from 1550 BCE that prescribes the use of hemp (a.k.a. cannabis) to alleviate pain and inflammation. What better way to maintain your reputation as a god among men than to return from a weeks-long battle looking as hale and hearty as the day you left?

It must have proven effective at treating his injuries, because Ramses the Great was one of the longest-reigning pharaohs in history, ruling for sixty-seven years and living to be at least ninety years old. So, it shouldn't be too surprising that when it was finally time for him to check out, he decided to pack some of his highest-quality medical marijuana in a ceramic jar to bring along with him.

Of course, cannabis wasn't the only tool that Ramses used to establish his reputation as a badass god in human form. He also relied on an extensive public relations campaign. His PR blitz began with the Battle of Kadesh in 1275 BCE, when he attacked the Hittite army in what is today a part of Syria. Ramses led a small force of twenty thousand men against a much larger force of fifty thousand men—and he didn't just win, he trounced them. He returned to Egypt a conquering hero.

Except it was fake news. In reality, the battle ended in a draw and he never captured the city. The war raged on for fifteen long

---

1. To quote *Star Trek* (and the animated classic *The Road to El Dorado*): "Gods don't bleed."

years, until both sides finally got sick of fighting and signed a peace treaty—actually, it was the first peace treaty in recorded history. But the people of Egypt didn't know any of that; they only knew what they were told, so he ordered poems to be written praising his victory and murals to be created depicting him as a military genius. But it was all propaganda. Ramses the Great understood at a young age that truth doesn't matter. History isn't written by the victors; it's written by the publicists.

That's why he constructed so many oversize monuments. If you are truly a god among men, there should be humongous monuments honoring your greatness; otherwise, there's no guarantee that subsequent generations will continue to remember your amazing achievements. Ramses constructed a series of staggeringly gargantuan monoliths up and down the Nile, from one end of Egypt to the other, each more physically imposing than anything that had come before. The Great Temple of Abu Simbel features four statues of Ramses himself, each sixty-five feet tall, towering over smaller images of his conquered enemies. They depict him as being, quite literally, larger than life. There is virtually no significant monument or site in all of Egypt that does not bear witness to the greatness of Ramses II.

The monuments are so ridiculously large that a bunch of people actually believe that aliens from outer space must have helped the Egyptians build them, because no ordinary humans could have accomplished something so miraculous. Ramses would have been thrilled by such conspiracy theories. He got exactly what he wanted: he got to control the narrative . . . well, almost.

For three thousand years, his plan worked perfectly—until that darn poet Percy Bysshe Shelley came along and ruined everything. You see, the pharaoh was known to his fellow Egyptians as Ramses II or Ramses the Great, but he was known to the ancient Greeks by a different name: Ozymandias. When a large chunk of an ancient

Ramses statue was unearthed in 1817 and shipped to the British Museum, the famous poet Shelley felt inspired to write a sonnet that forever changed how the world thinks of the once-great pharaoh:

> *"My name is Ozymandias, king of kings;*
> *Look on my works, ye Mighty, and despair!"*
> *Nothing beside remains. Round the decay*
> *Of that colossal wreck, boundless and bare*
> *The lone and level sands stretch far away.*

The name Ozymandias quickly developed a new meaning. It became synonymous with hubris, the selfish pride of a man who seeks to be remembered after he is gone but lacks the street smarts to understand that nothing can withstand the passage of time. Unfortunately for Ramses, this new, more cynical spin on his legacy took a firm hold in popular culture. For example, one of the most famous episodes of the television series *Breaking Bad* is titled "Ozymandias," and the official trailer for the final season features Bryan Cranston reciting this poem about the crumbling legacy of a once-great king.

Shelley's poem totally knocked the wind out of Ramses's legacy. Instead of evoking connotations of greatness, his name became synonymous with faded glory and narcissistic pride. The pharaoh became little more than a punch line—proof that overweening ambition achieves nothing.

But there's a twist: they say "life finds a way"—and sometimes so does ego. Thanks to the hard work of a plucky French ethnobotanist, the long-dead pharaoh has a brand-new fan base. Cannabis is the new legacy of Ramses the Great.

You see, when Arlette Leroi-Gourhan discovered those seven grains of cannabis pollen in the mummy's abdominal cavity, the mainstream media didn't talk about it very much. But it was super–big news in marijuana-related media. Websites that either sell cannabis and/or celebrate stoner lifestyles suddenly became extremely interested in reporting the latest news about ancient Egypt.

Basically, Ramses II is like any other celebrity who seeks to remain relevant over a long period of years: he's been forced to reinvent himself for a new audience. Nowadays, instead of being known as Ramses the Great because of the huge monuments he erected, he's probably more accurately referred to as Ramses the Baked—the pharaoh who loved weed so much that he tried to take it with him when he died.

At least he can rest in peace, knowing the modern world now fully appreciates that this pharaoh wasn't only mighty—he was *high* and mighty.

# CHAPTER 3

# Alexander the Great Was a Sloppy Drunk

Alexander the Great wasn't your ordinary teenager. When his dad went out of town on business, he didn't borrow the old man's car to go for a joyride. Instead, he borrowed his dad's soldiers to crush a rebel uprising. When his father was assassinated, he didn't pull a Hamlet and mope around the palace, paralyzed by indecisiveness. He took his army on a road trip and conquered Persia.

Alexander was great at many things. He was a gifted student who loved to learn (Aristotle was his tutor), a skilled orator who could galvanize an audience, and a charismatic leader who inspired loyalty and fearlessness in his men. Textbooks uniformly agree that he was one of history's most brilliant strategists and never lost a battle, even against armies larger than his own.

But there was at least one thing at which Alexander was not "great"—he couldn't hold his liquor.

Alexander's defining characteristic was that he was never satisfied—he always wanted more. From a military standpoint, it worked well for him. It explains why he didn't stop after conquering Persia in his twenties; he kept going. By the time he was thirty, he had conquered most of the known world, creating an empire that spanned three continents and encompassed two million square miles. One of the reasons he was able to grow his empire so quickly is that he didn't try to force Greek culture down the throats of the people he conquered. Instead, he let them hold on to their different beliefs and lifestyles, knowing that otherwise they would chafe under his rule and look for a chance to break free, and he'd end up fighting on too many fronts at the same time. He even adopted elements of these foreign cultures into his own life. By allowing conquered peoples to retain their local traditions, he encountered far less resistance, burnished his reputation as a wise ruler, and—most important from Alexander's point of view—freed up his army to race toward global domination at a pace never before witnessed in the history of mankind.

From a personal standpoint, however, always wanting more worked out very badly for him. His unquenchable thirst for everything life had to offer wasn't merely figurative; it was literal. He consumed an absurd amount of alcohol. He was the most notorious party animal in all of ancient Greece—and that's saying something, because folks in the fourth century BCE really knew how to party.

His drink of choice was wine, and wine in ancient Greece was much more potent than the wine we drink today. Refrigerators hadn't been invented yet, and while very rich people sometimes had their servants retrieve snow and ice from nearby mountaintops to chill their beverages, Alexander was usually on the road conquering stuff, so his wine was stored at room temperature. But it was stored with ridiculously high alcohol concentrations, sometimes as much as 40 percent—because the alcohol functioned as a preservative, allowing the wine to last longer.

Of course, you weren't supposed to drink it like that. You were supposed to add water so it wouldn't be so highly concentrated. The typical ratio was three parts water to one part wine.

But not Alexander. He insisted on drinking his wine "unwatered," as was the style in Macedonia, where he was born and raised. Plus, he didn't drink his wine out of a glass; he drank it out of a bowl. He would routinely drink unwatered wine, bowl after bowl, until he was utterly and devastatingly drunk. Who can say why? Maybe he considered wine to be a performance-enhancing drug because it obliterated any fear of dying in battle, or perhaps it was an aphrodisiac to fuel his notoriously vigorous sexual appetite for men, women, or both at the same time. Whatever the reason, Alexander would routinely drink bowlfuls of wine until he got blackout drunk.

You know how sometimes you're partying, and you think you're having a good time, but then you wake up in the morning and find out you did something really, really bad? That sort of thing happened to Alexander the Great on a regular basis. He might have been a genius on the battlefield, but, man, he did some stupid shit when he was drunk—like the time he impaled his good friend Cleitus the Black in 328 BCE.

Cleitus was one of his best officers and most trusted friends, having saved Alexander's life in battle a few years earlier (a fact Cleitus tended to bring up a little too often). One night, Alexander and Cleitus were sitting around, drinking heavily, and they got into a drunken argument, as friends sometimes do, and started yelling at each other. The rest of the group decided it was time to break it up before things turned ugly, so they pulled the two men apart and rushed them off in different directions. But at the last second, Alexander broke free, grabbed a spear, and impaled poor Cleitus, killing him instantly. When he finally sobered up and saw what he had done to his friend, he cried for three days straight.

You'd think that maybe, just maybe, Alexander would have learned his lesson and started to cut back on the booze, but of course that didn't happen. Also, as if that weren't bad enough, alcohol wasn't the only drug he was abusing.

He was also a big fan of opium.

Remember how I said that Alexander liked to adopt elements

from foreign cultures into his life? Well, opium was one of those. It was originally introduced into Greece via Egypt during the Bronze Age, and by the time Alexander became a dedicated opium enthusiast, it had been known to Greeks for almost a millennium. Opium did something for him that alcohol did not—it was a potent painkiller and sedative. Even though Alexander never lost a battle, he did get injured from time to time. When he was introduced to opium, he felt the gods had smiled on him by revealing a magical substance that was capable of making his pain disappear. Not only did he enthusiastically embrace opium for himself, he also strongly encouraged his troops to benefit from the drug's miraculous pain-relieving properties.

He quickly became the Johnny Appleseed of opium. He and his soldiers brought it with them on their road trips, spreading opium to Persia, India, and other parts of the world. Each time he conquered a new land, Alexander would introduce the local populace to opium, as if saying, "Hello there, this is opium, isn't Greek culture great?" Despite his keen intelligence, Alexander did not see any danger signs from his steadily increasing opium use—after all, he was still winning, still conquering, and it seemed obvious that no man on earth could possibly defeat him.

But wine and opium finally caught up with him in 323 BCE. He had conquered his way across the Middle East and much of the Indian subcontinent, and he probably would have kept conquering, but his homesick troops said "enough" and refused to go any farther. They demanded a break from all the nonstop winning so they could return home to see their families. Alexander reluctantly agreed and declared they would set up camp at Nebuchadnezzar's old palace in Babylon, where they would hold a grand memorial feast to honor the death of his close friend and lover Hephaestion. At the feast, he guzzled entire bowlfuls of unwatered wine. His troops cheered his massive alcohol consumption because in their minds, he was an unstoppable hero like the legendary Achilles.

But no matter how powerful, intelligent, or charismatic he was, Alexander was still a mortal man with a mortal man's liver. The party lasted all day and all night, and he continued to drink, bowl after bowl. Complaining he wasn't feeling well, he announced he was going to bed to recuperate a bit, but his condition steadily deteriorated. He was in tremendous pain, his fever wouldn't break, and he was experiencing convulsions and delirium. In the days that followed, his body grew weaker and weaker. After twelve long days of excruciating agony, he was so weak that he could barely move.

When his loyal soldiers demanded to see him and entered his tent, he was incapable of speaking. They filed slowly past his bed, and he could barely acknowledge them with a slight wave of his hand. Then he lapsed into a coma and died.

Rumors have swirled for thousands of years as to the cause of Alexander's death. Some have speculated he was poisoned by an enemy, but most historians have dismissed the idea of deliberate poisoning because he was savagely ill for twelve days, and assassins back then didn't have access to any slow-acting poisons. Others have theorized it was a disease, such as malaria or typhoid. At least one scholar has suggested that maybe he wasn't dead at all: a doctor from New Zealand has posited this might be an early example of pseudothanatos—a false diagnosis of death. Alexander might have been paralyzed, but still fully conscious, for six whole days after his doctors mistakenly announced that he was dead.

But the most likely explanation has always been that alcohol and opium pushed him over the edge. Sure, it's possible that he contracted a disease like malaria, but it's hard to believe the sudden downturn in his condition, coinciding with several days of massive drug consumption, was mere happenstance. Disease might have been a contributing factor, but the primary cause of his death was drug overdose and the complications thereof. With the benefits of modern medicine, we know people can do ruinous damage to their internal organs without appearing to be ill on the outside—but the ancient Greeks didn't know that. They assumed from his military victories that Alexander had been blessed by the gods, and thus could only have good fortune.

In classic Greek tragic fashion, it was Alexander's insatiable thirst for more that proved to be his undoing. It was said that no man on earth could defeat him—but it turns out there was one man who could, and it was Alexander himself. Although he never lost on the battlefield, his addiction to alcohol and opium finished him off at age thirty-two.

# CHAPTER 4

# Qin Shi Huangdi's Recipe for Immortality Backfired

———————

Chinese emperor Qin Shi Huangdi wanted to live forever. That sounds impossible, of course—but the fact is, he'd already accomplished one thing that should have been impossible. In 221 BCE, he conquered a part of the world that had been divided into rival warring factions for thousands of years and became the first emperor of a unified China.

How did he do it? By spilling unbelievably massive amounts of blood. He was an unapologetically ruthless guy. When unifying China, he didn't bother to use logic and reason to explain the benefits of having a single written language and a standardized system of currency, weights, and measures to facilitate trade. Instead, he chose violence. He annihilated his rivals and murdered anyone else who dared to get in his way. Similarly, a year later, when he decided to build a thick protective barrier around the Chinese empire to make it impossible for foreign invaders to attack, he didn't ask for volunteers. He forcibly conscripted an army of laborers to build the Great Wall, and when workers died—as four hundred thousand of them did—no one was allowed to stop working. Their bodies were dumped inside the wall and became part of the foundation.

He applied the same utter ruthlessness to his quest for immortality. He issued a decree to every town and village in China to locate the fabled "elixir of life." He commanded the local chieftains to drop everything they were doing and devote themselves entirely to the task. Whoever found the elixir would be rewarded handsomely, but anyone perceived as not trying hard enough would be sentenced to death. It was the classic "carrot and stick" approach—except in this case the "stick" was a razor-sharp blade to the neck.

Qin Shi Huangdi was obsessed with immortality for a very understandable reason. Everyone wants a job with upward mobility, right? But he was already an emperor, so there wasn't much room for advancement; he'd reached the top of his particular profession. But if he could discover the secret of eternal life, then he could break that glass ceiling. He'd become more than an emperor—he'd become a living god.

But living forever wasn't going to be easy, because people kept trying to kill him. Apparently, being a mercilessly murderous monarch doesn't breed warm and fuzzy feelings among the common folk. Assassins were always after him, so he took elaborate precautions to make sure no one knew where he was: covering windows with thick curtains so no one could see inside the rooms; building elevated walkways so he could exit one building and enter another without being exposed; digging underground tunnels and walling off roads so he could travel invisibly from town to town. He insisted on absolute secrecy about his movements, and anyone who dared to speak of the emperor's location was immediately put to death.

Unfortunately, achieving immortality requires more than dodging assassins. He needed to locate the elixir of life, or if no such thing existed, he needed someone to invent one. He tasked his advisers with finding the elusive recipe. The mission was of such paramount importance that he was willing to listen to anyone—alchemists, magicians, even charlatans. Finally, his advisers told him they had found the answer . . . liquid mercury!

The Chinese had long believed that mercury possessed supernatural properties. It seemed to defy the laws of nature because it was a metal—like iron or steel—but it wasn't a solid; it was a liquid that flowed like water. Whoa! Plus, it was shiny, silvery, and really cool looking. Ancient science always dictated that if something looked cool, it must definitely be magic.

The alchemists convinced the emperor that these mysterious, inexplicable qualities were proof that mercury possessed a special power that, if harnessed properly, would serve as the key ingredient in his elixir of life. Bottom line: if he drank precisely the right amount of liquid mercury, he would live forever.

Importantly, though, the alchemists didn't want him to drink mercury all by itself—because it would taste like crap. No one likes an immortality potion with a lousy aftertaste, so the alchemists took the liberty of adding a few other ingredients to improve the flavor.

By "ingredients," I mean drugs. They added wine (because alcohol makes everything taste better), and natural herbs and medicines, such as ephedra leaves to create a rush of energy, stimulate his heart rate, and reduce some of the nastiest effects of drinking poisonous metals. Thanks to the various drugs and herbs, whenever the emperor sipped this yummy concoction, he immediately felt exhilarated and revitalized. His advisers would smile and say, "That's how you know it's working."

Of course, anyone with a rudimentary knowledge of chemistry knows that mercury is highly toxic. It might look super rad, but it's extremely dangerous to drink, and even more dangerous to inhale. Liquid mercury vaporizes at room temperature, and those vapors are absorbed by the human body, starting in the lungs and spreading into the blood, organs, and brain. So, if you drink or inhale enough mercury, it will kill you.

You can probably guess the next bit: Qin Shi Huangdi died of mercury poisoning. But you've got to appreciate the irony, right? Here was a guy who was constantly being targeted for death by skilled assassins—yet, in the end, he wasn't killed by his enemies. He was killed (inadvertently) by those who worshipped him and wanted him to live forever.

And talk about the indignity of it all. He died while conducting a tour of his kingdom by carriage, and to hide the fact of his death for as long as possible, his lackeys placed cartloads of dead fish in front of and behind the royal carriage. They were afraid people would smell his decaying corpse and realize he was dead, so to cover up the smell, they concealed his body in a load of rotting fish—and that's how they delivered him to his tomb.

That's right, he had a tomb. It was his backup plan. He fully intended to live forever, but just in case things didn't pan out, he made sure he'd be laid to rest in a tomb of unprecedented opulence. He enlisted seven hundred thousand laborers to construct a scale model of China for the inside of the tomb, complete with replicas of famous palaces, monuments, and landscapes. Then he hired the finest artisans in all of China to construct eight thousand life-size terracotta soldiers, which would be stationed around the perimeter of the tomb to stand guard for him in the afterlife. The story goes that the emperor was so impressed by these magnificent clay soldiers that as soon as they were completed, he ordered the artists to be killed. He wanted them to be buried (while still alive) next to the soldiers they'd created. Why? To ensure they'd never create anything so spectacular for anyone else.

No one has ever seen the inside of Qin Shi Huangdi's tomb. Not because they can't find it—we know exactly where it is, that's not the issue. The problem is opening the tomb might kill tens of thousands of people. That's because the most amazing features of the tomb were reported to be replicas of the Yangtze River and Yellow River—but instead of flowing with water, the replicas are flowing with liquid mercury. It would be an amazing sight to behold, but, unfortunately, the tomb needs to remain sealed because the mercury levels in the surrounding soil are astronomically high. Unless and until someone figures out a way to vent those deadly mercury fumes, excavating the tomb would release enough toxic vapors to wipe out entire cities.

But there's one saving grace: while the death of China's first emperor by mercury poisoning was tragic, it served to put everyone on notice about the dangers of ingesting mercury. Subsequent emperors could learn from his example and avoid sharing the same fate. After Qin Shi Huangdi, no one in China would ever be foolish enough to think that drinking mercury could be the secret to eternal life—right?

Wrong. During the Tang dynasty alone, at least six more emperors died in exactly the same way. If you throw in nobles and other high-ranking government officials, the numbers escalate to the dozens. For more than a thousand years after Qin died, Chinese rulers and aristocrats continued to mess around with elixirs containing mercury, lead, arsenic, and a variety of other poisons, all in hopes of prolonging their lives.

But isn't repeating the same behavior over and over again and expecting a different result the very definition of insanity? Yes, it is—but bear in mind that royal alchemists had to justify their salaries somehow. They couldn't admit their whole profession was a sham. Instead, they convinced their bosses that mercury was, in fact, the secret to immortality, but crafting precisely the right elixir of life was an incredibly complicated task requiring the utmost knowledge, skill, and experimentation—and even then, it might not always work. In modern times, we don't blame the doctor if a patient who is suffering from stage-four cancer dies despite receiving the best treatments available—and achieving immortality is even harder than curing cancer.

Even though the alchemists failed time and again, Chinese rulers never lost hope. The pull of immortality was simply too strong.

They knew from the example set by Qin Shi Huangdi—the man who, against all odds, unified the rival warring factions of China into a single empire—that a person could accomplish the impossible. It was simply a matter of being utterly ruthless in pursuit of your dream and refusing to take no for an answer.

# CHAPTER 5

# St. John the Revelator Was Tripping on Shrooms

Try this conversation starter at your next cocktail party: "I heard the book of Revelation was written by someone on a bad drug trip. But he didn't take the drugs on purpose; it was more of a culinary misadventure."

Here's how it happened: The ancient Romans worshipped dozens of different gods, including household names like Jupiter, Apollo, and Mercury. They believed these gods were easily offended, and if the gods felt like they were being disrespected, they'd get pissed off and start causing trouble, so the government demanded that all Roman citizens honor and make sacrifices to these gods. This posed an obvious problem for the Jewish citizens of Rome, because the Jewish religion is monotheistic: Jews believe in one unitary, all-powerful God. The Jewish populace didn't like being told by a bunch of idol-worshipping pagans that they needed to pretend to accept Roman polytheism.

Then a new group emerged. In the first century CE, this new group launched an offshoot of Judaism that was still monotheistic but focused primarily on the son of God, who they believed had lived on earth as a mortal man named Jesus Christ, a.k.a. Jesus of Nazareth. The new group were called "Christians" or "Nazarenes." They didn't have many followers at first, but their movement was quickly gaining steam. Basically, these guys were Christians before it was cool.

The Romans were instantly fearful of this new religion. Maybe these Christians weren't directly advocating for the overthrow of the Roman government, but that sure seemed like the logical conclusion of their theology. If one accepted the premise that Jesus was the supreme being made flesh, it wasn't much of a leap to conclude that he should take precedence over any man-made empire, which meant the Romans shouldn't be the ones in charge anymore. In the minds of the ruling class, allowing Christianity to spread meant risking the downfall of the entire Roman Empire.

The Roman authorities cracked down brutally on the new sect, torturing and killing thousands of Christians. They were determined to wipe this new religion off the face of the earth. For more than two hundred years, until Emperor Constantine the Great finally embraced Christianity and made it the official religion of Rome, the earliest Christians were persecuted, killed, and martyred for their beliefs.

Those who weren't killed were banished. They were treated as ideological lepers who needed to be sent far away from Rome so they couldn't infect anyone with their dangerous beliefs. One of the places the Romans exiled these "thought criminals" was the tiny island of Patmos—a sparsely populated lump of rock in the Aegean Sea, forty miles off the west coast of Turkey. It was the perfect place to hide political prisoners.

One of these prisoners was a guy named John. He was a Christian activist who had been banished from Rome by Emperor Domitian in 95 CE and sent to live in exile on Patmos. He lived like a hermit, sleeping in a shallow cave, using a rock as a pillow. Roman authorities were confident that by sending him so far away, they had succeeded in ensuring that no one would ever hear from him again.

But there, in the middle of freaking nowhere, John did something incredible: he wrote the book of Revelation. He intended it as a clarion call to the early Christians, warning them of the persecution they would face, exhorting them to gird themselves for the upcoming battle, and revealing to them the ultimate victory that would come to them if they lived according to God's plan.

But what makes the book of Revelation so wild and unforgettable is that it's written as a first-person account of the apocalypse— as if John is standing right there in the middle of all this devastation and chaos, describing what's happening around him in real time. It reads like a hallucinatory fever dream and is light-years away from anything else in the Bible. What could possibly have motivated John to write it that way?

The answer is drugs—at least, that's what some historians believe. They have advanced the theory that John ingested a powerful psychoactive substance before writing his portion of the Bible. Specifically, they say he ate a fearsome fungus that causes hellish hallucinations—in other words, a magic mushroom.

There's a powerful psychotropic mushroom that grows on the island of Patmos. It has a very distinctive appearance: a red cap with white polka dots. (Actually, it resembles the red-and-white "power-ups" that Super Mario pops into his mouth when he needs a burst of energy.) This colorful mushroom might look fun and harmless, but those looks are deceiving; it's in fact extremely toxic. The mushroom's official name is *Amanita muscaria*, but it's commonly known as "fly agaric" because it was used to kill insects as far back as the thirteenth century. It was like Raid roach killer before the invention of chemical pesticides. Basically, it's poison.

Weirdly enough, this mushroom has a very long history of being used to induce religious experiences. Ancient Sanskrit texts from around 1500 BCE, known as the Vedas, describe a powerful drink called soma that allowed mortals to communicate directly with deities, and some scholars have concluded that *Amanita muscaria* was soma's key active ingredient. Similarly, Siberian tribes in the eighteenth and nineteenth centuries used the mushroom to achieve an "exalted state" in which their shaman could speak directly to the gods—but, get this, they didn't eat the mushroom itself because they knew its poison would cause all sorts of disturbing neurological side effects, like convulsions, emesis, and loss of bowel control. Instead, they would feed the mushrooms to a deer, then drink the deer's urine (yikes!) because that was actually *less* disgusting—they'd get the benefit of the mushroom's psychoactive properties without any of the vomiting, diarrhea, and seizures.

The theory is that John of Patmos ate these superpowered mushrooms before writing his masterpiece. Given the nightmarish images he describes, it isn't hard to believe he might have had some pharmaceutical assistance. In the book of Revelation, John watches as the sun turns black, the moon turns to blood, and stars literally fall out of the sky. A massive earthquake levels the mountains, a heat wave causes the sun to scorch people with fire, and a woman who's about to give birth is chased around by a red dragon with seven heads. Then Jesus returns with an army from heaven, and there's this epic battle royale between good and evil. The army of heaven wins, and they throw Satan and his hell-beasts into a flaming lake of fire.

Pretty intense, right? No one turns the other cheek in this section of the Bible.

But what about the seizures, vomiting, and diarrhea? It's difficult to believe that John of Patmos would voluntarily suffer these consequences just because he thought it might give his writing some extra oomph. I know there are artists who are willing to suffer for their craft—but, c'mon, man, people have been known to die from eating *Amanita muscaria*.

The theory is that he ate them by accident. That's because *Am-*

*anita muscaria* isn't the only kind of mushroom that grows on Patmos. There are several different species, and most are harmless. In fact, one of them is *Amanita caesarea*, known as "Caesar's mushroom." It's considered a real taste treat, a delicacy comparable to modern truffles. The theory goes that John was gathering mushrooms for his dinner and accidentally scooped up a few of the nasty hallucinogenic ones.

No one is saying the mushrooms told John what to write. He was a Christian activist; that's why he was banished. He would have written the book of Revelation regardless. But the mushrooms amplified his imagination—cranked the dial up to eleven—so that as he wrote, he was seeing these nightmare images play out in Technicolor on a movie screen in his head. It probably felt to him like he was actually there, watching the apocalypse happen, and he wrote down what he saw in words that were vivid and unforgettable.

Some say that John even admits in the book of Revelation that he was tripping. There is a line at the beginning where he says it was the Lord's Day and he was "in the Spirit" when he heard a loud voice like a trumpet telling him to write down what he was about to see. They say "in the Spirit" is code for being intoxicated or tripping.

That seems like a stretch. It's more likely that "in the Spirit" means he had achieved a state of religious ecstasy—but that raises the question, how did he achieve this sacred state of religious ecstasy? Maybe he nibbled on some *Amanita muscaria* and it helped him get there. Remember, this notorious mushroom has a documented history of being used to induce religious experiences. It allowed the authors of the Vedas and an assortment of Siberian shamans to speak to their gods. Perhaps by ingesting the same mushrooms (either deliberately or by misadventure), John of Patmos gained the ability to speak directly to his Savior, because that's exactly what happens. The book of Revelation ends with Jesus himself reading John's writings and proclaiming to everyone that "these words are trustworthy and true."

We will never know for sure whether John wrote the book of Revelation while tripping on drugs. But there are three facts we do know: (1) he wrote the book while living on the island of Patmos; (2) the mushroom known as *Amanita muscaria* grows on Patmos; and (3) Revelation is by far the trippiest book of the Bible.

Everything else is speculation—and fun cocktail party banter.

# CHAPTER 6

# Marcus Aurelius's Sleepy-Time Medicine

Y ou know how famous people like to surround themselves with sycophants and yes-men to tell them how amazing they are? The Roman emperor Marcus Aurelius was just the opposite. The story goes that people kept stopping him on the street to tell him how awesome he was, but he was so determined to stay grounded that he had a servant follow him around and whisper in his ear, "You're only a man, you're only a man."

Admittedly, this would be a more uplifting story if it weren't an enslaved person who was forced to follow him around, and instead he actually paid someone to do the job—but, hey, as all-powerful emperors go, Marcus Aurelius seems to have been a pretty cool guy.

Before Marcus came into power, Rome had some really awful emperors. In the first century CE, Emperor Caligula hosted depraved orgies at his palace, demanded that people worship him as a god, and delighted in forcing parents to watch as their children were murdered in front of them. He famously said, "Remember that I have the right to do anything to anybody." A decade or so later, Emperor Nero set a fire that burned down a huge chunk of Rome, lied about it by blaming the Christians, and then devised sadistic ways to torture and kill these Christians for a crime he knew they hadn't committed. As if that weren't enough, he also murdered his mother, his first wife, and very possibly his second wife as well. Nero was not a nice guy.

Marcus Aurelius, on the other hand, was an extremely good emperor. By all accounts, he was wise, patient, and strove to make Roman laws less brutal and capricious. He was a strong military commander who won many great victories, and even his enemies recognized that he was fair and even-handed. His reign, from 161 to 180 CE, is regarded as part of the golden age of the Roman Empire, a time of internal peace, economic growth, and rational governance. Best of all, Marcus Aurelius didn't selfishly pursue power, glory, or wealth for himself. Instead, he was a benevolent "philosopher king" who cared only about making just decisions and improving the lives of his people. He was about as far from Caligula and Nero as you can get.

It's likely a more vain or arrogant emperor might have been tempted to declare himself a god—as Caligula had done. But Marcus Aurelius was determined to stay humble at all costs. That's why, as a boy, he wore a simple tunic made of coarse wool instead of a silken cloak and slept on the ground instead of in a comfy bed—and why, as the emperor, he ordered an enslaved person to whisper in his ear constant reminders of his own mortality.

Luxury and vanity were antithetical to the Stoic philosophy by which Marcus Aurelius governed his life. Being a Stoic meant critically examining all the decisions he made each day, to ensure he only did things that were right and just—even if he knew he'd be criticized or insulted for doing them. Marcus was a big fan of the teachings of Epictetus, who was born a slave but had gone on to become a great philosopher. Epictetus said: "If anyone tells you that a certain person speaks ill of you, do not make excuses about what is said of you, but answer 'He was ignorant of my other faults, else he would not have mentioned these alone.'"

If you go to the philosophy section of any bookstore, you'll see that Marcus Aurelius wrote the definitive text on Stoic philosophy; it's called *Meditations*. But here's the weird part: he never intended for it to be published. He didn't write it for others to read; he wrote it for himself. Basically, he was into journaling way before journaling was a thing. Writing notes to himself was how he examined the decisions he made. He jotted them down all day long on scraps of paper or parchment or anything else that was lying around, looking back on the events of his day and reflecting on whether he had made the right decisions, reminding himself of the values he held important, and upbraiding himself when he occasionally missed the mark. After his death, these scattered notes were collected and published as a book.

There's never been a book quite like it: the innermost thoughts of the world's most powerful man. Marcus scrutinized his every deed under a microscope to make sure he was living up to his own ideals. He judged all his actions and emotions, logically and dispassionately, every single day of his life. He was, undeniably, the epitome of clear thinking and sober reflection.

Oh, wait, did I mention he drank opium at night?

That's right, Emperor Marcus Aurelius, the master of mindfulness, used drugs on a regular basis. The historical record is crystal clear on this point. His opium habit was noted in writings by ancient scholars, including the doctor who prescribed it to him, the legendary physician Galen of Pergamon. Naturally, though, because this was Marcus Aurelius, there was a logical reason for his drug use.

You see, Marcus was strong in mind and spirit—but not so much in body. He was physically frail and sick for most of his life, was plagued by chronic pain (believed to be from stomach ulcers and chest issues), and had almost no appetite for food. His poor health was a constant source of worry for his adoring subjects.

In 175 CE, a rumor circulated that he had passed away. The rumor was so widespread and credible that one of his senior generals stepped forward to proclaim himself the new emperor. When the news reached Marcus, he was understandably displeased. He got ready to march against the would-be usurper, but it turned out he didn't have to. As soon as people heard that Marcus was still alive, the rogue general was killed by his own troops. That's how much people liked Marcus Aurelius.

Despite his poor health, Marcus didn't waste time feeling sorry for himself. That's not what Stoics do—they don't engage in self-pity. Sickness and poor health are just like everything else in life, facts to be dealt with logically and rationally. You can't choose what happens to you, but you can control how you respond to it.

Marcus's response to his situation was to take opium. That's because the ailment that bothered him the most was his inability to sleep. It wasn't a symptom that stemmed from the weakness of his body but rather from the strength of his mind. His brain simply refused to stop working. He was always thinking, always evaluating, always reexamining—and as a result, he couldn't fall asleep at night.

Applying his unparalleled critical thinking skills to the task, Marcus logically concluded that his ability to function as emperor would inevitably suffer if he was continually sleep-deprived, so he turned to his trusted medical professional, Galen, for an effective way to hit the pause button on his endless rumination. Based on his doctor's response, there must not have been a lot of other sleep aids on the market in ancient Rome, because Galen told him he needed to drink the milk of the poppy.

Opium was fairly well-known by this point in history. Legendary figures such as Alexander the Great had demonstrated its effectiveness as a painkiller and sedative, but the risk of addiction was also quite familiar. Even thousands of years ago, it was impossible not to notice that people who took opium on a regular basis got hooked on it—which is why Marcus needed to invoke his Stoic values of restraint, self-control, and discipline to ensure he did not fall into this all-too-common trap. He administered the drug in a carefully measured dose under the watchful eye of his doctor—just a tiny spoonful—and it worked. He was able to sleep.

But, at some point, it worked a little too well. The opium was making him drowsy at times when he needed to be awake and alert. So he stopped taking the poppy juice for a while—but then he couldn't sleep at all and was forced to resume taking it. At least one scholar who has closely studied Galen's notes points out that the doctor attributed the emperor's inability to sleep after he stopped taking opium to something he called "dry humors"—but this scholar suggests that modern doctors would call it a symptom of opium withdrawal. He believes Marcus was hooked on opium and couldn't kick the habit.

Some historians disagree. Most seem to believe the dosage was too low to create a physical addiction. But even if he was psychologically addicted, everyone seems to agree that Marcus did not take opium recreationally, and his opium use did not impair his job performance as emperor.

Countless geniuses and visionaries throughout history have used drugs for one reason or another, and too often it turned out badly for them. Marcus Aurelius was an exception. He didn't take opium to get high, and he took only the smallest amount needed to turn off his brain at night. Sure, it might be fun if there were wild stories I could share with you about the crazy shit he did while he was on opium, but there aren't any. He is one of the rare historical figures who used drugs but did not allow drug use to define his life or to control it. Instead, opium was a tool he employed for a specific purpose, and with great success.

Marcus Aurelius was truly a Stoic. He understood that too much of a good thing can kill you and was able to exercise the necessary self-control. But, for what it's worth, maybe he wasn't always as "sober-minded" as the history books might suggest.

# PART 2

# MEDIEVAL HIGHS

# CHAPTER 7

# The Hashashin, the Devout Killer Potheads

Here's a crazy true story: in the late eleventh century, a religious man named Hasan-i Sabbah organized the world's first league of assassins. He convinced a group of idealistic young men to devote their lives to three things: studying the Quran, striking down their enemies, and eating an insane amount of hashish—so much, in fact, that the group was actually named for the stuff: the Hashashin.

They didn't start off as killers. They began as a small (but scrappy) religious sect that disagreed with the two predominant branches of Islam over a pretty important issue: who should have succeeded the Prophet Muhammad after his death. The Sunnis believed a successor should have been selected by the Muslim community at large, while the Shias believed it should have been limited to the closest person in Muhammad's direct bloodline. But this tiny splinter group said "you're both wrong" and instead supported the seventh person in the line of succession, a man named Ismail bin Jafar. They were thus dubbed "Ismaili Shias" or "Seveners."

The Sunnis and Shias didn't like being told they were wrong by a bunch of arrogant upstarts. They branded this new sect heretics, which effectively painted a target on their backs. These Seveners were at serious risk of being hunted down and killed—until they developed an unusual way of fighting back against their much more numerous and more powerful religious rivals.

They became assassins.

Their leader, Hasan-i Sabbah, established their headquarters in an impregnable castle at the top of a mountain in Persia. Then, in the basement of the castle, he trained his followers in the dark art of assassination. He taught them how to disguise themselves to look harmless, how to speak foreign languages so they could infiltrate enemy encampments, and most important, how to kill someone in hand-to-hand combat. When their training was complete, he would identify a target, and the assassins would set out to learn everything they could about their intended victim. They'd watch his movements, study his routines, and find his weaknesses. Then, when their victim least expected it, the assassins would strike.

They soon became the dominant military force in the Middle East—which was amazing because, keep in mind, they didn't have an army, just this elite group of assassins. They carried out their attacks in broad daylight, in public places, with people clustered all around, because they wanted everyone to see. They used daggers to kill their targets, which meant they had to be standing right in front of them (or behind them—they were totally fine with stabbing someone in the back). And they weren't concerned about escaping. They fully expected to die after completing their mission, because they knew their utter disregard for their own safety made them even more intimidating. They were like old-world Terminators: they would never stop and never turn back, even if their target surrounded himself with dozens of bodyguards.

But their most distinguishing trait was their fanatical loyalty to their leader. One time, a rival commander said to Hasan, "I'm not afraid of you, I've got ten times as many men." Hasan shrugged, pointed to one of his men, and told him to jump off the roof of the castle. The man did not hesitate. He ran straight off the roof and plummeted to his death. The rival commander just stared at Hasan with his jaw on the floor.

How did he inspire such blind loyalty? Drugs, very powerful drugs.

His men trained every day in a dark, windowless basement, abstaining from all of life's pleasures. Then one day Hasan would appear before them, holding a potion for them to drink. (Accounts suggest it was a blend of opium, hashish, and lysergic acid amide, a naturally occurring precursor to LSD.) The men would immediately fall asleep—but when they awoke, they'd find themselves in a magical garden filled with palm trees, flowers, exquisite food and wine, and lovely young maidens playing music for them and caressing their skin. They couldn't believe their good fortune.

Then they'd drink the potion again and wake up back in the basement. Shit!

That was paradise, Hasan explained. He'd offered them a brief glimpse of what awaited his truest followers in the afterlife. So long as they pledged their unconditional loyalty to him and performed every task he assigned them without hesitation or delay, he would ensure they returned to paradise—permanently, this time—when they died. His men were sold; no further convincing was required. They were like, "Screw it, who do I have to kill?"

Of course, drinking that magical potion wasn't the only time they used drugs. Consuming hashish was an integral part of their training—because being an assassin is stressful work. To infiltrate an enemy camp, they'd have to pretend to be someone else and maintain that cover story for days or weeks at a time. If people saw them acting nervous and jittery, their cover would be blown. Luckily, the psychotropic effects of hashish were strong enough to lift them up and take them out of themselves. They were able to detach from their emotions and disassociate from any sense of fear.

To murder a man in broad daylight, when he's surrounded by bodyguards, knowing those bodyguards will rip you apart after you've killed their employer, takes more than being detached from your emotions. You have to be out of your freaking mind. You need to achieve a state of ecstatic fury that is so insanely over-the-top that absolutely nothing and nobody can stop you. Once again, Hasan's followers relied on the psychotropic effects of hashish. They would consume enough of the drug to transform themselves into ferocious killing machines that would feel no pain and no fear until their mission was completed—imagine John Wick wearing a hooded robe instead of a black suit.

At first, the Hashashin targeted the leaders of rival Muslim sects. But when the Crusades started in 1095 CE, they quickly shifted their attention to the invaders from Europe. In the twelfth century, the Christian Crusaders captured Jerusalem and attempted to install one of their own as king, Sir Conrad of Montferrat—but only four days after he started his new job, as the king was walking through a public square surrounded by a squad of armed soldiers, two men dressed as monks suddenly threw off their robes, pulled daggers, and stabbed him repeatedly in the chest and back. Within seconds, the would-be king of Jerusalem was dead, proving once again there was no one the Hashashin could not reach.

Admittedly, there's some disagreement among scholars as to whether these highly trained killers actually carried out their missions while stoned on hashish. But we know one thing for sure—the famous thirteenth-century explorer and writer Marco Polo certainly believed it was true. He traveled to the region where their fortress was located and wrote down everything he learned about them, including how their leader earned their loyalty by drugging them and giving them a glimpse of "paradise," and the way they attacked their targets while under the influence of drugs. In fact, the story goes that their constant drug use is what gave them their name. Because they carried out their missions under the influence of hashish, and they murdered people in the name of Shia Islam, people began referring to them as the "Hashishia." Later, when foreign explorers heard of their exploits, they westernized the name a bit, calling them "Hashashin." Over time, "Hashashin" gradually morphed into a word we know today: "assassin." (Today, of course, anyone who performs a targeted killing is called an assassin, even if they weren't stoned at the time.)

But other scholars aren't so sure. No one denies the league of assassins existed, but some historians believe the Hashashin did not actually carry out their assignments while under the influence of drugs. Instead, these historians believe the whole "killing people while stoned" story was a slanderous lie spread by people who feared and hated the group. As much as I'd love to offer you a definitive answer one way or another, given this all happened more than a thousand years ago, no one can say for certain which story is true—but I can tell you without any hesitation which story is more fun. I choose you, Marco Polo!

If all this "ancient league of assassins" stuff is starting to sound like a video game you're familiar with, there's a very good reason for that. *Assassin's Creed* features a fictionalized version of the Hashashin. It depicts an order of assassins that, in the mythology of the game, has existed throughout all of recorded history. In real life, however, the Hashashin lasted for only about three hundred years. As fearsome and dominant as they once were, they vanished into legend after the thirteenth century, because that's when the Mongols invaded the Middle East and laid waste to anyone who opposed them, including the Hashashin.

Yes, it took the arrival of the dreaded Genghis Khan before the Hashashin finally encountered an enemy more terrifying, lethal, and formidable than them. And even though almost eight hundred years have passed since the Hashashin vanished from the face of the earth, their reign of terror was so notorious that the legend of the deadly killer potheads endures even today.

# CHAPTER 8

# William Shakespeare Was a Stoner

William Shakespeare was in danger of being canceled. He was a big fan of mind-altering drugs—especially cannabis. But the Church of England looked down on live theater because of its "unwholesome" moral content and was keeping an eye out for plays to shut down; plus, city officials had to approve plays before they could be performed within the city limits. So, if Shakespeare had dared to admit publicly that he smoked cannabis, it might have ended his career.

That's right, Shakespeare was a stoner. I'm not making this up—they found the evidence in his backyard. Back in 2001, some anthropologists got permission from a museum to borrow twenty-four clay pipe fragments that had been dug up in the small town of Stratford-upon-Avon, where Shakespeare used to live. Using state-of-the-art forensic technology, the anthropologists discovered cannabis residue on eight of them—including several from Shakespeare's backyard garden—that dated back to the late 1500s/early 1600s, around the time he actually lived there.

Professor Francis Thackeray has written extensively about the findings. This guy is legit: he's got a PhD from Yale University, and he personally participated in the forensic tests. He says they also found traces of coca leaves (that's where cocaine comes from) and myristic acid (a hallucinogenic drug derived from nutmeg) on some of the pipe fragments. Unlike the cannabis residue, however, the coca leaves and myristic acid weren't found directly in Shakespeare's garden (although they were found nearby)—but it opens the door to the tantalizing possibility that Shakespeare might have been into all sorts of mind-altering drugs.

Technically, the evidence is circumstantial. Pipes with cannabis residue were dug up in Shakespeare's garden, but that doesn't necessarily mean Shakespeare is the one who put them there. (Hey, maybe they were planted in his garden by Sir Francis Bacon, right?) So Professor Thackeray, being a smart and thorough scientist, decided to obtain conclusive proof. He asked the Church of England for permission to exhume Shakespeare's corpse and run the necessary tests in order to answer, once and for all, the question of whether Shakespeare smoked pot. Guess what the church said. No way, not a chance, that's not a question they want answered.

But if Shakespeare was a stoner, he faced a thorny dilemma. On the one hand, he enjoyed using drugs and wanted to include depictions of drug use in his plays. On the other hand, he didn't want the church to ban his plays for immoral content. So how did the greatest writer of all time resolve this dilemma?

The answer is he wrote about drugs, but without saying what they really were. His plays are filled with characters who ingest all manner of fantastical pharmaceutical concoctions. For example, in *A Midsummer Night's Dream*, Oberon, the king of the fairies, tells Puck to fetch an exotic magical flower so that he can extract its juice to formulate a love potion—but it's pretty obviously opium. We know for a fact that Shakespeare was familiar with opium because he says as much in *Othello* (emphasis added):

> *Not* poppy, *nor mandragora,*
> *Nor all the* drowsy syrups *of the world,*

> *Shall ever medicine thee to that sweet sleep*
> *Which thou owedst yesterday.*

Similarly, in *Romeo and Juliet,* the young heroine, Juliet, is distraught because her parents are forcing her to marry someone other than Romeo. She begs the friendly Friar Laurence to help, and what's his genius idea? That she drink a sleeping potion that will knock her out so completely and convincingly that the whole world will believe she's dead for two days. Juliet actually takes his creepy advice. Basically, she roofies herself—Shakespeare might just as well have been talking about GHB.

But the fact that Shakespeare wrote about love potions, sleeping potions, and other fanciful elixirs isn't conclusive evidence. It's the nature of dramatic storytelling: writers invent peculiar concoctions to give their characters a reason to act in ways they wouldn't normally act. That doesn't prove Shakespeare was a drug user. You can scour through every single one of his plays looking for passages that might or might not refer to drugs, but you won't find a *Da Vinci Code*–like secret that unlocks a hidden drawer containing a signed confession from William Shakespeare admitting that he smoked cannabis.

Although one of the sonnets he wrote comes pretty close. Professor Thackeray, the same anthropologist who performed the pipe analysis, points to Shakespeare's Sonnet 76, which talks in part about the act of writing (emphasis added):

> *Why is my verse so barren of new pride,*
> *So far from variation or quick change?*
> *Why with the time do I not glance aside*
> *To new-found methods and to* compounds strange?
> *Why write I still all one, ever the same,*
> *And keep invention in a* noted weed,
> *That every word doth almost* tell my name . . .

The wording in Sonnet 76 is pretty convincing. Many scholars believe the "noted weed" in which the author finds "invention" is a reference to cannabis and its ability to stimulate creativity. Some also think the phrase "every word doth almost tell my name" is a sly reference to the fact that "shake" (as in *Shake*speare) is another word for cannabis—specifically, the scraps left over after cannabis buds have been plucked and packaged.

But what about "compounds strange"? The sonnet says a writer whose writing has become "barren" could potentially turn "to new-found methods and to compounds strange," but the author suggests he has chosen *not* to go that direction. Does that mean Shakespeare wasn't a drug user? Not necessarily. Professor Thackeray believes the passage could mean Shakespeare used cannabis ("a noted weed") for his creative inspiration, and chose to avoid using other, more dangerous drugs, such as cocaine, because they were "compounds strange" that could prove harmful.

As you might guess, Shakespeare scholars tend to get a bit defensive when someone starts to suggest that maybe the Bard enjoyed cannabis. They feel like it's an attempt to undercut his achievements—but that isn't the case at all. I'm not saying if Shakespeare was smoking pot when he wrote *Hamlet*, it somehow makes the play less great—or worse, that anyone who was smoking pot could have written it. Heck, writers have been using cannabis for four hundred years since Shakespeare died, and so far no one has managed to come close to replicating the man's genius.

To put a twist on one of his most famous lines: I come to praise Shakespeare, not to bury him. He was a uniquely gifted writer who told stories in a compelling and enjoyable way. Basically, he was the Walt Disney of the sixteenth and seventeenth centuries. Everyone loved his plays. He didn't write only for kings, queens, nobles, and other snooty rich people. Sure, they attended his shows and appreciated his work—but his most enthusiastic fans were the lowly commoners who flocked to the Globe Theatre to occupy the standing-room-only section. They were known as "groundlings," and they'd hoot and holler at his ribald jokes and raunchy banter. It was almost like having a mosh pit at his plays.

The stories he told weren't necessarily original. Shakespeare borrowed plotlines from books and adapted folktales from other cultures—*Hamlet*, for example, is based on an old Scandinavian tale. His real genius lay in retelling these stories in a way that appealed to a much broader audience than the original source material—just like Disney didn't create the plots of *Cinderella*, *Mulan*, and *The Little Mermaid*, but instead took existing source material and transformed it into audience-pleasing, world-spanning megahits.

His real gift was language: puns, rhymes, clever wordplay, and memorable turns of phrase. If he were alive today, Shakespeare might be a rapper because of how easily the words seemed to flow from his mind. Do we have cannabis to thank for that? Maybe, at least in part. Many authors (and rappers) have used mind-altering drugs to enhance their creative process and boost their productivity—and no one can deny that Shakespeare was insanely productive, given that he wrote 37 plays and 154 sonnets in the span of his twenty-three-year career.

In addition to writing plays and sonnets, Shakespeare created words themselves. He's credited with adding roughly 1,700 words to the English-language lexicon. While the total number is probably exaggerated—experts believe some of the words were already being used in everyday conversation and Shakespeare was simply the first person to write them down—the fact remains that he invented at least a few hundred new words.

But wait, how were audiences able to follow what the characters were talking about if he kept making up new words? This was part of Shakespeare's genius. Like the plots of his plays, the words he invented weren't cut from whole cloth; they were adapted from familiar source material.

One of his favorite tricks was to take two existing words and join them together, as he did with "bare-faced" and "blood-sucking." At other times, he took a noun and turned it into a verb ("elbow-ed"). He changed nouns into adjectives ("cat-like"), verbs into adjectives ("revolt-ing"), and verbs into nouns ("excite-ment"). He also liked to add prefixes, taking words like "formal" and "educated," and giving them a twist, creating "in-formal" and "un-educated." Or he'd add a suffix, creating words like "disgrace-ful" and "distrust-ful." When all else failed, he'd take a Latin word and anglicize it a bit, yielding words like "tranquil" and "articulate."

The result is that Shakespeare's plays are filled with words that never existed before, and yet their meaning was immediately clear. And yes, a few of his new words sound like they might have been invented by someone who was high at the time—words such as "trippingly" and "moonbeam," and "zany" and "swagger." In fact, Shakespeare was the person who first coined the word "addiction"— but he also created the word "transcendence."

So did Shakespeare smoke cannabis? The scientific evidence suggests he probably did, but this doesn't make him any less of a genius. He's still regarded by many as the greatest writer who ever lived. If cannabis helped him get there, it doesn't tarnish his legacy. Maybe his real genius was knowing what worked for him.

# COLONIAL CHAOS

# CHAPTER 9

# George Washington's Terrible Teeth

Everyone knows that on his sixth birthday, little George Washington received a hatchet as a gift and was so excited he used it to chop down a cherry tree. When his father discovered his prized cherry tree had been chopped down, he got angry and demanded to know who was responsible. That's when brave little George stepped forward and confessed, saying, "I cannot tell a lie." His father immediately forgave his son and gave him a big hug, because his honesty was worth more than a thousand trees.

It's a heartwarming story—but it's a complete lie. It never happened. The cherry tree incident was invented by the man who wrote Washington's biography, a religious bookseller named Mason Locke Weems, to sell more copies of his book. Because Weems was a minister, he was always looking for ways to promote virtuous behavior, so he decided to imbue the father of our country with a few more virtues than he actually possessed.

In fairness, George Washington did achieve some remarkable things. He took an inexperienced, poorly equipped civilian army and, in 1776, led it to an improbable victory over what was, at the time, the most powerful empire in the world. He was elected president of the United States unanimously, by all sixty-nine electors who cast votes, and he repeated the feat four years later when he was unanimously elected to a second term. No other president has ever won the Electoral College unanimously—and yet Washington did it twice. Then, amazingly, he chose to walk away from the job. There was no rule preventing him from running for a third term, and remember, the early Americans were totally used to monarchy. People expected, even wanted him to keep going, but he chose to voluntarily relinquish the job, deciding it was more important to establish a precedent that the United States was going to operate differently from other countries, thus ensuring the smooth transition of power that has become the hallmark of American democracy for over two hundred years.[1]

So, yes, George Washington was a truly impressive person—but he was no saint. Like everyone else, he had flaws, and a few of them were pretty damn bad.

For one thing, he owned slaves. Washington became a slave owner at age eleven, when his father died and left him 10 slaves in his will. But that wasn't the end of his slave ownership. He bought and sold numerous slaves over the years, whipped them when they disobeyed, and hunted them down when they ran away. Plus, when he married his wife, Martha, her dowry included 84 slaves. By the time Washington died in 1799, a total of 317 enslaved people were living at his Mount Vernon estate.

You might think, well, that's how things were back then. He was a product of his time—and besides, the historical record reflects that Washington was never entirely comfortable with the notion of slavery.

But here's the thing: he was the most powerful man in the country. He'd already proven that he wasn't afraid to defy expectations if he believed something was truly important. That's why he voluntarily chose to walk away from a third term as president, be-

---

1. There were a few hiccups on January 6, 2021.

cause he felt it was the right thing to do. That means he could have voluntarily walked away from slavery, too—but he didn't. Instead, he left instructions in his will that, at some point far off in the future, after he and Martha were both dead, his slaves should eventually be emancipated. (For the record, only half of them were actually freed; the other half remained enslaved for a couple of decades.) So he wasn't exactly an icon of racial harmony and tolerance.

But wait, it gets worse. Not only did he own slaves, he stole teeth from them. You see, George Washington had terrible teeth; they were all cracked and broken. He started losing teeth in his early twenties because he wouldn't stop using them to crack Brazil nuts. By the time he became president, he had only one real tooth left in his mouth. In order to speak and be understood, he needed to have teeth, so he wore extremely primitive dentures.

I know what you're thinking—you learned all about Washington's terrible teeth in grade school. You know he wore fake teeth and they were made of wood, right?

Wrong. That's another myth. The ugly truth is that his teeth were a Frankenstein-esque nightmare. A set of Washington's dentures is on display at the George Washington Presidential Library at Mount Vernon, and trust me, it is not a pretty sight. I apologize for what you are about to see:

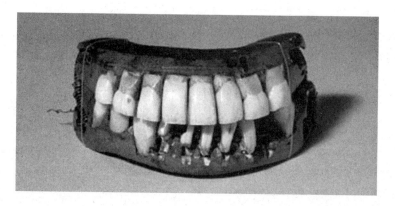

Horrifying, right? The top row of Washington's false teeth were actually horse and donkey teeth, which are larger than human teeth. But the bottom row came from real people. They were cobbled together from a collection of extracted human teeth—some from corpses (which is gross), and the rest from enslaved people (which is even worse). This is a proven historical fact. It's hard to believe this monstrosity was ever placed inside a human mouth, let alone the mouth of the president of the United States. The primitive dentures disfigured his face, causing his cheeks to bulge, his lips to protrude, and his mouth to appear swollen and misshapen. But he felt it was necessary to wear them, especially when he was speaking to the American people. As a University of Virginia research specialist put it, "George Washington probably gave his inaugural speech with teeth that were from people who were enslaved. It's grim."

It gets even worse. There was a thriving market for human teeth back in the 1700s. Desperate people could sell their teeth as a way of earning money. Newspaper ads from the time show the going rate was two guineas apiece, but historians discovered entries in Washington's personal ledger showing he paid only a fraction of this amount to his slaves. This means either his slaves were so incredibly fond of their owner that they gave him a "friends and family" discount—or, alternatively, they had no real say in the transaction and were forced to surrender their teeth at cut-rate prices, just so Washington could sleep better at night, telling himself he didn't actually "steal" their teeth, he bought them. Even the George Washington Presidential Library admits that "while Washington paid these enslaved people for their teeth it does not mean they had a real option to refuse his request."

Okay, this is all extremely depressing, but what does it have to do with drugs? The answer is Washington's crude dentures were incredibly painful to wear. To prevent them from falling out of his mouth, they needed to be anchored to the one real tooth he still possessed. This meant the dentures would grind against that tooth every time he spoke or moved his jaw, so wearing them hurt like hell. Washington was in constant pain.

That's why he took opium.

Our foremost Founding Father drank a spoonful of opium every night to cope with the never-ending pain caused by his creepy Frankenstein teeth.

This isn't something you'll find in a textbook—the local PTA wouldn't be too happy if teachers were telling their kids that George Washington was a big-time druggie, so this fact has been omitted from the history books. "Censored" might be a more accurate word to describe it—but it is absolutely true. Washington's doctors advised him to take a drug called laudanum, which is a tincture of opium. For those unfamiliar with the term, a tincture is a medication that's typically found in solid form but has been suspended in a liquid solution. In this case, the solid medication was opium, and it was suspended in very-high-proof alcohol. As you can probably guess, the combination of opium and alcohol packed quite a punch. In fact, only a few decades later, addiction to laudanum would become an epidemic among rich and powerful people in England.

That said, there's no evidence that Washington was *addicted* to laudanum. It was quite simply the most advanced medicine available two hundred years ago for someone suffering from acute dental pain. While it was known to involve some risk of dependency and overdose, there are no stories reported of his overindulging or using it recreationally. Washington wasn't taking laudanum to get high or to cope with the stress of leadership; he was using it to manage his pain. Per his doctor's instructions, he consumed daily doses of opium to control his pain level so he could do his job as president of the United States.

Of course, I'm not saying Washington was always sober. Far from it; he was extremely fond of alcohol. His personal favorite was

Madeira, a Portuguese wine that was "fortified" (meaning it had extra alcohol added). He drank anywhere from four glasses to multiple bottles of Madeira over the course of a day. In fairness, back in his time, drinking water wasn't necessarily safe, so it was common for everyone—men, women, even children—to drink wine on a daily basis. But Washington was reportedly so fond of his Portuguese wine that he didn't like to share. He was known to complain loudly that he believed his slaves were drinking up his supply. (Perhaps they needed something to numb the pain from their wrongfully extracted teeth.)

Like I said, he was no saint. The good things Washington accomplished were eminently laudable—but some of the bad things he did were just plain awful. He owned slaves throughout his entire life. When he lost teeth due to a weird addiction to Brazil nuts, he extracted replacement teeth from his slaves—apparently against their will. He drank regular doses of opium and super-alcoholic Portuguese wine to help him navigate his day. And, just so we're perfectly clear on the point, he didn't chop down a goddamn cherry tree when he was six years old.

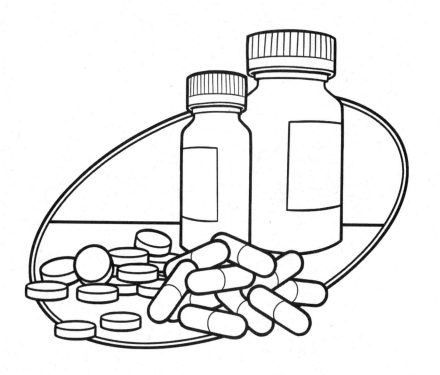

# CHAPTER 10

# Andrew Jackson Was a Mean, Crazy, Racist, Murderous Drunk

T here are a bunch of insane stories about Andrew Jackson, and they're almost all true. Like the time he almost killed a would-be assassin. It was 1835, and Jackson was leaving a funeral when a guy pointed a single-shot derringer pistol at him and pulled the trigger—but the gun didn't fire. Jackson was sixty-seven years old at the time and walked with a cane, but that didn't stop him from charging at the poor schmuck. Panicked, the guy reached for a second pistol and pulled the trigger—but that one misfired, too. Now it was Jackson's turn. He raised his cane and started bashing the guy with it, even after the man had been knocked to the ground and was no longer a threat. A crowd of horrified onlookers, including the legendary Davy Crockett, had to physically pry the president of the United States off the hapless assassin; otherwise Jackson would surely have killed him.

Jackson fought in more than a hundred duels. He was notoriously quick-tempered and astonishingly thin-skinned. Whenever he felt someone had impugned his honor (which was all the freaking time), his go-to move was to challenge the guy to a fight to the death. His most notorious duel was in 1806 against a man named Charles Dickinson, who had the temerity to accuse Jackson of reneging on a horse race bet. Jackson's strategy for the duel wasn't what you might expect—he didn't turn and shoot as quickly as possible. Instead, he waited for the other guy to shoot first. Jackson deliberately wore a bulky, oversize coat that day to disguise the shape of his body. He stood like a crazed madman as Dickinson's bullet struck him squarely in the chest, but he refused to fall down. Dickinson, an expert marksman, stared in disbelief, wondering if he had somehow missed—but he hadn't. Jackson simply absorbed the bullet, clamped his hand tightly over the wound, then took his sweet time carefully lining up a shot at his now-unarmed opponent. But when he pulled the trigger, the hammer stopped halfway. According to traditional dueling rules, a misfire counts as a shot, so the duel was officially over. But Jackson decided screw that. He re-cocked the gun, fired again, and this time killed Dickinson.

He cheated, but he won. However, the bullet that Dickinson had fired was lodged so close to Jackson's heart that surgeons couldn't take the chance of trying to remove it, so Jackson carried that bullet inside him for the rest of his life—and that wasn't the only one. This was a man who'd fought in two wars and over a hundred duels. Legend has it, he had so many bullets inside him, he actually clanked when he walked. He was always looking for an excuse to kill somebody, and he didn't need much of one. By any modern standard, Jackson would probably be labeled a serial killer, given all the deaths for which he was responsible.

He was no less murderous in his politics. He gleefully instituted the so-called Indian Removal Act of 1830, in which soldiers systematically rounded up Indigenous people and violently coerced them to vacate their homes and march thousands of miles to much worse land on the western frontier. The removal program was notorious for its mistreatment of Native Americans and a near-total lack of food and medical care for them. The forced exile turned into a series of tragic death marches, leading to the loss of as many as ten thousand Indigenous lives among the Cherokee, Creek, Choctaw, Chickasaw, and Seminole peoples. It became known as the Trail of Tears and today is widely regarded as genocide. But, of course, the thousands of deaths didn't bother Jackson in the slightest, because he got what he wanted—valuable real estate he could use to bribe poor white voters, who were hungry for land they could claim as their own.

Jackson had absolutely no regard for the lives and dignity of Indigenous peoples. In 1830, when the Cherokee discovered gold on land that was guaranteed to them by treaty, the State of Georgia attempted to strip the suddenly valuable land away from them. The Supreme Court ruled in favor of the tribe, but President Jackson sided with the State of Georgia. He flatly ignored the Supreme Court's ruling and said snarkily about the chief justice: "John Marshall has made his decision; now let him enforce it." Then he sent federal troops to forcibly evict the Cherokee from their homes.

It probably won't shock you to learn that Jackson drank constantly. In the nineteenth century, water wasn't necessarily safe to drink. It was cloudy, was unfiltered, and could make you sick. Alcohol, on the other hand, was antibacterial, so it wasn't unusual for people to drink more whiskey than water over the course of a day. Jackson, however, was in a class of his own. He installed a distillery at his plantation home. He began drinking whiskey when he got up in the morning and continued until he went to sleep at night. Drinking all day didn't interfere with his daily routine—heck, it *was* his daily routine.

With some people, their entire personality changes when they drink—but that wasn't the case with Jackson. If anything, drinking simply made him *more* Andrew Jackson. It potentiated his personality, making him even more intensely himself. His penchant for physical violence, his seeming immunity to pain, his bravery to the point of recklessness, his ferocious anger, and his instinctively populist aptitude for knowing how to pander to the common man—all these qualities were bolstered when he was swigging his favorite whiskey.

When he decided to run for office, he took whiskey on the campaign trail with him. He threw drunken parties for his supporters, which proved to be an effective way to get people who didn't otherwise care about politics to pay attention to him. He basically invented populism, discovering that offering booze to poor white men, who'd long been excluded from the electoral process, while simultaneously fueling their bigotry toward Black voters and Native Americans, would get these troglodytic males to cast their votes for him and to support his racist policies of stomping on civil rights and inflicting genocide on Indigenous people. Whiskey turned out to be the catalyst that transformed prickly and unlikable Andrew Jackson into a "man of the people."

This explains his wild inauguration party. On March 4, 1829, Jackson threw a gigantic blowout at the White House and opened it up to anyone who wanted to attend. Twenty thousand of his rowdiest supporters showed up, including shabbily dressed farmers and frontiersmen, with their trousers tucked into their boots and wearing pistols on their belts. Many were first-time voters who wanted to shake the new president's hand, so they went tromping through the White House in their muddy boots to look for him. It was an uncontrolled free-for-all that got totally out of hand when the drunken crowd began climbing on top of the furniture to get a better view, rummaging through cabinets looking for fine china and other souvenirs to steal, and generally smashing stuff in the White House. The inauguration was on the verge of turning into a full-fledged riot—and what did "man of the people" Andrew Jackson do? He fled the White House by climbing out an open window.

Meanwhile, his servants were desperately trying to get his sloshed supporters to exit the White House before they destroyed the place, but the mob had no interest in leaving. Until the servants got the smart idea to move the alcohol outdoors, trusting that the plastered partygoers would follow—and they sure did. Punch bowls the size of bathtubs were filled with whiskey and juice on the White House lawn, the inebriated partygoers quickly moved outside, and disaster was avoided. It took several weeks to repair all the damage to the building, but once it was done, Jackson officially moved into the White House—and proceeded to enjoy his whiskey in private from then on.

As much as Jackson loved to offer booze to people, there was one group he fought hard to exclude: Native Americans. He signed a piece of legislation in 1834 that officially banned distilleries on Native American land because of his condescending view of Indigenous people—he believed they were uncivilized, incapable of resisting the lure of alcohol, and would only get themselves into trouble. Everyone else was allowed to drink, but not them.

Despite his cornucopia of abhorrent behavior, Jackson's face appears on the twenty-dollar bill. This is because, even though he was a mean, crazy, racist, murderous drunk, he was popular, not only with voters but also with other presidents. Abraham Lincoln was a big fan of Jackson; so was Franklin D. Roosevelt. They admired him because he grew up poor and uneducated yet worked his way up to become president of the United States. They viewed him as the personification of the American Dream. So, for the past ninety-five years or so, the nation has been stuck with a racist douchebag on its currency.

The only thing that makes it bearable is that Jackson would have hated it. He detested the idea of paper money, saying it was worthless, insisting that only precious metals, such as gold, silver, and coins, should be used as legal tender. Luckily for him (and everyone else), the Treasury Department has finally decided to boot Jackson off the twenty-dollar bill and replace him with someone far more deserving—Harriet Tubman.

So long, jackass.

# CHAPTER 11

# Andrew Johnson Was Blackout Drunk

A ndrew Johnson gave the most disastrous inauguration speech in American history—and he's got hard liquor to thank for it.

Here's the story: On March 4, 1865, Abraham Lincoln began his second term as president, and Andrew Johnson was sworn in as his new vice president. Everyone understood adding Johnson to the ticket was a calculated political move. Lincoln knew he'd have a hard time getting reelected with the Civil War raging, so he wanted a Southerner as his running mate, but only if he could find one who wasn't in favor of secession. That meant choosing Johnson, because he was the only senator from a Southern state who didn't quit the Senate when the Civil War started. Lincoln was convinced Johnson was the right pick—not because the two men shared the same values or temperament (they absolutely didn't) but because adding a Southerner who opposed secession would help him win reelection and, hopefully, keep the United States in one piece. Lincoln was right; he won the election. Bringing in Johnson was a stroke of genius—until Johnson opened his mouth and started speaking.

Johnson was drunk off his ass. He was recovering from a bout of typhoid fever and decided to "cure" himself by drinking whiskey— always a smart decision. He'd gotten plastered the night before the inauguration, and then he drank another three tumblers of hooch in the morning, just before giving his speech. When the moment of truth arrived, he rose unsteadily from his chair, swaying precariously, and delivered an impromptu, semi-incoherent, utterly belligerent speech that shocked everyone in the room. He harangued the crowd about his own humble beginnings, reminding them he grew up poor and uneducated, then bragged about his triumph over the rich and powerful in the room and how much he hated the aristocratic elite. "I am a plebeian," he slurred. "I glory in it."

Then he pointed his finger at the individual cabinet members who were sitting flabbergasted in front of him. He went down the row, insulting each one by name—except he couldn't remember some of their names and had to ask for help in a cringe-inducing stage whisper. Everyone in the room—congressmen, Supreme Court justices, diplomats, even Lincoln himself—was horrified. They buried their faces in their hands and prayed he would stop talking. A friend of Johnson's tugged repeatedly on his jacket, trying to get him to sit down, but Johnson blundered on for another twenty minutes. As one senator wrote later to his wife, "I was never so mortified in my life, had I been able to find a hole I would have dropped through it out of sight."

Johnson's insane rant went viral—which was hard to do in the nineteenth century. The speech made headlines around the world and embarrassed the entire nation. Some senators called for Johnson to resign; others threatened to impeach him. Several weeks went by, and people were still furious about the incident. You'd think another, newer scandal might have grabbed the headlines away from this one, but no such luck.

Then, on April 13, 1865, it got even worse. The New York newspaper the *World* published an incredibly detailed, blistering account of Johnson's drunken speech, recounting everything he'd said, blow by blow, written by a British journalist who'd witnessed the debacle firsthand. The article said flat-out that Johnson was no better than a common lowlife drunkard lying facedown in the gutter, and quoted a US senator as saying that if Johnson ever somehow became president, the United States would "sink to a lower depth of degradation than was ever reached by any nation since the Roman emperor made his horse a consul." (That's right, history buffs, the senator was comparing Andrew Johnson to Caligula.)

This was the death blow. Johnson's political career was truly over. Any future he might have imagined for himself in government was now permanently and unalterably foreclosed. He had humiliated the United States of America and every one of its citizens. One thing was absolutely certain: Andrew Johnson would never become president.

But the very next day, Lincoln was assassinated. Johnson, as his vice president, was suddenly catapulted into the presidency. Only twenty-four hours after the *World* published an article that should have sealed his doom forever and guaranteed that he would never again hold any political office, Johnson was being sworn in as the president of the United States.

Everyone knows where Lincoln was on the night of the assassination. He and his wife went to Ford's Theatre to see a play. John Wilkes Booth surreptitiously entered their private box, shot the president, and then leapt from the balcony down to the stage. Scholars have researched the assassination exhaustively and can account for every movement Lincoln made that night.

But what was Johnson doing on the night of the assassination? Well, it depends whom you ask, because there are two very different narratives: One narrative says Johnson was asleep in his bed, when suddenly he was awakened in the middle of the night and summoned to Lincoln's bedside. This narrative assumes he was somber and dignified in the room with the dying president but was unable to stay more than a few minutes because Mrs. Lincoln was asking to see her husband again. Everyone present knew she was not fond of Johnson, and given the incredible stress she was under with her husband lying there on his deathbed, they all agreed the vice president should quickly exit stage left.

But the other narrative is a whole lot more scandalous. An acclaimed expert on the facts of the Lincoln assassination says that, at the time, rumors were circulating that Andrew Johnson was blackout drunk on the night the president was shot. White House staffers tried to rouse him but couldn't because he was so totally out of it. They had to physically lift and drag him to the boardinghouse where the dying president was lying in bed. Johnson showed up with bloodshot eyes, matted hair, filthy clothes, and a beard caked with mud. Mrs. Lincoln took one look at him, shrieked in horror, and demanded that he be physically removed from her husband's presence. Frantic staffers tried their best to clean him up. They snipped off his soiled clothing, sheared away chunks of matted hair, and slapped a fresh new suit on him—then watched in horror as this wreck of a man, still woefully inebriated, was sworn in at ten a.m. on April 15, 1865, as the new president of the United States.

We'll never know for sure which narrative is accurate—but historians are quite certain which narrative Mary Todd Lincoln claimed was true. She told anyone who would listen that Johnson was a "miserable inebriate," and she continued to believe until the day she died that he was somehow involved in the assassination plot against her husband. "As sure as you and I live," she wrote, "Johnson had some hand in all this."

Once he became president, Johnson was an unmitigated disaster. Lincoln had wanted to help Black Americans make the transition from slavery to freedom, but Johnson didn't give a damn about that. He only cared about reincorporating Southern states into the Union and was willing to do pretty much anything to achieve that result. He handed out pardons like they were candy, including to high-ranking Confederate officials. He allowed unrepentant Southern states to elect brand-new governments and to do everything they could to suppress Black votes in those elections. The new state governments then enacted so-called Black Codes, which restricted the rights of freedmen to hold certain jobs, earn decent salaries, and own property. The penalties for violating the Black Codes were incredibly severe, including forced plantation labor—that is, bringing back slavery under a new name.

Johnson was an unrepentant white nationalist. He believed only white men should be allowed to hold power, declaring in 1866: "This is a country for white men, and by God, as long as I am president, it shall be a government for white men." When Congress tried to enact new laws to protect freed slaves, such as the Civil Rights Act of 1866 and the Freedmen's Bureau Act, Johnson immediately vetoed them. He undermined Reconstruction at every turn, and when Congress overrode his vetoes, he turned on Congress. When Congress passed the Fourteenth Amendment, granting equal protection of the law to all citizens, including to former slaves, he went on a road trip, visiting every Southern state, in person, to urge them not to ratify it.

Finally, Congress said "enough." The House of Representatives impeached Johnson, making him the first president in US history to be impeached. Sadly, a two-thirds majority of the Senate was required to convict and remove him from office, and Johnson survived, but just barely. He avoided conviction by the narrowest of margins—one vote. He won the right to finish out the last few months of the term that he had taken over from Lincoln, but seeing the writing on the wall, he did not run for reelection—thus making him one of only a handful of people in history to serve as president of the United States without ever having been *elected* president.

Here's the takeaway: as embarrassing as it was for the nation that Johnson showed up plastered at his own inauguration, and as profoundly disgraceful as it was to show up blackout drunk at the deathbed of President Lincoln, by far the worst thing Andrew Johnson did was his undermining of Reconstruction. His utter disregard for the rights of freed slaves set back the civil rights movement by at least a hundred years and inflicted lasting damage on the United States of America.

# PART 4

# VICTORIAN DECADENCE

CHAPTER **12**

# Samuel Taylor Coleridge's Trip Wore Off

Y̲ou know how sometimes you wake up in the middle of a dream, and things that seemed crystal clear and unforgettable disappear in an instant? That happened to the nineteenth-century British poet Samuel Taylor Coleridge, except it wasn't a dream he woke up from—it was a drug trip. Coleridge was addicted to laudanum—remember that stuff, from the George Washington chapter? It was a potent old-timey mixture of opium and alcohol, which at the time was available over the counter. Coleridge used it both for relief and for creative inspiration. During one of his drug-induced, mind-bending, trippy reveries, he was struck with the inspiration to write his masterpiece, *Kubla Khan*.

The way Coleridge tells it, one night in 1797, he gulped down some laudanum and fell asleep reading a book that mentioned Xanadu, the legendary palace constructed by Kubla Khan. When he woke up a few hours later, there was a fully formed poem in his head. It was two hundred to three hundred lines long, and it was unbelievably great. He started writing it down as quickly as he could, which was pretty quickly because, remember, it was already sitting there in his brain, fully completed. He didn't have to think about what to write; he was merely transcribing something he'd already composed while dreaming.

He was interrupted by a knock at the door—damn it! The laudanum-chugging poet was staying in the English countryside at the time, and someone from the nearby village of Porlock dropped by unannounced on some sort of "business." Coleridge never said what this mysterious business was—maybe he was too high to remember—but in his intoxicated state it took him a full hour to get his unexpected visitor to hit the bricks.

When he went back to the poem, the drugs had worn off. The transcendent masterpiece he'd pictured so clearly in his mind's eye when he was high off his ass had trickled away like sand in an hourglass. Knowing Coleridge, he undoubtedly tried getting high again in hopes of reclaiming what he'd lost, but it was to no avail. The train had left the station; he'd forgotten the rest of the poem.

It kept nagging at him for almost twenty years, but the hundreds of verses that he'd pictured so distinctly in his head never came back to him. Finally, in 1816, he gave up and published the small number of verses he'd managed to jot down before the party pooper from Porlock showed up. *Kubla Khan* is only fifty-four lines. Literary critics say it's one of best things he ever wrote, but Coleridge dismissed it as a mere "fragment" of the grander work he'd envisioned. He said it wasn't worthy of study as a piece of literature but rather only as an object of "psychological curiosity."

The *Kubla Khan* anecdote is a microcosm of Coleridge's career. On the one hand, he was so tremendously talented that he was capable of doing great work even while super messed up. On the other hand, he was held back from reaching his full potential by his crippling drug dependency. Opium inspired him, but it also made him more likely to get distracted or completely forget what he was doing. Would you want Coleridge as your poet laureate? Yes, absolutely. But would you ask him to feed your cat while you went away for a few weeks? Hell no, the man would forget and your cat would die.

Coleridge became addicted to laudanum in the same way that many modern Americans become addicted to pain pills: he started taking opioids for legitimate medical purposes, but chronic use caused him to become physiologically dependent on them. He was an unathletic, bookish, anxious youth who suffered from chronic pain and what at the time was called "nervous illness" but today would probably be called anxiety, depression, or any of a host of other similar disorders.

In the late eighteenth and early nineteenth centuries, when Coleridge lived, laudanum was considered to be a miracle drug of sorts. It took the edge off even the sharpest pain. It was the go-to treatment for almost any conceivable medical condition, including very minor maladies such as toothaches, insomnia, and hangovers. Even infants and children were routinely given laudanum: if your crying baby was teething, just give them a couple of drops of laudanum, and suddenly no more tears.

But Coleridge continued to imbibe laudanum for the next forty years, consuming larger and larger quantities of the drug. The recommended dosage was only a few drops—one or two for a child, up to a maximum of twenty-five drops for a full-grown adult—but, of course, no one was enforcing these recommended dosages. As a lifelong addict with an insanely high drug tolerance, Coleridge routinely drank four to five *ounces* of laudanum per day. The more he took, the higher his tolerance became, meaning he needed to ingest even more obscenely large amounts to achieve the same result. Coleridge confided that on at least one occasion, he drank nearly a full *pint* of laudanum.

At some point, he metamorphosed into a recreational drug user. He wasn't taking opium to remove pain but rather to produce euphoria. He wrote to his brother, saying: "Laudanum gave me repose, not sleep; but you, I believe, know how divine that repose is." He wasn't alone in this. Lots of people in the nineteenth century took laudanum for recreational purposes, including a great many literary luminaries, including Charles Dickens, Percy Bysshe Shelley, Elizabeth Barrett Browning, and Lord Byron. Even if Coleridge realized his consumption was getting out of hand, no one was going to stop him from buying his drug of choice—and why should they? The concept of laudanum addiction didn't really exist back then. Laudanum was ubiquitous. Barbershops, tobacconists, wine merchants, even candy stores—everyone sold this liquid form of opium.

When you read his work, it makes perfect sense that Coleridge was heavily drugged when he was writing. His poems unfold in a trippy, surreal, impressionistic way, with a stream of stimuli flowing through the speaker and overwhelming the senses, as in this passage from *Kubla Khan*:

> *And from this chasm, with ceaseless turmoil seething,*
> *As if this earth in fast thick pants were breathing,*
> *A mighty fountain momently was forced:*
> *Amid whose swift half-intermitted burst*
> *Huge fragments vaulted like rebounding hail,*
> *Or chaffy grain beneath the thresher's flail:*
> *And mid these dancing rocks at once and ever*
> *It flung up momently the sacred river.*

In addition to writing evocative poetry, Coleridge produced insightful literary criticism. In fact, his insights helped to repopularize Shakespeare's *Hamlet*, which had fallen into disrepute. Many critics said *Hamlet* wasn't a great play because the lead character thinks and thinks all the time but doesn't do squat. In a lecture Coleridge gave in 1818, he explained this was a deliberate choice by Shakespeare that proves his "deep and accurate science in mental philosophy." Shakespeare was depicting the consequences of a man being out of balance—by thinking too much, he becomes a "creature of mere meditation, and loses his natural power of action." Critics agreed with this perceptive analysis and suddenly liked *Hamlet* again. (While Coleridge's literary criticism often tended to ramble and go off on tangents—quite likely due to his laudanum consumption—he managed to get away with it due to his tremendous intellect and talent.)

While Coleridge's goal in using laudanum was to relieve stress and make him happy, his drug use also brought along its own distresses. It caused painful constipation that required an embarrassing series of nonstop enemas and sapped his productivity. He often left projects unfinished or abandoned them altogether. Plus, being high all the time caused him to act in really weird ways that alienated his friends and family—like the time he stayed at the Wordsworths' house and insisted salt wasn't good enough for his eggs; he could only eat them with cayenne pepper and served out of a teacup. That's the sort of behavior that doesn't get you invited back.

Coleridge ended up unable to live alone. Despite his immense talent, he understood he needed constant supervision or he'd be swallowed up by his opium dependency. In April 1816, at age forty-three, he moved into the Highgate home of Dr. James Gillman for depression and laudanum addiction—it was basically an early version of rehab or inpatient addiction treatment. But Gillman's supervision wasn't designed to keep him drug-free, just drug-*lite*. The goal was moderation, not abstinence.

Coleridge remained in that quasi-rehab living situation for the next eighteen years, until his death in 1834. While his official cause of death was an unnamed lung disease, it is widely believed that his long-term opium and alcohol abuse were major contributors to his premature death at age sixty-one. It wasn't until several decades later that laudanum addiction was recognized as the danger it truly was, leading to the passage of laws such as Britain's 1868 Pharmacy Act, which restricted the availability of laudanum.

If Coleridge had been born later, maybe he would have been able to get better medical care. At a minimum, there would have been safeguards in place to stop him from acquiring such ungodly quantities of laudanum. Instead, he was born at a time when consumption of laudanum was wholly unrestricted.

We'll never know how much more he could have achieved if he hadn't been held back by his addiction. Even the small portion of *Kubla Khan* he was able to remember is a masterpiece, yet it's only a fraction of what it was meant to be. It's an allegory for his career: impressive as it was, it could have been so much more. Like his famous poem, Coleridge's life was cut short, so we'll never know how it was supposed to—

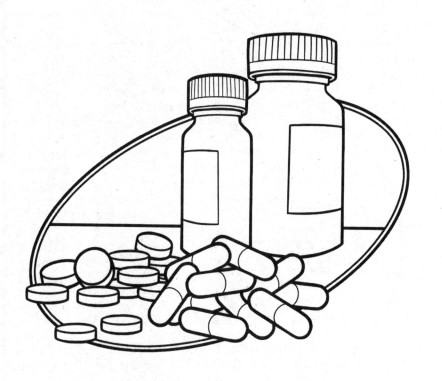

# CHAPTER 13

# Queen Victoria Was the Biggest Drug Dealer of All Time

Who was the most notorious drug kingpin of all time? You might think it was Pablo Escobar, or maybe El Chapo—but you'd be wrong. More than one hundred years before those guys were born, there was an incredibly powerful woman who controlled a drug empire so vast and so unimaginably lucrative that it made Escobar and El Chapo look like low-level street dealers. Plus, she wasn't forced to live in a remote jungle compound surrounded by gun-toting thugs, because no one was coming after her. And she didn't have to conceal her ill-gotten gains from the government tax collectors, because the proceeds from her drug operation were funding the entire country. And she didn't have to worry about being thrown in prison because everyone with the authority to punish drug crimes was already on her payroll. She was Queen Victoria and she was running the British Empire.

Queen Victoria was a huge fan of drugs. That's probably not what you'd expect from a stodgy old queen, but that's a popular misconception. People tend to think of Queen Victoria as being super old, but in reality, she was only eighteen when she ascended the throne, and she routinely enjoyed using a wide variety of pharmaceuticals.

Opium was one of her favorites—but she didn't smoke it in a

pipe. In nineteenth-century Britain, the more fashionable way to ingest opium was to drink it in the form of laudanum. (Remember our old pal laudanum, from the George Washington and Samuel Taylor Coleridge chapters?) This heady one-two punch of opium and alcohol was widely used to knock out pain or discomfort, whatever the cause. It was sort of like aspirin before there was aspirin—respectable doctors even recommended it for toddlers who were teething. Queen Victoria drank a big swig of laudanum every morning, believing it was the perfect way for a royal teenager to start her day.

Cocaine was another of her darlings. It wasn't illegal; it was brand-new, and Europeans were just starting to experiment with it. They'd stumbled across it in South America, where Spanish explorers had witnessed Indigenous peoples working at extremely high elevations on the slopes of the Andes Mountains. This backbreaking work should have been thoroughly exhausting, but the locals were always chewing dry coca leaves, and it seemed to give them inhuman amounts of energy and stamina. European scientists decided to extract the active ingredient from the coca leaves and transform it into something their own citizens could use.

There were plenty of fun and exciting ways to consume cocaine back in the 1800s, but Queen Victoria's personal preferences were chewing gum and wine. Cocaine chewing gum was perfect for soothing toothaches and sore gums from horrendous nineteenth-century British dentistry, plus it gave the chewer a powerful blast of self-confidence, which was great if you were a young, inexperienced queen trying hard to project a strong, assertive image. She wasn't the only high-ranking British official to try it—on at least one occasion, she shared cocaine chewing gum with a young Winston Churchill. The cocaine wine she drank was called Vin Mariani, a psychoactive concoction that was hugely popular with celebrities and world leaders (not to mention a certain elderly Pope, but we'll get to him in the next chapter). Queen Victoria was so fond of Vin Mariani that she wrote an anonymous review praising it and sent her review to the local newspaper—the nineteenth-century equivalent of a five-star Yelp review.

She used a few other drugs, too. Per her doctor's instructions, the queen sipped a liquid form of cannabis to relieve her monthly menstrual symptoms. And to cope with the agonizing pain of childbirth, Victoria enthusiastically embraced chloroform. She held a soaked handkerchief to her face for fifty-three minutes and described the experience as "delightful beyond measure." Maybe that's why she ended up having *nine* children—it was a good excuse to get knackered. As historian and author Tony McMahon summarized it in *Smithsonian* magazine: "Queen Victoria, I think by any standard, she loved her drugs."

Of course, this only proves she was a drug user, not a drug dealer. Her personal consumption was prodigious, but surely not enough to make her a bigger kingpin than Pablo Escobar and El Chapo. But that's the wonderful thing about Queen Victoria; it wasn't all about her. The adolescent monarch insisted on sharing her love of pharmaceuticals with the world—whether they wanted it or not.

From the moment she was crowned in 1837, the young queen inherited a king-size problem: British people drank too much tea. It wouldn't have been a problem, except the tea was coming from China. The average London household was spending 5 percent of its income on Chinese tea, but Britain didn't have anything to trade to China in return. The Chinese were being extremely picky; they looked down their noses at British goods, saying they were inferior and unnecessary. With nothing to trade, Britain was forced to pay for Chinese tea with its precious silver. Britain was almost literally pouring silver into China's treasury and racking up massive trade deficits in the process. China was getting rich, and Britain was growing resentful. The Brits were desperate to find something—anything—that Chinese people craved.

How about opium? It ticked all the boxes. The Brits had tons of it because it grew abundantly in India, which was essentially under British control thanks to the powerful East India Company's domination of the Indian economy. It was an amazingly effective pain-killer, which meant the Chinese were willing to pay insanely high prices for it. And most important, it was super addictive; people who used opium got hooked almost immediately, which meant the Brits could jack up the price even more. Britain had been shipping opium to China for years, but the amount grew exponentially once Queen Victoria assumed the throne.

Thanks to the miracle of opium, the trade imbalance was reversed overnight. China was forced to return all the silver the British had spent on tea, plus a great deal more. Now it was China, not Britain, that was racking up ruinous trade deficits.

China tried desperately to halt the opium trade. Opium was already illegal in China, but the laws were rarely enforced, so now the Chinese government started cracking down severely. But the British Empire wasn't ready to give up its lucrative drug operation. If they couldn't sell opium legally, they'd hire drug mules and third-party cutouts, pay off corrupt officials, or do whatever else it took to keep the money pouring in. They even offered free samples of opium to Chinese citizens in a craven attempt to get as many people addicted as possible. From their point of view, it wasn't personal, it was business—and business was booming. Opium sales were now responsible for 15 to 20 percent of the British Empire's entire annual revenue.

The emperor of China assigned his top man to the job. The guy's name was Lin Zexu, and he was a scholar, philosopher, viceroy, and all-around teacher's pet. His mission was to stop the flow of opium at all costs. He tried diplomacy, but it didn't work. He wrote a letter to Queen Victoria, politely pointing out the immorality of what she was doing: China was shipping goods to Britain that were beneficial and useful, such as tea, silk, and pottery—so why was Britain responding by sending China poisonous drugs that were turning millions of innocent people into opium addicts?

The queen didn't bother to read the letter. This meant the doggedly persistent Lin Zexu needed to find another way to get her attention—so, in the spring of 1839, he intercepted a fleet of British ships, seized a massive shipment of opium, and ordered his soldiers to dump it all into the South China Sea.

This time, the queen noticed. Remember, she was only twenty years old and had lived a pretty charmed life so far. She was used to things going her way. So when Lin Zexu and his men dumped 2.5 million pounds of British opium into the sea, she reacted like any all-powerful imperial teenager would: she declared war on China.

It's known as the First Opium War. (That's right, there was a *Second* Opium War a few years later.) British forces laid waste to the Chinese army and slaughtered tens of thousands of Chinese citizens. The emperor had no choice but to capitulate. He signed a blatantly one-sided so-called peace treaty that handed over Hong Kong to the British, opened up even more ports for opium to flood into the country, and granted immunity to British citizens who were living in China—meaning that the British could (literally) get away with murder.

Even worse, the whole world watched it happen. The Chinese empire had long been regarded as fearsome and indomitable, but not anymore. A petulant teenage queen had demonstrated to the world that China could be defeated, and fairly easily. China was now perceived as ripe for invasion and subjugation by other nations.

The façade had been ripped away; everyone wanted a piece of the pie. Thus began the period referred to in textbooks as China's "century of humiliation."

And that's how a bullying teenager brought an esteemed ancient civilization to its knees. To the young queen, the only thing that mattered was what served her interests. It was fine with her if untold numbers of foreigners halfway around the world died, so long as silver kept flowing into Her Majesty's coffers. It was this ruthless, unabashed self-interest that made her the most successful drug kingpin of all time.

One final note: Because she genuinely believed that cocaine was a safe, healthy energy booster with no ill effects, Queen Victoria refused to sell it to the Chinese. She was happy to sell them all the opium in the world—whether they wanted it or not—but they'd better not touch her cocaine.

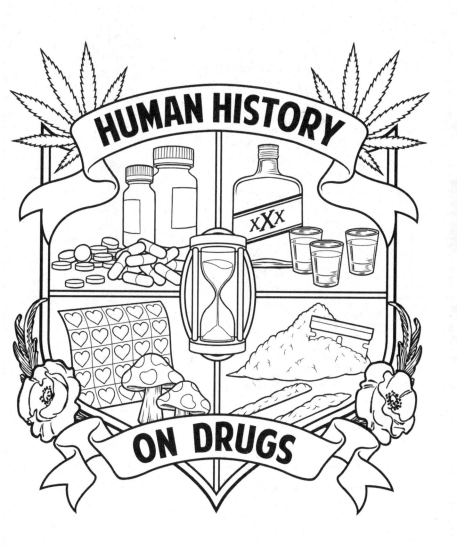

# CHAPTER 14

# The Pope Who Loved Cocaine Wine

If you aren't a devout Catholic, you might guess the history of the Popes is probably pretty dull. But trust me, you'd be wrong—it's amazing. The history of the Catholic Popes is filled with fascinating characters, beginning with the very first Pope, St. Peter. He was sentenced to be crucified by the Roman emperor Nero (who hated Christians), so Peter asked to be crucified *upside down* because he felt unworthy of dying in the same way as Jesus. Some of the Popes who followed were truly bizarre and outrageous—such as Stephen VI, who dug up his predecessor's corpse, put it on trial, found it guilty, hacked off its fingers, and threw it into the Tiber River; and John XII, who murdered several people in cold blood, gambled with church offerings, and was killed by a man who found the Pope in bed with his wife. And who can forget Urban VI, who complained he didn't hear enough screaming when the cardinals who had conspired against him were being tortured to death? Or Alexander VI, who bribed a bunch of cardinals to get the job of being Pope, engaged in countless orgies, and fathered nine illegitimate children? After his death, his unattended corpse became so bloated and swollen that it couldn't fit into its coffin.

Of course, there have been plenty of good Popes, too. One of them was Leo XIII.

One of the longest-serving Popes, Leo XIII was the head of the Catholic Church from 1878 to 1903. He was a forward-thinking intellectual who aimed to reinvigorate Catholicism at a time when many Europeans felt the Church was stuck in the past and had become irrelevant to their day-to-day lives. Leo sought to convince a skeptical world that religion was compatible with modern life. He spoke passionately about many of the same issues that progressive politicians today speak about—fair wages, safe working conditions, and the importance of labor unions. He was a skilled diplomat who succeeded in improving relations with a host of countries, including Russia, Germany, and the United States, and he wholeheartedly embraced science and technology. In fact, he was the first Pope whose voice was recorded on audio, and the first to be filmed by a prototype movie camera (which he blessed while it was filming him).

But he's best known for his amazing productivity. Pope Leo wrote more encyclicals than any other Pope in history. In case you don't know the term (and seriously, why would you?), an encyclical is a letter from the Pope to all the bishops in the Roman Catholic Church. Basically, it's how the Pope announces his official viewpoint on important topics. Encyclicals are deep, thoughtful, and expansive, which means they tend to be pretty darn long. Since the beginning of the Catholic Church, a total of about three hundred encyclicals have been issued—and Leo wrote approximately ninety of them. (That's right, this one guy churned out nearly one-third of all encyclicals ever written.) His encyclicals covered all sorts of topics, from big, overarching concepts such as liberty, marriage, and immigration to eleven letters focused wholly on the subject of rosaries.

Scholars have always been amazed by his prodigious output. Bear in mind he was appointed Pope shortly before his sixty-eighth birthday and served well into his nineties. He was a really old dude—and yet, despite his advanced age, he remained a tireless workhorse the whole time. Where the heck did he find all that energy?

*It was probably the cocaine.*

Popes have always loved wine. Forward thinker that he was, Leo brought something new and edgy to the mix. He drank wine laced with cocaine. At the time, it was an actual product you could buy in grocery stores—the magical elixir known as Vin Mariani, which you might remember from the Queen Victoria chapter.

You see, cocaine wasn't always on the naughty list. Back in the late 1800s, it was brand-new and people were quite high on it (literally). It was neither illegal nor stigmatized, and it was viewed with wonder and awe by the medical establishment.

Cocaine was added to all sorts of products to make them more appealing, including toothache drops, cigarettes, margarine, and especially drinks. If you wanted to create an energy drink in the late nineteenth century, adding a bump of cocaine was the obvious way to go. Each ounce of Vin Mariani contained between 6.5 and 7.2 milligrams of cocaine (meaning up to 200 milligrams of cocaine per bottle). But the beverage was even more potent than it sounds because when cocaine and alcohol combine in a person's liver, they form a new drug called cocaethylene that produces psychoactive effects similar to cocaine—but with even *more* euphoria.

The inventor of the wine, Angelo Mariani, must have been a genius, because 150 years before the invention of Instagram and TikTok, he was already using celebrity influencers to peddle his product. He gave away free bottles of his cocaine wine to any famous person he could find, and it paid off big-time for him. A bunch of famous writers loved his Vin Mariani, including Sir Arthur Conan Doyle, Jules Verne, Alexandre Dumas, Henrik Ibsen, and Robert Louis Stevenson. World leaders loved it, too—everyone from Queen Victoria to the shah of Persia.

Even better, a bunch of these famous folks went public with their support: Emile Zola wrote glowing testimonials that were later reprinted in Vin Mariani advertisements. Thomas Edison said it helped him stay awake longer, and Ulysses S. Grant said he drank it while writing his memoirs. But my personal favorite is Frédéric-Auguste Bartholdi—he was the French sculptor who designed the Statue of Liberty and said if he'd been drinking Vin Mariani at the time, he would've made her several hundred meters taller.

Thanks to his effusive celebrity fan base, Angelo Mariani became the world's first cocaine millionaire. Vin Mariani was seen not only as a health tonic, but as a prestigious and sophisticated beverage on par with fine vintage wine. Advertisements boasted that Vin Mariani was a "veritable scientific fountain of youth" and could cure a host of medical ailments, from brain exhaustion to malaria.

But Pope Leo XIII didn't care about all that. The only thing that mattered to him was the sudden burst of energy he got from Vin Mariani. It was the papal equivalent of Popeye eating a can of spinach—it was the power-up he needed to get the job done. Drinking cocaine wine kept Pope Leo perpetually in the mood to philosophize and pontificate, allowing him to write those ninety encyclicals in twenty-five years.

Leo wasn't shy about professing his love for the stuff. He'd proclaim to anyone who would listen that he carried cocaine wine in a hip flask at all times—"to fortify himself when prayer was insufficient." (Yes, he actually said those words.)

In fact, he loved cocaine wine so much that he decided he needed to honor the man who invented it. He summoned wine-maker Angelo Mariani to Rome and presented him with an official Vatican gold medal for his remarkable achievement in the field of cocaine vintnery.

At this point, you're probably thinking I've gone too far. A coked-out Pope is a funny idea, and maybe there are some dubious rumors scattered around the internet that His Holiness (or, as one writer dubbed him, "His Cokiness") enjoyed the taste of cocaine wine, but surely there's no actual proof he did so—and he certainly didn't hand out a gold medal to his drug dealer. After all, it's not like he appeared in a full-page advertisement touting the benefits of cocaine wine.

Oh, wait, he totally did.

Angelo Mariani printed up posters advertising the gold medal he'd received from the Pope. These ads featured a huge smiling image of Pope Leo, alongside text that stated: *His Holiness the Pope writes that he has fully appreciated the beneficial effects of this Tonic Wine and has forwarded to Mr. Mariani as a token of his gratitude a gold medal bearing his august effigy.*

That's right, the Pope knowingly appeared in a full-page advertisement for cocaine wine.

Things were simpler back then.

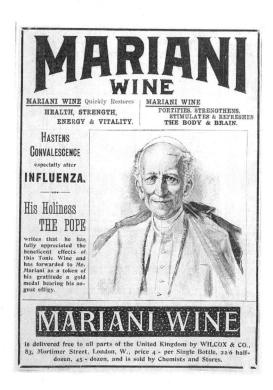

Of course, Vin Mariani didn't stick around forever. Governments around the world finally began noticing that large numbers of their citizens—men, women, and even children—were getting hopelessly addicted to cocaine-infused products. It dawned on them that maybe cocaine wasn't the innocent energy booster they'd originally believed it to be, and they started banning the drug. Angelo Mariani fought these bans for as long as he could, but finally, in 1914, more than ten years after Pope Leo died (at age ninety-three), Vin Mariani was permanently taken off the market.

But there's a happy ending to the story. Angelo Mariani's cocaine wine is directly responsible for the creation of another famous beverage that's still being sold today. Back in its heyday, Vin Mariani was so enormously popular that it inspired copycats. One of these copycats was a man named John Pemberton, who lived in Atlanta, Georgia. He started bottling his own cocaine wine, and he added a new ingredient—caffeine—to give it an even bigger energy boost. He called it Pemberton's French Wine Coca. Unluckily for him, the city of Atlanta and surrounding Fulton County enacted an early version of Prohibition, thirty-four years before the federal government did the same thing, meaning he couldn't sell French Wine Coca anymore because alcohol was now illegal—but cocaine was still perfectly fine!

Pemberton didn't want to give up on his fledgling business, so he swapped out the wine and replaced it with sugar. Then he changed the name of the beverage from French Wine Coca to Coca-Cola. He advertised it as "Coca-Cola: the temperance drink," perfect for everyone who wanted the double boost of energy from caffeine and cocaine—but without all that nasty alcohol. And the rest is soft drink history.

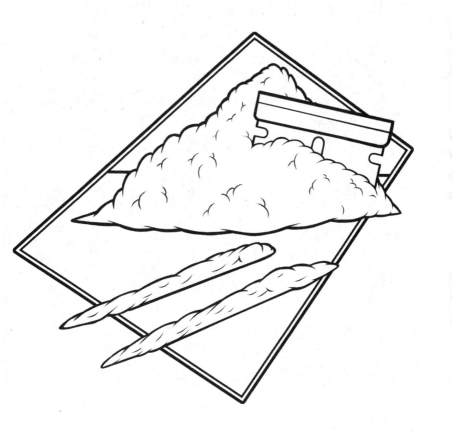

# CHAPTER 15

# Friedrich Nietzsche Thought He Was Jesus

here's a fine line between genius and madness—and self-medicating with chloroform probably isn't the best way to stay on the right side of that line. This is the sad tale of philosopher Friedrich Nietzsche.

He was a wunderkind. At age twenty-four, he was appointed the chair of classical philology at the University of Basel, even though he hadn't yet written a dissertation, taken his final exams, or earned a teaching certificate. His ideas were so groundbreaking that they gave him a doctorate and put him in charge of the entire department.

Nietzsche said human beings created God, not the other way around. He believed God was an artificial construct designed to trick humans into accepting their suffering by telling them they would be rewarded later in a fairy-tale afterlife. He announced, "God is dead," and sought to replace him with his own creation, the Übermensch, a superior man of the future who would bring a new code of ethics that was better than Christianity. Nietzsche also said there was no such thing as objective reality, that truth was a matter of perspective: "There are no facts, only interpretations." His theories were radical and subversive—and made lots of people angry—but it's impossible to deny his influence on modern thought and belief.

Although he was a genius, he flirted with madness from the

very start. His father had died of a brain disease at a young age, and Nietzsche inherited all sorts of strange afflictions of his brain and body. He suffered from crippling migraines, insomnia, dizzy spells, unexplained visual disturbances, and horrible gastric distress. Things only got worse when he served as a volunteer medical orderly in the Prussian military in 1870. Within one month, he contracted three terrible diseases—syphilis, dysentery, and diphtheria. He was never in good health again.

Drugs became a major part of his life. He started using opium to relieve his pain. To treat his insomnia, he chose a drug that he'd learned about as a medical orderly: chloroform. He began using a variant—chloral hydrate (a.k.a. "knockout drops")—to put himself to sleep at night. Essentially, he was chloroforming himself over and over again. He took dangerously high doses of both drugs, opium and chloral hydrate, and it became a vicious cycle. The more drugs he took, the worse his headaches, insomnia, and intestinal pain got, and he responded by taking even more drugs. Finally, in 1879, his health deteriorated to the point where it became impossible for him to continue teaching at the university.

He became a wandering scholar, roaming from city to city. Living off a small pension and money borrowed from friends, he drifted aimlessly for ten years, spending a few months here and a few months there. He no longer had a home. He'd renounced his Prussian citizenship because he believed no one should owe loyalty to a specific nation-state, so he remained stateless for the rest of his life, living as a nomad who wandered the globe.

He cut ties with countless people and organizations, usually because he disagreed with their beliefs. He broke with Richard Wagner because the famous composer pandered to German nationalism, and Nietzsche couldn't abide nationalism. He also broke with his longtime book publisher because he was disgusted by the man's anti-Semitism. This meant he no longer had a financial backer for his books, so he had to pay out of his own pocket to publish his later works.

Most significant, Nietzsche had a huge rift with his sister, Elisabeth. When she got engaged to an anti-Semitic agitator in 1885, he flat-out refused to attend the wedding. He despised anti-Semitism and was never one to hide what he was thinking. When the newly married couple announced they were traveling to Paraguay to start a "pure-blooded" Aryan utopia called New Germany, Nietzsche openly mocked the idea. (Elisabeth would ultimately have the last laugh, but we'll get to that in a minute.)

Despite being a homeless nomad who was half blind and in nearly constant pain, he remained a genius. He published a new book almost every year for the next decade, including his four-part masterpiece, *Thus Spake Zarathustra*. However, due to excessive drug use and his continually deteriorating mental and physical condition, the quality of his work was wildly inconsistent. Some of the books were great; others not so much. He had occasional bursts of manic energy in which he did tons of writing, but many of his works remained unfinished.

One reason his condition kept deteriorating was that he was self-medicating. Nietzsche had a doctorate but wasn't a medical doctor—yet he was writing prescriptions for himself and signing them as "Dr. Nietzsche." He was living in Italy at the time, and the pharmacies didn't bother to question his qualifications. This allowed him to ingest obscene amounts of opium and chloral hydrate, far more than any sane physician would permit.

Nietzsche suffered a full-scale mental breakdown on January 3, 1889. While wandering the streets of Turin, he witnessed a horse being whipped by its owner and was so horrified by the wanton cruelty that he ran up to the horse, threw his arms around its neck to shield it from harm, began to sob uncontrollably, and then collapsed to the ground in an almost vegetative state.

He was placed in a mental asylum. He had become psychotic and utterly detached from reality. At times, he was convinced he was Jesus Christ. At other times, he thought he was the Greek god Dionysus—and sometimes he was Buddha. How do we know what he was thinking? Because he put it in writing. From his locked room in the asylum, he wrote a series of deranged letters to his few remaining friends.

They are known as the Madness Letters. In one, he proclaimed that he (Jesus) had returned to earth, jailed the Pope, and ordered the execution of the German rulers. Translated into English, his letter to Fräulein von Salis reads: "The world is transfigured, for God is on the earth. Do you not see how all the heavens rejoice? I have just now taken possession of my kingdom, am casting the Pope into prison, and am having Wilhelm, Bismarck, and Stocker shot. Signed, The Crucified."

In several other letters, he claimed to be Dionysus, the god of wine and pleasure. For example, he wrote to one friend: "I come as the victorious Dionysus, who will make the earth a festival."

In what might be the strangest of the letters, he lists all the numerous historical figures that he believed he had become: "Among the Hindus I was Buddha, in Greece Dionysus—Alexander and Caesar were incarnations of me, as well as the poet of Shakespeare, Lord Bacon. Most recently I was Voltaire and Napoleon, perhaps also Richard Wagner . . . I was also hung on the cross."

No one was able to pinpoint the exact cause of his derangement. Some believed he was in the advanced stages of syphilis, which can cause insanity; others suspected a brain tumor. Without knowing the true cause, it was impossible for doctors to help him—and his long-term abuse of opium and chloral hydrate only made the situation more confusing. Ultimately, he was released to the care of his mother, but by that point, his mind was in tatters.

He spent the last ten years of his life as a madman. His genius had vanished entirely. All that remained was his reputation—but he soon lost that as well. When his mother died in 1897, he was transferred to the care of his sister, Elisabeth. As you recall, she and her anti-Semitic husband had pinned their hopes on building an Aryan utopia in Paraguay. Shockingly, that gambit failed, and her husband committed suicide. Sad and embittered, Elisabeth blamed her brother for all the unhappiness in her life—and now she was becoming his sole caretaker.

That's when she exacted her revenge. Remember all those works that Nietzsche began writing during his nomadic years but never completed? She finished them for him—but not in any way that he would have approved of. She diabolically cut, pasted, rewrote, and forged his work, so it appeared to promote her own ultra-nationalist agenda and the horrifying anti-Semitic beliefs of her dead husband.

Nietzsche died in 1900, but his sister outlived him by thirty-five years. She used those years to radically twist his words and undermine his legacy. Despite the fact that Nietzsche hated nationalism and anti-Semitism, his sister's malevolent rewriting of his works led to his being embraced as the muse and intellectual mouthpiece of the Nazi Party in the 1930s and '40s. It took many years before scholars finally uncovered the fact that his writings had been faked by Elisabeth. By then, however, the damage was done; it was impossible to put the genie back in the bottle. Even today, many people continue to believe that Nietzsche was a raging anti-Semite.

Genius and madness are two sides of the same coin. If Nietzsche had left it to chance, his story would have had an equal possibility of ending happily or unhappily. But when he made the decision to write his own fake prescriptions for opium and chloral hydrate, he put his thumb on the wrong side of the scale.

# CHAPTER 16

# Vincent van Gogh Ate Yellow Paint

Plenty of people know that Vincent van Gogh loved the color yellow—but did you know he loved it so much that he ate yellow paint? Questions about Van Gogh eating paint come up so often that the subject is addressed head-on in the FAQ page of the official Van Gogh Museum website. Some people believe the artist ate yellow paint because he thought it would make him more cheerful. Others, including Van Gogh's psychiatrist, believed he ate paint because he was trying to kill himself. The truth is more elusive—even Van Gogh didn't know why he ate paint. He wrote in a letter to his brother, "It appears that I pick up filthy things and eat them, although my memories of these bad moments are vague." So what's the real reason—why the heck did Van Gogh eat yellow paint?

Scientists now believe he had a biochemical craving for something called terpenes. To put it simply, terpenes are chemical building blocks found in nature, most often in plants. They give plants their distinctive aromas. Why do roses smell different from pine needles? That's terpenes, baby! Cannabis enthusiasts might be familiar with the term because terpenes are what produce the wide variety of aromas found across different strains of weed.

But here's the thing: terpenes are pretty potent, so they're usually found in very small concentrations. It doesn't take a ton of terpenes to give a plant its distinctive scent. It's like when you put on perfume or cologne—a little spritz of musk might draw people toward you, but if you use too much, their eyes are going to start watering and you'll end up driving them away. Van Gogh had a strong nose for terpenes and sought them out relentlessly. But the twist is, he didn't do it consciously. He had no idea what terpenes were or why he was drawn to them—he only knew that he wanted them.

That's why he drank absinthe. Absinthe is a froufrou alcoholic beverage derived from wormwood and other plants. It's emerald green in color, smells pungently woodsy, and contains a terrifyingly high concentration of liquor. Nicknamed "the green fairy," it typically clocks in at 60-something percent alcohol by volume. Absinthe is supposed to be heavily diluted before you drink it—in fact, there's a whole stylized ritual you're supposed to follow: First, you pour a shot of absinthe into a glass. Then you lay a slotted spoon across the top of the glass and gently place a sugar cube into the spoon. Then you drizzle ice-cold water onto the sugar cube—this dissolves the sugar, and the sugar-water solution drips through the slots in the spoon and mixes with the absinthe. This imbues the liquid with a foggy green murk, and that's when you drink it. Not pretentious at all, right?

Absinthe was super popular in France in the late 1800s, when Van Gogh lived there. When it was originally developed, absinthe was regarded as the drink of the intelligentsia and was consumed mostly by highbrow artist types. But in the 1880s, a disease infected the French vineyards, making wine ultra-expensive and absinthe a cheaper alternative, so absinthe quickly became the preferred beverage for the poor and downtrodden. This was ideal for Van Gogh because he was both a highbrow artist type *and* extremely poor and downtrodden. He craved the terpenes in absinthe and thus drank an insane amount of the stuff, far more than any human should. Unfortunately, while absinthe contains a ferocious amount of alcohol, it contains only a tiny amount of terpenes, so absinthe alone wasn't sufficient to satisfy his terpene-related cravings.

He got the rest of his terpenes from even less salubrious sources. Some terpenes get processed into consumer products, such as perfumes, pesticides, and cleaning solvents. Obviously, this stuff isn't meant to be eaten, but that didn't stop Van Gogh. It's a psychiatric condition known as pica—the unnatural compulsion to consume nonfood objects. Van Gogh was a painter, so his studio was equipped with a wide selection of art supplies that were positively teeming with terpenes, such as paint and turpentine. In fact, the word "terpene" is derived from an old, now-disused spelling of "turpentine." The good news for Van Gogh was that paint and turpentine contain lots of terpenes; the bad news was they are highly poisonous and ingesting them causes brain damage.

Consuming too many terpenes causes mood swings, seizures, blackouts, hallucinations, and all sorts of psychotic behavior. No sane person would choose to suffer these dire consequences, so why did Van Gogh keep doing this to himself? Well, as you've probably guessed by now, someone who is eating paint and drinking turpentine might not be a paragon of rational thinking. Van Gogh made a host of poor life decisions—he smoked too much, drank too much, and visited brothels all too frequently, exposing himself to a cornucopia of sexually transmitted diseases, including syphilis, which can cause brain damage. On top of his already über-unhealthy lifestyle, he was eating paint that contained high levels of lead and other toxins, and drinking an industrial-grade solvent used to thin and strip paint. Things were not going to end well for this man.

Pica wasn't Van Gogh's only mental disorder. Doctors have spent decades trying to diagnose the exact nature of his mental illness. There are dozens of different theories, including epilepsy, schizophrenia, bipolar disorder, syphilis, borderline personality disorder, cycloid psychosis, delirium tremens, manic-depressive disorder, even sunstroke—but his exact pathology remains unknown. Clearly, he had some sort of episodic psychotic disorder, meaning he experienced fits of madness during which he behaved in unpredictable and dangerous ways. It became a recurring pattern in Van Gogh's life: he would black out and do something horrible; then, when he finally started recording memory again, people would stare in horror at him, but he'd have absolutely no clue what he had done.

The most notorious example is the time he sliced off his left ear. Everyone knows Van Gogh cut off his ear in a fit of rage, but do you know what crazy thing he did after cutting it off? He went to the brothel he frequented to deliver the lopped-off ear as a gift to an underage maid named Gabrielle, who was responsible for cleaning the rooms at the brothel. Of course, when he was later questioned at the hospital, Van Gogh didn't remember anything about the event. Quite memorably, though, he painted a bunch of self-portraits that depicted bandages wrapped around his head, covering his now-missing ear.

As a result of his increasingly self-destructive behavior, Van Gogh realized he couldn't live independently. He had himself committed to a mental institution, and it was definitely the right move, because just before he entered the asylum, he had to be restrained from drinking a quart of turpentine directly from the bottle. He moved into the asylum on May 8, 1889, at age thirty-six, a few months after the infamous ear-cutting incident, with his wound still healing and his neighbors still terrified of him. He remained there for slightly more than a year, and the asylum and its gardens became the subject of most of the paintings he created during that time. Notably, it was during his stay at the asylum that he painted

*Starry Night*—one of his most famous and beloved works. For the most part, life in the institution provided him with peace and stability, and because his commitment was voluntary, he was occasionally permitted to paint outside the grounds and to travel to Brussels and Paris for art shows.

Unfortunately, one year after checking into the asylum, Van Gogh changed his mind, said he felt trapped, and insisted he needed to live independently. The asylum allowed him to leave (since he was there voluntarily) and he moved to a small village north of Paris, where he planned to reside in the country, paint all day, and live happily. As a safeguard, a sympathetic doctor named Paul Gachet, who lived nearby, agreed to keep an eye on him. However, Gachet's occasional supervision was entirely ineffective at dealing with Van Gogh's unpredictable bursts of insanity. Everything seemed to be going well for Van Gogh in the village—but on July 27, 1890, only two months after he left the asylum, he was struck by another fit of madness. This time he shot himself in the belly with a revolver. Even though he missed his vital organs and received medical care soon after, it wasn't enough to save him. The injury site became infected, and he died two days later. His final words were: "The sadness will last forever."

Today, Van Gogh is regarded as one of the most talented artists who ever lived, and his paintings are worth hundreds of millions of dollars. During his lifetime, however, he experienced almost no success. He was a madman who died broke and unappreciated, saying in a letter to his brother: "I can't change the fact that my paintings don't sell."

Maybe if he'd lived longer, he would have eventually found fame, and possibly even a small degree of happiness. But it wasn't to be. The weight of his insanity was too heavy to bear; he simply couldn't escape his fits of madness and self-harm. Even in modern times, it would be challenging to treat someone like Van Gogh, but at least there would be medications and therapies that might give him some degree of control over his actions. But in the time period in which he lived, there was no way for doctors to give him what he most desperately wanted—a peaceful life in the French countryside, where he could paint and feel happy.

# CHAPTER 17

# Sigmund Freud Was Wrong About Cocaine

Sigmund Freud was massively wrong about cocaine. In 1884, he was a nervous, obsessive-compulsive twenty-eight-year-old research assistant at the University of Vienna, eager to make a name for himself in the burgeoning field of neuroscience. He'd heard tales of a new drug that had been discovered in the Andes Mountains of South America. Indigenous people living there had been chewing on coca leaves for a thousand years, and it appeared to supply them with unlimited energy and endurance. Drug companies had now extracted the effective ingredient from coca leaves, had refined it, and were selling it under the name "cocaine hydrochloride."

Freud was salivating at the possibilities. This might be the big break he'd been hoping for. He wrote to one of the drug companies and explained he was interested in learning more about their product. The company sent him a few free samples of cocaine and—as a selfless man of pure science—Freud decided he must try some for himself.

He fell in love with it right away. He took cocaine orally at first, dissolving the powder in water. He wrote in a letter to his fiancée, "A small dose lifted me to the heights in a wonderful fashion." Soon, he began taking it nasally (i.e., putting it up his nose), because the nostrils are lined with mucous membranes, which makes the effects of the cocaine even more intense.

Freud was convinced his groundbreaking work with cocaine would make him famous. He was going to be single-handedly responsible for introducing this miraculous new drug to the medical establishment of Europe. But first, he needed to get his hands on everything that had been written on the subject and become the world's foremost expert on cocaine. He explained to his fiancée, "I am just now busy collecting the literature for a song of praise to this magical substance."

In July 1884, he published *Über Coca*. It was his first major scientific publication and it was focused entirely on the glory of cocaine. He described feeling "a most gorgeous excitement" upon first consuming it, which soon transformed into "exhilaration and lasting euphoria." It was the perfect drug for a hardworking scientist because it "wards off hunger, sleep, and fatigue and steels one to intellectual effort." Freud praised cocaine as a "miracle cure" that could be used to treat a multitude of maladies—everything from indigestion and flatulence to seasickness and impotence.

But he missed a big one. Freud somehow failed to notice that cocaine was a super-effective anesthetic—the only use for which it is still approved today. Only a few months after Freud published *Über Coca*, one of his colleagues who worked at the same hospital, a young ophthalmologist named Carl Koller, presented a paper about cocaine's value as an anesthetic for eye surgery. Koller immediately received international acclaim for his discovery—and Freud was devastated. He fell into a deep depression and the only thing that could lift him out of it was—well, you guessed it: more cocaine.

Freud was using cocaine almost constantly at this point. As a scientist, he understood what mattered most wasn't the size of the dose but rather the frequency. His favorite trick was to overlap doses. Every time the effect of one dose began to fade ever so slightly from its peak, he would consume another dose to make sure he was always getting the maximum effect. It's a scientific technique known as titration, and if done correctly, it meant he would always be high and never crash.

Freud was still dead set on becoming famous. He decided the best way to accomplish that was to expose even more people to the wonders of cocaine. He gave small bags of the powder to his friends and began dispensing it to his patients. He knew in his heart that once people had experienced firsthand the benefits of this amazing drug, they would understand how truly miraculous and life-changing it was.

He proclaimed to the world that cocaine was safe and nonaddictive. "Even repeated doses of coca produce no compulsive desire to use the stimulant further," he wrote. Because it was so safe, he believed it was the perfect way to cure people who were addicted to dangerous narcotics, such as morphine. Simply swap out the morphine for cocaine; get the patient accustomed to taking this new, much safer drug instead; then discontinue the cocaine—which the patient would be totally fine with, because cocaine isn't addictive.

Freud was so confident in his I'll-use-cocaine-to-replace-morphine-because-I'm-a-genius theory that he experimented on one of his closest friends, Ernst von Fleischl-Marxow. Ernst had long been addicted to morphine, but Freud swore he could wean him off it within a matter of weeks. After twenty-one days of cocaine therapy, Freud happily announced that his friend was cured. Of course, Ernst was not cured at all. He'd become hopelessly addicted to cocaine. He was spending huge sums to purchase the drug, then injecting it directly into his veins and telling Freud that he felt like snakes were crawling under his skin. Ernst was dead by age forty-five.

Freud remained stubbornly convinced that cocaine could cure almost anything. One of his female patients was experiencing painful menstrual cramps, and Freud thought to himself: "I know how to fix this." Like some doctors of the time, he believed the nose was a microcosm of the entire body, which meant almost any malady could be cured if you applied medicine to the proper spot in a person's nostrils. Accordingly, Freud treated the woman's menstrual pain by packing her nose with pure cocaine. To the surprise of absolutely no one, the cocaine burned through her nasal tissue and caused one side of her face to collapse in on itself.

The universe was clearly trying to send a message to Freud to knock it off with all the cocaine—but he still didn't get it. Despite all the evidence to the contrary, he remained utterly confident that cocaine was great stuff. How could he be so blind, you might ask? *Because he was on freaking cocaine!*

As much as I enjoy mocking Freud—and, trust me, I enjoy it a lot—I admit that he transformed what people know about the human mind. Before he came along, scientists believed synapses firing in the brain and tiny neurotransmitters carrying chemical messages from one neuron to another were responsible for determining whether a person was happy or unhappy. There was a competing school of thought that said everything a person felt was a fairly obvious manifestation of their hopes, fears, and desires—so, if you sat back and did even a little bit of introspection, you'd pretty quickly be able to figure out exactly what was motivating your behavior.

Freud pointed out (correctly) that both theories were inadequate. He announced there was an unconscious mind at work, and a person's behavior is shaped by important events from their childhood of which they often remain wholly unaware. Only by engaging in exhaustive psychoanalysis can these buried memories be brought to the surface and confronted head-on, thereby allowing the patient to process these traumatic events from their childhood in a healthy, productive way, so the past will finally release its grip on them.

So, yes, Freud is the father of psychoanalysis, I'll give him that. But here's the funny part: he believed cocaine was essential to psychotherapy. That's because psychotherapy is a "talking cure"—and nothing gets people talking like cocaine. Freud wanted his patients to say everything that popped into their heads—free association, random memories, pointless rambling, anything they could think of—without holding back due to feelings of guilt or shame. But most people won't do that. There's a natural tendency to filter what you say, to avoid being judged. But when Freud gave his patients cocaine, that filter was magically removed. It loosened their tongues and unlocked their minds. Once he gave them cocaine, he couldn't shut them up.

Ultimately, Freud got what he wanted—today, he is a household name. Terminology that he invented has become part of everyday conversation. People regularly throw around terms like "wish fulfillment," "defense mechanism," "libido," "repression," and "denial," and everyone pretty much understands what they mean.

Sure, a few of his theories have attracted a bit of skepticism over the years, and maybe even some snickering (I'm talking about you, penis envy). But there is no denying the impact that Freud's theories have had on Western thought. At the same time, there's no denying the impact that cocaine had on Freud.

He might be the "father" of psychoanalysis—but cocaine was Father's little helper. He used cocaine ultra-aggressively for twelve years, but it wasn't until 1895 that he finally admitted to himself that he'd become addicted. "I need a lot of cocaine," he wrote to a friend. He had been taking larger and larger doses over the years, and more than once, the membranes in his nose had become so inflamed and congested that a surgeon had to use a heated blade to open up his nasal passages so he could breathe.

He finally stopped using cocaine in 1896. But up until then, he was the world's biggest cheerleader for the drug, ever since he published *Über Coca* in 1884. For more than a decade, he had been proselytizing others to try his wonder drug, and he succeeded in converting a huge number of people into cokeheads. In the words of an author who has traced the entire three-thousand-year history of cocaine, from Indigenous tribes in the Andes Mountains to large-scale drug traffickers in Colombia: "If there is one person who can be held responsible for the emergence of cocaine as a recreational pharmaceutical, it was Freud."

Sigmund Freud was a really bad doctor.

# PART 5

# WARTIME FOGGINESS

# CHAPTER 18

# Adolf Hitler Was Tweaked out of His Mind

---

veryone knows that Adolf Hitler was one of the worst mass murderers of all time, but not everyone knows the role that drugs played in fueling his genocidal viciousness and hunger for world domination.

Long before he became "der Führer," Hitler was a low-level infantryman in World War I. He was a loner. During the lulls between battles, other soldiers would huddle together to tell stories, complain about the food, or talk about women. But not Hitler; he'd sit alone, reading a book or painting a landscape with his watercolors. The other soldiers in his unit regarded him as a little odd but overall not a bad guy. It's like when someone turns out to be a serial killer and the neighbors say, "Gee, I never would have guessed. He was so quiet and kept to himself."

But when a battle started, Hitler's personality transformed. He was no longer meek and quiet. He became insanely zealous, volunteering for all the most dangerous assignments. He was a dispatch runner on the front lines in 1914, carrying instructions from headquarters to the units taking heavy fire. He was running unprotected from bunker to bunker, completely exposed, with bombs exploding all around him and enemy soldiers shooting at him.

Of course, it's entirely possible these reports of Hitler's behavior in World War I are German propaganda—that his bravery has been wildly exaggerated to make him appear more heroic than he actually was. However, there is also an extremely plausible one-word explanation for why Hitler might have acted so fearlessly in the face of danger: *cocaine.*

The German military passed out cocaine like candy at Halloween. It was a stimulant for the troops, viewed as no more dangerous than tobacco. It was routinely included in the soldiers' rations to keep them awake and alert during long nights on watch, to suppress their pain and hunger, and most important, to fuel their fighting spirit. In the early 1900s, cocaine wasn't regarded as dangerous or addictive; it was simply a tool to help make a soldier's job easier.

Hitler absolutely loved the stuff. The rush he got from cocaine made him feel vital and invulnerable. He would get cranked up on the drug and run headfirst toward the front lines. Sure, he got shot at constantly, was exposed to poison gas attacks, and narrowly avoided death dozens of times. But fear and pain were nothing to him when he was blitzed on cocaine. He took part in some of the fiercest battles of the war—including one in which almost his entire regiment was wiped out—but he was coked out of his mind and loved every minute. He described his time in World War I as "the greatest of all experiences."

Twenty years later, when World War II began, cocaine had fallen out of favor. It was now dismissed by the German government as "degenerate poison." The German military had a new drug of choice: crystal meth. I'm not making this up. The Nazis claimed to be antidrug, but they made a special exception for methamphetamine because it fit nicely with their deluded belief in their own superiority. On meth, their soldiers were stronger, faster, hypervigilant, and didn't need to eat or sleep—they were practically superhuman.

The brand name was Pervitin. It was being sold as an energy pill over the counter in pharmacies, no prescription necessary, and it was wildly popular. The German high command added Pervitin to the soldiers' daily rations, sometimes in pill form, but also embedded in chocolate bars. We aren't talking about individual soldiers popping pills in secret; this was a systematic doping of an entire army by its government. The Nazis' goal was to create chemically enhanced supersoldiers. When Germany invaded France in May 1940, they used a "blitzkrieg" strategy—the army doled out thirty-five million Pervitin pills and ordered the troops to stay awake and constantly moving for three days and three nights. Thanks to the Pervitin, sleep was no longer needed and their plan worked. The Nazis succeeded in capturing more territory in one hundred hours than they had during the entire four-year span of World War I. Altogether, between 1939 and 1945, German soldiers consumed more than two hundred million of these miracle meth pills.

If crystal meth was good enough for the troops, it was certainly good enough for their drug-fueled Führer. There is footage of Hitler at the 1936 Olympics, rocking faster and faster in his chair as if he'll explode if he doesn't keep moving. This is classic tweaker behavior—he's visibly cranked up on something very strong, and the obvious culprit is meth. Ernst-Günther Schenck, who was formerly Heinrich Himmler's "nutrition adviser," confirmed that Hitler was a big fan of Pervitin and gulped down the pills on a regular basis.

But unlike his soldiers, Hitler wasn't limited only to meth. He took all sorts of additional drugs. He wanted to feel virile and full of energy at all times, so in 1936, he hired Dr. Theodor Morell as his personal physician. Morell was a shady celebrity doctor who specialized in giving what he euphemistically called "vitamin shots," but his injections contained a great deal more than vitamins—they also contained, at various times, steroids, testosterone, veterinary stimulants, sex hormones, and substances derived from bull testicles, bull prostates, and bull semen-producing glands. In other words, Hitler was doping. Soon, he was getting multiple injections every day, and before every speech he got an additional "power injection" to give him a little extra oomph. That's why video footage of Hitler's speeches shows him with his cheeks flushed, screaming, gesticulating wildly, slamming down his fists, looking like a bomb ready to explode.

He added even more drugs as time went on. In 1941, it was opioids. He got sick one day and missed a briefing, which he deemed unacceptable—he couldn't afford to show the slightest bit of weakness. He ordered his doctor to give him something to make him feel better instantly. Dr. Morell gave him an opiate called Dolantin, which immediately perked him up, causing Hitler to tell the doctor (and I'm paraphrasing now), "Wow, that's good shit, we're definitely keeping that in the rotation." Two years later, in 1943, Dr. Morell upgraded to an even stronger opioid with the brand name Eukodal—but you probably know it by its generic name: oxycodone. Hitler became an enormous oxycodone enthusiast.

A year later, he incorporated yet another powerful pharmaceutical—his old buddy cocaine. In July 1944, Wehrmacht officers tried to assassinate Hitler with an exploding briefcase—it was called Operation Valkyrie. Hitler was only slightly injured, except that both his eardrums burst. To treat his ear pain, he summoned an ENT doctor, who administered cocaine nose swabs. Hitler loved the feeling so much that he got fifty cocaine swabs in seventy-five days. When he expressed some mild fear of becoming addicted, his doctor reassured him (again, I'm paraphrasing): "Don't worry, dude, you only get addicted if you snort dry cocaine, but I'm applying a liquid cocaine solution directly to your mucous membranes, where it's absorbed directly into your bloodstream, so you're totally fine." Hitler was ecstatic.

Hitler was so astronomically high that when the Germans

started losing the war, he didn't know it. In 1943, the Nazis were losing battle after battle, the Allies were advancing from the west, and the Russians were blazing a path of destruction through the east. Yet Hitler remained massively confident the whole time. His top generals began to wonder if he knew something they didn't know—did he have a secret weapon he hadn't told them about? Nope, it was just the unholy trinity of meth, oxy, and cocaine that he was pouring nonstop into his body. He was stuck in a fantasy dream world where everything was going his way. He'd lost the ability to understand what was happening in reality.

Meanwhile, the Nazis were trying to convince the world that Hitler was a teetotaler. It had been true for a while, many years earlier, but certainly wasn't anymore. Norman Ohler explains in his illuminating book *Blitzed: Drugs in the Third Reich*, "It was an important part of Nazi propaganda to merge Hitler's body with the body of the German people, and to show that body was healthy and pure." So, the Nazi propaganda machine worked overtime to cover up Hitler's drug use. They insisted he did not drink, only ate vegetables, and did not permit any toxins to enter his body, not even coffee. In reality, however, der Führer was a total junkie. Dr. Morell's records show he gave his patient more than a thousand injections in the final eight hundred days of the war. Hitler's arms were literally covered in track marks.

Everything came crashing down at the end of 1944. British warplanes started bombing the crap out of the factories that manufactured Hitler's drugs. By New Year's Day in 1945, it became impossible for Dr. Morell to obtain new supplies of meth, oxycodone, and cocaine—which meant Hitler couldn't get his fix. He shouted at his doctor to give him drugs, but with the factories all but wiped out, there simply weren't any drugs to give him.

Hitler went through withdrawal, and it was brutal. He was rambling, incoherent, often delusional, and his body wouldn't stop shaking. Even worse, his blinders had been removed. With the drugs gone, he'd been yanked out of his fantasy dreamworld in which Germany was winning the war. The truth hit him like a brick—the Third Reich had lost. This sudden realization caused him intense pain; he felt like every last piece of him was being utterly demolished.

That's when he issued the so-called Nero Decree. He ordered the complete destruction of Germany—all roads, bridges, canals, harbors, infrastructure, landmarks, financial institutions, cultural monuments, everything. He wanted it all blown to hell, a scorched-earth policy, leaving nothing behind for the invaders. To quote Norman Ohler in *Blitzed*: "He wanted to raze Germany to the ground like he was being razed."

As his enemies closed in on him from all sides, Hitler finally reached his breaking point. If it had been possible to do so, he would have taken an overdose to ease his way out. But with no drugs available, he was forced to use a bullet instead. He retreated into his bunker and shot himself in the head.

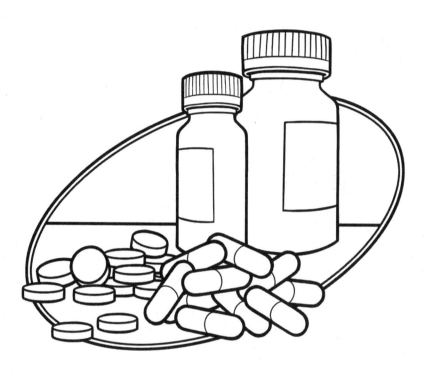

# CHAPTER 19

# Bill W. Took LSD to See God

The story of how Alcoholics Anonymous got started is absolutely insane. You probably think the guy who started AA must have been a doctor, psychologist, scientist, or something like that, given that he created a treatment program that's been used by tens of millions of people—but he wasn't. AA was born out of one man's drugged-out vision of God.

Bill Griffith Wilson (known more commonly as "Bill W.") was an average Joe who, like many of us, struggled with depression and anxiety. He dropped out of military college due to a series of panic attacks, but in 1915, when the United States sent troops to Mexico to hunt down Pancho Villa, the army desperately needed manpower, so they reinstated him. Many of his classmates liked to go out carousing at night, but Bill's crippling social anxiety kept him from joining in the fun—until he took a drink for the first time.

He'd always steered clear of alcohol, afraid of what it might do to him. But when one of his peers suddenly thrust a drink into his hand, he felt too self-conscious to say no. He gulped it down, and said later it was like flipping a switch: "Then, lo, the miracle! That strange barrier that had existed between me and all men and women seemed to instantly go down. I felt that I belonged where I was, belonged to life; I belonged to the universe; I was a part of things at last. . . . I became the life of the party."

Chasing that feeling consumed his whole life. He tried attending law school but didn't graduate because he was too drunk to take his final exam. He tried his luck in the stock market and demonstrated real skill as a securities analyst—but he was falling-down drunk most of the time. His Wall Street buddies were willing to put up with it as long as he was making money for them, but when the stock market crashed in 1929, they cast him out into the wilderness. He became a full-time alcoholic, despairing and despondent. By 1933, Bill was drinking half a gallon of cheap rotgut whiskey a day, he had no job and no friends, and his wife was pleading with him to get help.

Towns Hospital in Manhattan specialized in treating alcohol addiction. Bill checked in three different times but always ended up drinking again. The fourth time he checked in, the doctor in charge knew he had to try something different. Dr. William "Silky" Silkworth was ahead of his time in one way—he understood alcoholism was a medical condition, not a moral failing, which was pretty damn progressive for 1934. But in other ways, Silky was horrendously backward, because the treatment he prescribed for Bill was deeply deranged.

It was called the Belladonna Cure. He drugged Bill with powerful hypnotics (chloral hydrate and morphine) to plunge him into a trancelike stupor. Then, every hour, attendants would wake Bill up and force him to drink a scary blue solution that contained actual poison (belladonna, also known as deadly nightshade) and a deliriant called "insane root." Bill was required to drink this noxious concoction every hour *for fifty consecutive hours*—and, as if that weren't bad enough, they also gave him a small amount of strychnine (i.e., rat poison) every four hours. The entire purpose of the

Belladonna Cure was to make the patient so violently ill that he would "puke and purge" all the toxins out of his body.

Silkworth claimed his Belladonna Cure had a 90 percent success rate—but what that really meant was nine out of ten patients who'd endured the horrible experience never came back to see him again. (Thanks for nothing, doc!) So, at his mad doctor's orders, Bill spent the next fifty hours vomiting, defecating, and hallucinating—not knowing whether he was awake or asleep, alive or dead. It was hell on earth.

But then something incredible happened. In the midst of his drug-induced delirium, Bill had a divine revelation. In agonizing pain and despair, he shouted to the heavens: "I'll do anything! Anything at all! If there be a God, let Him show Himself." Suddenly, a blinding light filled the room and he felt a wave of ecstatic euphoria. From that moment on, he knew with absolute certainty there was a higher power in the universe that could save him from his addiction, and he never took another drink for the rest of his life.

This experience was the impetus for Bill to create AA—not the Belladonna Cure (that would be crazy, and probably illegal), but rather the mystical-higher-power part. In 1935, a few months after checking out of Towns Hospital, Bill met Dr. Bob, a Dartmouth-educated surgeon, and together they started Alcoholics Anonymous. It was built on the premise that people can free themselves from alcoholism if they admit they are powerless over their addiction and turn over their lives to a higher power.

But there's a threshold issue—not everyone believes in a higher power. Many alcoholics try to follow the Twelve Steps, but when it comes to the "higher power" mumbo jumbo, they just don't get it. They're going through the motions, but they don't actually feel a connection to a force greater than themselves—heck, even Bill didn't feel that connection until he drank poison for fifty hours straight.

Bill understood this was a problem. He wanted to help his members have a spiritual experience so AA could work for them. But how to do it? After twenty years, he finally came up with a really bizarre solution: LSD.

LSD was legal in the early 1950s. It was new on the scene, and doctors, scientists, and philosophers were excited by its possibilities. When someone suggested that maybe LSD could be used to treat alcoholics, Bill at first dismissed the idea—he wasn't going to ask AA members to substitute one addiction for another. But when he tried LSD for himself in 1956, under medical supervision at the Los Angeles Veterans Administration hospital, his skepticism disappeared. This stuff was awesome!

Bill said the spiritual experience LSD triggered in him was a "dead ringer" for the one he had experienced with the Belladonna Cure—which meant LSD might be the key to making AA work for everyone. For atheists and cynics who didn't believe in God, taking LSD would awaken them to the supernatural mysteries of the universe.

When AA's board of trustees heard rumblings about Bill talking up the benefits of LSD, they were pissed off. They were an organization whose whole mission was to cure addicts—they couldn't start handing out drugs; the idea was insane. Now it was Bill's turn to get angry—he'd already stepped down as the head of AA specifically because he wanted the freedom to explore psychedelics on his own time, so how dare the board of trustees stick their noses in his personal business. In a strongly worded letter in 1958, Bill wrote: "The public today is being led to believe that LSD is a new psychiatric toy of awful dangers. It induces schizophrenia, they say. Nothing could be further from the truth. . . . The cases have been studied from the biochemical, psychiatric, and spiritual aspects. Again, no record of any harm, no tendency to addiction. They have also found that there is no physical risk whatsoever. The material is about as harmless as aspirin."

What happened next is unclear: AA's official position is that Bill "gracefully" decided to walk away from his LSD experiments in 1959. But c'mon, really? This guy was all in for acid. Did he stop taking it—or did he just stop talking about it? More important, without LSD (or something like it), does AA still work?

The answer seems to be no. Sure, there's plenty of anecdotal evidence that AA has helped people, but there's also plenty of anecdotal evidence going the other way—how many times have you scrolled through entertainment news on your phone and seen TMZ reporting on yet another celebrity fresh out of rehab who's gone on a bender? The problem is, there's no hard data to look at because AA chapters operate independently, they don't keep records of who attends their meetings, and everyone is anonymous. But a retired Harvard psychiatry professor crunched all the data he was able to gather and concluded that AA's actual success rate is extremely low, probably only 5 to 8 percent.

How does that compare to other treatments? Not so well, it turns out. A comprehensive 2003 study ranked treatment methods according to their effectiveness, and AA finished thirty-eighth out of forty-eight. That means thirty-seven other approaches were more effective than AA. Cognitive behavioral therapy was one of them, and another was a medication called naltrexone, which blocks the brain receptors that derive pleasure from drinking—so you can drink, but it won't make you feel good. Plus, there are more aggressive medicines that actually make you feel nauseated if you take a drink. Controlled laboratory studies have proven that each of these approaches actually works.

The bottom line is, AA offers a support structure that helps many people—but it's not real medicine. Bill Wilson understood alcoholism was a medical condition, so it might actually require a medical solution. He thought LSD might be the answer. Maybe if he were alive today, Bill would think the answer was naltrexone, or one of the three dozen other treatment methods that have proven more effective than AA. But given that addiction is a disease, it's probably time to start treating it like one.

# CHAPTER 20

# Jean-Paul Sartre's Really Long Bad Trip

Jean-Paul Sartre took a massive amount of drugs every single day. He had all these ideas he wanted to share with the world, and he'd pop amphetamines like crazy so he could write nonstop, without any breaks. When he finished writing for the day, he was too revved up to sleep, so he'd swallow barbiturates to knock himself out. When he woke up the next day, his brain was still foggy from the barbiturates, so he'd pop even more amphetamines to cut through the fog so he could start writing again. On top of all that, he consumed tons of alcohol, caffeine, and nicotine—anything to keep his body going so he could keep writing.

What sort of ideas was he eager to share with the world? You know, fun, upbeat stuff, such as: There's no God. There's no higher power deciding our fate. We're born alone, we die alone, and everything we do in between is determined by us alone. Human beings are cursed with freedom of choice, which means we can (and should) be judged on the choices we make. Every success and every failure rests squarely on our shoulders—and it's a crushing weight. We live in anguish and despair because we desperately wish there were a higher power making decisions for us—but, too bad, there isn't. Human beings are "condemned to be free." Existentialism, baby!

He didn't write only about existentialism. He wrote all sorts of stuff: novels, plays, screenplays, journalism, literary criticism, art criticism, psychological studies, and biographies. He was so hooked on writing that in 1973, when he went almost totally blind and could no longer use a typewriter, he started using a reel-to-reel tape recorder instead. Nothing was going to stop him from getting his ideas out there.

Of course, when you're as brilliant as Sartre was, you're bound to win a few awards. He won the Nobel Prize for Literature in 1964—but he turned it down. He decided that writing books was stupid—or, at least, no longer sufficient on its own. Sitting alone in a room, banging out ideas on a typewriter, was no substitute for taking action in the real world: "For a long time I looked on my pen as a sword; now I know how powerless we are." It was time to boldly leave his apartment and effect meaningful change.

He almost got blown up for it. He loudly protested the French government's use of torture and concentration camps during the Algerian war of independence. A group of offended far-right paramilitaries responded by planting bombs in his apartment building—not once, but twice! Sartre survived both assassination attempts—and wisely decided it was time to move to a better neighborhood.

He advocated Marxist ideals. He insisted capitalism was a trap designed to convince people they needed to earn money so they could buy stuff, but that in reality, possessions only weighed you down—they were an excuse not to live an authentic life. He embraced Marxism because he thought it would allow people to stop focusing on money. In 1960, he went to Cuba and hung out with hard-core Marxist icons like Fidel Castro and Che Guevara. He said later that he couldn't entirely get behind Castro because of the Cuban government's persecution of gay people, but he was enormously impressed by Che, whom he praised as "not only an intellectual, but also the most complete human being of our age."

Championing far-left causes got him into trouble with the law—but luckily, being super-famous was like having a get-out-of-jail-free card. When Sartre was arrested for civil disobedience in 1968, French president Charles de Gaulle pardoned him, saying, "You don't arrest Voltaire." He was arrested again in 1970, at age sixty-five, for publishing a Maoist newspaper called *La cause du peuple.* The prior publishers had been jailed for provoking violence, so Sartre happily agreed to take over, wanting to strike a blow for freedom of expression. He stood on a street corner handing out free copies of the outlawed publication, actively hoping the police would arrest him so he could embarrass the French government. But as soon as the police realized who he was, they released him. He was too much of an icon to put behind bars.

But if Sartre truly believed a man was defined by his actions, how did he justify his wildly excessive drug use? Did consuming ungodly amounts of uppers, downers, and everything in between somehow help to effect change in the world? It helped boost his productivity in the short term, but as one of his biographers, Annie Cohen-Solal, points out, the long-term effects were devastating to his health: "His diet over a period of twenty-four hours included two packs of cigarettes and several pipes stuffed with black tobacco, more than a quart of alcohol—wine, beer, vodka, whiskey, and so on—two hundred milligrams of amphetamines, fifteen grams of aspirin, several grams of barbiturates, plus coffee, tea, heavy meals. . . . Did he know that he was pushing himself to the brink, and past it? Did he realize that his behavior was a form of suicide?"

The truth is productivity wasn't the only reason he used drugs. When he was a young man, Sartre was excited to experiment with psychedelics because he wanted to break the shackles of conventional thinking. He sought to strip away the artifice and see the world as it truly was. Basically, he wanted to trip the light phantasmic.

That's why he injected mescaline. In 1935, at the age of twenty-nine, while writing a book about the imagination, Sartre asked a longtime friend, a doctor, to let him try the psychoactive drug. He was affirmatively hoping to hallucinate. He wanted to undergo a new adventure that ordinary life could not provide. The good news is he succeeded; the bad news is he got much more than he bargained for.

Mescaline is one of the most potent hallucinogens ever found in nature. Indigenous Americans have used mescaline in the form of peyote (which Sartre called "the plant that fills the eyes with wonder") since before the start of recorded history, extracting it from specific species of cactus and going on psychedelic trips as a way of communicating with the spirit world. This inspired university biochemists to experiment with mescaline, which was legal at the time and regarded as a safe entry point into the world of psychedelics. Users would typically consume it orally, either in powder form or in gel capsules, and the effects would last for an average of four to twelve hours.

Sartre decided taking mescaline orally was lame and scoffed at the notion of starting with a small dose. He persuaded his doctor friend to inject a colossal amount of the drug in liquid form directly into his veins. He shot up with one of the strongest psychedelics ever to occur in nature, then waited to see what would happen—and what happened was he almost lost his mind.

The mescaline reactivated his childhood fear of sea creatures—crabs, lobsters, octopuses. He hallucinated that hundreds of crabs with sharp claws were surrounding him, swarming him, and crawling all over his body. It was an intensely bad trip—so much so that he never repeated the experience. The drug wore off after a few hours, but the hallucinations didn't go away. He had injected so much mescaline into his system that the hallucinatory effects of the drug lingered for an unbelievably long time.

The coterie of crabs followed him everywhere. For days, weeks, months on end, the shellfish stalkers shadowed him—and yet, miraculously, didn't harm him. He knew they weren't real. He understood perfectly well that they were figments of his imagination, yet every morning when he woke up, the phantom crabs were waiting for him.

Gradually, he became accustomed to their presence. He even came to think of them as friends and spoke to the crabs when he was alone. As he said in a 1971 interview: "After I took mescaline, I started seeing crabs around me all the time. They followed me in the streets, into class. I got used to them. I would wake up in the morning and say, 'Good morning, my little ones, how did you sleep?' I would talk to them all the time. I would say, 'OK, guys, we're going into class now, so we have to be still and quiet,' and they would be there, around my desk, absolutely still, until the bell rang."

Finally, after spending a full year with his crustacean compadres, he began to fear that maybe he was having a nervous breakdown and decided to see a psychiatrist. "I began to think I was going crazy, so I went to see a shrink," he said. They concluded that it was "fear of being alone, fear of losing camaraderie of the group," that caused him to see the crabs. Once the doctor diagnosed the reason for their presence, the crabs went away—they were gone in an instant. But they had been at his side for such a ridiculously long time that when they finally disappeared, he sort of missed them.

Sartre said human beings should be judged on the choices they make, so how should we judge him? While he undeniably had significant flaws, he was the most well-known philosopher of the twentieth century, he was a household name in France when he died, and at his funeral fifty thousand people followed his coffin through the streets of Paris—so I guess he must have done something right.

# CHAPTER 21

# Richard Nixon Wanted to Nuke Everyone

A lcohol is a straight-up hard drug. That's not a moral judg-ment; it's a scientific fact. On a biochemical level, alcohol affects the brain in the same way as Valium, Xanax, Ambien, GHB, and Quaaludes. All of them act on the GABA receptors in the brain and thus qualify as a type of drug called a GABAergic. Taking these drugs in small quantities can produce positive feelings and relax-ation, but consuming too much can seriously mess you up. In fact, GABAergics can become so physically addictive that, in extreme cases, attempting to quit cold turkey can kill you.

But thanks to the wonders of advertising, people don't think of alcohol that way. The beverage industry has spent billions of dollars to brainwash people into believing that drinking booze is fun and harmless: it's how cool people socialize. Drinking makes you more popular and more confident, and if you play your cards right, it might even get you laid. As a result of this industrial-level gaslight-ing, it's not uncommon for politicians to publicly proclaim that recreational drug use is morally repugnant and a blight on society—while simultaneously, those same politicians drink alcohol all the damn time.

No one illustrates this jarring disconnect better than President Richard Nixon. At his core, Nixon was a balled-up agglomeration of bitterness, anger, and resentment. He felt that life had screwed him. As a high school senior in 1930, he won a scholarship to Harvard, but he couldn't go because his mom needed him to stay home to help care for his brother Harold, who was sick with tuberculosis. Nixon attended Whittier College instead, which was much closer to home but far less prestigious. This unfairness ate away at him for the rest of his life.

Since fate had denied him what he so richly deserved, he felt entitled to take what he wanted by any underhanded means he could devise. At age twenty-nine, he joined the navy and spent four years as a card shark, taking other people's money and leaving the service $10,000 richer (which went a lot further in 1946 than it does now). He used his poker winnings to finance his political career, winning four consecutive elections in 1946, 1948, 1950, and 1952, mostly by slandering his opponents—he branded them Communists even though he knew they weren't. As Adlai Stevenson said, "Nixonland is a land of slander and scare, of sly innuendo . . . the land of smash and grab and anything to win."

The higher he climbed up the ladder of American politics, the more cutthroat he became. He would sandbag his enemies, smear their names, and stack the deck against them by any means necessary, no matter how immoral or illegal. It's no surprise that when running for reelection as president in 1972, he sent burglars to break into the Democratic National Committee headquarters at the Watergate Hotel, looking for dirt he could use against his opponents. That was totally par for the course for the man known as "Tricky Dick."

Even stone-cold sober, Nixon was a maniac. In 1969, he made the calculated decision to present himself to the world as an insanely violent psychopath who was ready, willing, and able to do literally anything to destroy those who dared to challenge him. This was his deranged strategy for how to end the Vietnam War. He would drop millions of tons of bombs on Vietnam—as well as neighboring Cambodia and Laos (even though the United States wasn't at war with them)—to prove he would enthusiastically annihilate anyone who opposed American military might or sought to provide aid and comfort to the Communists. Nixon dubbed it the "madman theory"—he would deliberately exceed all rational limits, raining down death and destruction on Southeast Asia, until his enemies finally backed down. He was weaponizing game theory to achieve a political result.

But when Nixon was drinking, the threats got even more extreme. What could be more extreme than carpet-bombing large swaths of Southeast Asia? Dropping nuclear bombs on them, that's what. He talked about it all the time. Whenever he got intoxicated, his go-to move was to order a nuclear strike. He used to drunk-dial his cabinet members in the middle of the night and order them to nuke Cambodia—"Bomb the shit out of them!" he'd yell into the phone. That's also how he wanted to end the Vietnam War. An aide overheard a drunk Nixon saying to Henry Kissinger in 1968: "Henry, we've got to nuke them." And when North Korea shot down a US spy plane in 1969? You guessed it—nuke them, too.

It was no idle threat. The Pentagon got involved and started picking out targets. Fortunately, Secretary of State Henry Kissinger persuaded the Pentagon to hold off until Nixon sobered up in the morning. (BTW, you know your country is in trouble when Henry Kissinger is the voice of reason.) Nixon's late-night nuclear strike orders became such an ongoing problem that his secretary of defense, James Schlesinger, issued a standing order to the military not to act on any commands given by the White House, unless and until those orders had been cleared by either Schlesinger or the secretary of state. As Kissinger once said, "If the president had his way, there would be a nuclear war every week."

Political enemies weren't the only targets of Nixon's drunken invective; his loyal staffers received similar treatment. He berated and hectored them constantly, and after a few drinks, he'd fire any-one who told him something he didn't want to hear. But he wouldn't remember it the next day, so people pretended it never happened. Numerous high-level staffers were fired multiple times by the president, but they kept showing up for work each day, realizing he would never know the difference.

It seems too crazy to be true: Nixon was the most powerful man in the world—with the world's largest nuclear arsenal at his fingertips—yet much of the time he was in office, he was drunk off his ass. And it didn't take much to get him drunk; he was a total lightweight. Journalists Bob Woodward and Carl Bernstein revealed in their book *The Final Days* that everyone in his inner circle knew he couldn't handle more than one drink. After two drinks, he'd start slurring his words, and after three drinks, the paranoia and self-pity would kick in.

Despite being a drug addict himself, it was Nixon who gleefully launched America's "war on drugs." On June 17, 1971, he announced to the nation that drug use was "America's public enemy number one" and declared he was going to wage an "all-out offensive" against it. He was determined to punish not only those who manufactured and distributed drugs but also those who used drugs.

In reality, Nixon's war wasn't about drugs at all. That was merely a ruse. It was a war against his political opponents. Nixon was running for a second term as president and he proved, once again, there was no limit to how low he would sink to win an election.

When he ran (and won) in 1968, Nixon had pioneered the despicable "Southern Strategy"—a cynical ploy designed to lure white voters in the South to vote Republican instead of Democrat, by stoking their fears about desegregation and the civil rights movement. Every time he opened his mouth, Nixon reminded these voters that he was a staunch proponent of "law and order" and "states' rights." He was sending out dog whistles that integration and people of color were dangerous, and only a strong Republican president could keep them safe. He was feeding on and amping up their racism and hatred for his own personal gain.

The War on Drugs was another deeply cynical ploy. In 1972, he'd identified two core groups of people that were trying to stop him from getting reelected: war protesters and Black people. So he made up lies about both of them. He was weaponizing game theory all over again—these two groups were threatening his position, so he needed to remove them from the board.

One of the architects of his devious plan has admitted to the whole thing. Here's an actual quote from John Ehrlichman, Nixon's top adviser on domestic affairs:

The Nixon White House . . . had two enemies: the antiwar left and Black people. You understand what I'm saying? We knew we couldn't make it illegal to be either against the war or Black, but by getting the public to associate the hippies with marijuana and Blacks with heroin, and then criminalizing both heavily, we could disrupt those communities. We could arrest their leaders, raid their homes, break up their meetings, and vilify them night after night on the evening news.

Did we know we were lying about the drugs? Of course we did.

Fifty years later, the War on Drugs is still raging. Even though it's been revealed that it's based on a lie told by an immoral politician so he could persecute his enemies, police still arrest more than a million people each year for drug crimes, including possession of very small amounts, and the United States continues to have one of the highest incarceration rates in the world.

And Richard Nixon was the drug addict who started it all.

# CHAPTER 22

# John F. Kennedy Was on All Sorts of Drugs

—————

**J**ohn Fitzgerald Kennedy was sick for damn near his entire childhood. It started when he was only two years old and came down with a potentially life-threatening case of scarlet fever. He had to be isolated in a sterile hospital room for two months. From then on, his young life was repeatedly interrupted by bouts of illness that landed him in the hospital alarmingly often. He suffered from mumps, measles, chicken pox, bronchitis, ear infections, whooping cough, and back pain that wouldn't go away and would only grow worse over the course of his life. To pass time while convalescing, he read voraciously. He was especially fond of histories of heroic figures, as well as the mythical stories of King Arthur and the Knights of the Round Table.

In a fascinating twist on the usual "rich kid" scenario, he actually had to use his family connections to get *into* the military instead of to stay out. The first time John tried to enlist, he was classified as 4-F because of his back problems, ulcers, and asthma. But he got his wealthy father to pull some strings so he could bypass the official navy doctors and find a less rigorous physician to examine him. Without his dad's intervention, John never would have been able to serve in the military.

But serve he did, and with distinction. During World War II, he was put in command of PT-109, one of a small fleet of patrol boats monitoring coastal regions for Japanese warships. On August 2, 1943, a Japanese destroyer rammed his boat, cleaving it in half, igniting the fuel tanks, and throwing John and the rest of the crew into an ocean that was literally on fire. John, who'd been on the Harvard swim team, bravely helped rescue his shipmates and pull them to safety, saving lives even though he had been injured himself. The incident made him a war hero.

Of course, the full story of PT-109 was far more complicated. John made mistakes that night, and so did the rest of his crew—but all that was quickly swept under the rug. John's father massaged the facts with the media to position his son as a flawless white knight.

John's father, Joseph Kennedy Sr., was a sketchy guy. He made his fortune as a stockbroker in the 1920s through insider trading (before the stock market crashed and that sort of thing became illegal) and by flooding the United States with booze the moment that Prohibition ended in 1933. He was supremely rich and powerful, but what he craved most was legitimacy—and what better way to achieve legitimacy than to make sure his son became president of the United States?

Amazingly, this intense and overbearing man was actually the more loving of John's two parents. John's mother, Rose, seemed to have little to no interest in him and basically zero warmth. And while you might expect an old-school hard-ass like Joseph Sr. would insist on micromanaging every detail of his son's upbringing, he was actually fairly indulgent and laid-back toward young John.

But there was a reason for that—John wasn't the son that Daddy was grooming to be president. That was John's older brother, Joseph Jr. He was the full package—star athlete, Harvard Law grad, and World War II bomber pilot. From 1915 to 1944, Joseph Sr.'s sights were laser-focused on his eldest son; he raised him from birth with the expectation that he would one day become president. So it didn't really matter if his younger son John was frail, was sickly, and screwed up a lot, because Joseph Sr. didn't have his hopes and dreams built around little Johnny.

Everything changed on August 12, 1944, when Joseph Jr. died unexpectedly. The experimental bomber plane he was flying exploded in midair. If Joseph Sr. still wanted a son of his to become president—which he desperately did—he needed to switch to his backup plan. John once told a reporter that "it was like being drafted." His father now demanded that John go into politics.

If you're trying to become president, the natural first stop is Congress. John was only twenty-nine years old when he first ran for office, and he beat his Republican opponent by a mile. He won three terms in the House of Representatives, followed by two terms in the Senate—but all those elections were nothing more than a test run for his presidential campaign, which he launched in January 1960, as the junior senator from the state of Massachusetts.

Importantly, John insisted on hiding the truth about his medical problems during all these elections. As bad as his health was before the war, it was even worse after. His actions on PT-109 made him a hero but also made his back problems worse than ever. His back pain was so severe that he couldn't even put on his shoes or pick up his kids without substantial amounts of medication. He was in pain, or at least in significant discomfort, almost constantly. In addition to his ulcers and colitis, he'd been diagnosed with a rare, potentially lethal endocrine disorder called Addison's disease. Fairly or unfairly, voters might have felt that someone experiencing so many different maladies was simply incapable of governing.

To mask his symptoms, John took tons of pharmaceuticals on the campaign trail—and the façade worked perfectly. Thanks to the hard-core drugs he was taking behind the scenes, he projected a healthy, relaxed, smiling demeanor when he appeared on camera—in stark contrast to his sweaty, awkward, perpetually angry Republican opponent, Richard Nixon. John charmed the voters and won the election—and he was only forty-three years old at the time, making him the youngest person ever elected president of the United States.

But America now had a president who was a functioning drug addict. He was taking opioids, steroids, amphetamines, barbiturates, antibiotics, and antipsychotics—often all at the same time. Then, in addition to all the drugs he was taking for legitimate medical reasons, he was recreationally using cocaine, marijuana, and meth, the latter of which he had injected directly into his throat. The guy was essentially a walking pharmacy. Robert Kennedy once joked, "If a mosquito bites my brother, the mosquito dies."

The president of the United States couldn't buy drugs on the street, so he had to find his own personal drug dealer. That was Dr. Max Jacobson, also known as "Miracle Max." Max was a shady German doctor who was popular with numerous celebrities of the era, including Truman Capote, Cecil B. DeMille, and Tennessee Williams. He specialized in unconventional, controversial, and frankly deranged medical treatments. Max liked to inject his patients with so-called vitamin shots to boost their energy levels and make them feel great. The main ingredient of these vitamin shots was amphetamines (a.k.a. speed), which he accompanied with a wild mix of chemicals, including animal hormones, enzymes, bone marrow, painkillers, tranquilizers, steroids, placenta, and—just to keep things interesting—a few actual vitamins. Not surprisingly, the Federal Bureau of Narcotics and Dangerous Drugs didn't like him very much.

Max quickly became the "Dr. Feelgood" of the Kennedy White House. His vitamin shots might not have been FDA-approved, but they got the job done. As John put it: "I don't care if it's horse piss.

It works." (Years later, in the mid-1970s, Max's medical license was revoked after he got patients hooked on speed, became sloppy and erratic in his treatments, and caused the death of a wealthy client from amphetamine poisoning.)

The insane array of drugs the president obtained from Max kept him functional, which was good—but his private life became an absolute mess. From an early age, John had become habituated to the idea that drugs make you feel better (because he needed so many chemicals to treat his various medical ailments). But as he got older and his physical condition worsened, he needed even more powerful drugs to remain productive. It's hardly surprising that, given all the drugs he was already taking out of sheer necessity, he eventually started using them for pure recreational purposes, especially with a shady doctor like Max being ready, willing, and able to give him anything he wanted.

Unfortunately, the same drugs that dulled John's pain and boosted his energy level also fueled his increasingly reckless behavior. Hedonism is a fairly common means of escape from chronic pain and suffering—especially for those with the financial means to indulge themselves. Being president gave John the opportunity to travel far and wide, and to sleep with an extremely large number of women who were not his wife, many of them celebrities themselves. Marilyn Monroe is probably the most talked-about of these mistresses, but there were many other women with whom John had affairs. They included wealthy socialites as well as strippers and prostitutes—and even two White House secretaries, who were given the demeaning code names Fiddle and Faddle by the Secret Service. John's rampant infidelity was fully enabled by the Secret Service, which helped him to meet up with his paramours in privacy and to hide his inveterate cheating from his wife and the rest of the world.

Perhaps the most amazing fact about John F. Kennedy is that

despite myriad illnesses and medical conditions that he kept hidden from the voters, all the dangerous pharmaceuticals he took on a regular basis, and his absolute mess of a personal life, he somehow managed to do a pretty damn good job as president. While he engaged in rampant hedonism on a personal level, he always maintained a strong moral sense for the nation as a whole. This was the man who created the Peace Corps in 1961, signed the Equal Pay Act of 1963, and supported what became the Civil Rights Act of 1964—although tragically he was assassinated before it was signed into law. And he was the person who began the massive expansion of the US space exploration program that ultimately led to a successful moon landing in 1969.

Despite his many personal struggles, John F. Kennedy showed that a forward-thinking government can make a positive difference in people's lives. That's why he is regarded today as a truly great president, and both historians and the general public remember him fondly—even though he lied his pants off to everyone and covered up the truth about his wildly excessive drug use.

# CHAPTER 23

# Audie Murphy Was the Real-Life Captain America

Did you know America's greatest war hero was only five feet five inches and weighed 112 pounds? Audie Murphy was the real-life Captain America: a scrawny kid from a small town in Texas, but with the heart of a hero. At age sixteen, he was obviously too young to join the military, but after the Japanese bombed Pearl Harbor on December 7, 1941, nothing was going to stop him from defending his country—so he falsified his birth certificate.

No one who looked at this baby-faced teenager could possibly have thought he was old enough to enlist, but there was a war to fight and the army needed as many soldiers as it could get. So, thanks to his forged birth certificate, Audie Murphy succeeded in joining the US Army on his seventeenth birthday. He must have been the youngest and smallest kid in his unit—but, against all odds, he quickly became legendary for his valor, bravery, and amazing combat skills.

At age nineteen, he single-handedly held off an entire battalion of German soldiers and tanks. Here's the situation: German troops had knocked out his regiment's heavy-duty tank destroyer and set it on fire. Murphy told the other men in his unit to run into the trees for safety, so they wouldn't get killed by the Germans. Then he climbed atop the burning tank destroyer (which could have blown up at any second), grabbed the .50-caliber machine gun that was bolted there, and began firing at the Germans. He was alone and totally exposed to enemy fire—and he'd already been wounded in both legs—but he kept firing that machine gun at the German troops to protect his men.

But, wait, there's more: He used his field telephone to summon an air attack—and even as American firepower was raining down from the skies onto the enemy troops, he stayed put on top of the burning tank destroyer for nearly an hour, feeding one ammunition belt after another into the machine gun. Only after he'd thoroughly and successfully repelled the German attack did he finally slide down from the tank destroyer and limp away from the huge conflagration. That's when he noticed his right leg was throbbing and his pants were soaked in blood. Moments later, the tank destroyer he'd been standing on exploded.

You remember that scene in *Rambo* where Sylvester Stallone climbs on top of a burning armored vehicle and mows down hundreds of enemy soldiers with a .50-caliber machine gun? That was directly inspired by what Audie Murphy did in real life. The author of the novel *First Blood* (on which the Rambo movies are based) has publicly stated that the supersoldier Rambo was based on Audie Murphy.

Murphy became the single most decorated war hero in American history, earning a slew of medals, including two Bronze Stars, two Silver Stars, the Distinguished Service Cross, and the Medal of Honor. Basically, he won every American military medal there is (some more than once) and was so unbelievably awesome that foreign countries like France and Belgium gave him medals, too. He earned a grand total of fifty-four medals, awards, and other honors for his remarkable valor—and he hadn't even turned twenty-one by the time the war ended.

When he returned home in 1945, he was the closest thing to a superhero anyone had ever seen. Parades were thrown in his honor, photographers followed him everywhere he went, and his youthful smiling image was plastered on the cover of *Life* magazine. He even wrote a memoir about his experiences in the war, which he called *To Hell and Back*. Several years later, Universal Studios turned his book into a movie—and guess who starred in it. He did. But get this: the studio had to tone down some of the amazing stuff he did during the war because they were afraid audiences might think it was too impossibly over-the-top heroic to have actually happened. That's how amazing his real-life exploits were. The film was a smash hit in 1955. In fact, it made so much money that it remained Universal's most profitable movie for twenty years, until it was finally dethroned in 1975 by Steven Spielberg's *Jaws*.

Audie Murphy was a bona fide movie star for more than two decades and appeared in nearly fifty films, mostly westerns and war movies, including classics such as *The Red Badge of Courage*, *The Unforgiven*, and *No Name on the Bullet*. He was so massively popular that, at one point, he was getting more fan mail than almost any other actor. The public adored him because no matter how famous he became or how crazy things were around him, he was always preternaturally cool, calm, and collected. To his millions of fans, he was the American Dream personified.

What people didn't know was that beneath his perpetually self-assured façade, he was a terrified young man whose war experiences had scarred him for life. The term "PTSD" didn't exist back in the 1940s, '50s, and '60s. People assumed that because he returned from the war as a "hero," it meant Murphy had come back unscathed. In public, he always seemed relaxed and calm. But in truth, he'd been deeply traumatized by the horrors of war. At night, he slept with the lights on and a loaded gun hidden under his pillow.

When the studio first offered him the lead in *To Hell and Back* he turned it down. He didn't want to be perceived as cashing in on his war exploits—but that wasn't the only reason: reliving his war experiences was deeply painful for him. He was plagued by insomnia and horrible nightmares.

It wasn't long before he developed an addiction to sleeping pills. The brand name was Placidyl. They were meant to be taken only at bedtime, but Murphy took them at all times of the day and night. He'd be posing for photographs to promote his latest movie, with flashbulbs going off all around him and people shouting his name, and he'd surreptitiously pop a few Placidyls to remain uncannily calm and repress his flashbacks of the war. The pills were effective, but they later became infamous for widespread abuse, including by other famous individuals such as Elvis Presley, Steven Tyler, and Supreme Court chief justice William Rehnquist. (The manufacturer finally stopped making Placidyl in 1999.)

Murphy went public about his drug problem in the mid-1960s. He confessed to his fans that he'd developed a crippling dependence on sleeping pills. Then, badass that he was, he quit taking the pills in the most difficult way possible—by going cold turkey even though he was a hard-core addict. He locked himself away in a hotel room for a week, totally alone, without any Placidyl or other drugs to prop him up, suffering through the debilitating symptoms of withdrawal until he was finally rid of the addiction.

That should have been the end of his problems—but instead, it was only the beginning. Once he stopped taking Placidyl, his PTSD flared up and intensified. He was angry, depressed, and violent. He withdrew from everyone around him, felt alone and lost, and was prone to bouts of deep depression, wild mood swings, and other serious psychological problems.

But that's when Audie Murphy proved his heroism once again.

He did something that other movie stars of the era would never have dreamed of doing—he confessed that he was suffering from mental illness. He became a passionate activist for mental health in the late sixties and early seventies, determined to use his platform as a celebrity to help others who were experiencing the same pain as he was, including the shell-shocked soldiers returning from Korea and, later, from Vietnam. The medical profession at the time tended not to pay much attention to mental problems faced by soldiers, dismissing them as symptoms of what they called "battle fatigue," but Murphy helped people understand it was much more serious than that. He spoke openly about his struggles with post-traumatic stress and lobbied the government to devote more mental health resources to returning service members. His efforts were especially brave because they came at a time when the subject of mental health was never publicly addressed and mental illness was regarded as shameful.

Murphy hit rock bottom financially. He developed a serious gambling problem and squandered the fortune he'd earned from starring in movies. Any money he didn't lose gambling was lost in a series of monumentally bad business investments. But even though he was having a tough time making ends meet, he refused to sell out. He was repeatedly offered starring roles in TV commercials for alcohol and cigarettes, which would have easily solved his money problems. But he turned them all down because he knew those commercials would set a bad example for the millions of kids who looked up to him as a role model.

Tragically, Audie Murphy's career as a mental health activist was cut short when he died in a plane crash at age forty-five. He was buried at Arlington National Cemetery in 1971 and given full military honors. That same year, Congress voted to name a brand-new Veterans Administration facility after him because of his stead-fast advocacy on behalf of veterans. The Audie L. Murphy Memorial Veterans' Hospital opened in 1973. Even today, Murphy's grave site remains one of the most frequently visited graves at Arlington National Cemetery, second only to that of President John F. Kennedy.

While Audie Murphy is most often remembered as a war hero who became a beloved movie star, he deserves even more credit for his remarkable bravery and tireless work to shine a light on the psychological toll of war, and for openly discussing his own personal struggles with addiction and mental illness.

# PART 6

# SHOWBIZ BLUES

# CHAPTER 24

# Howard Hughes, the Drug-Addled Billionaire

There have been lots of bad movies, but Howard Hughes made one so toxic it actually gave people cancer—it was called *The Conqueror*. In one of the worst casting decisions of all time, he hired iconic movie cowboy John Wayne to play Genghis Khan, and painted his skin yellow and gave him a Fu Manchu mustache so he'd look more like a thirteenth-century Mongol warlord. Of course, it wasn't the cringeworthy racism that gave people cancer—it was the shooting location. Hughes found out he could save a few bucks if he filmed in the desert not far from an active nuclear test site, where a year earlier the US government had detonated eleven atomic bombs. Hughes didn't make the connection that fallout from the bomb tests had traveled downwind and irradiated the shooting location. Of 220 cast and crew, 91 got cancer, and 46 died—including John Wayne.[1]

But this was just one thread in the rich tapestry of deranged behavior that characterized Hughes's life. He pioneered the image of the eccentric celebrity billionaire who stubbornly follows his

---

1. John Wayne also smoked several packs of cigarettes a day, so technically it's impossible to know whether his cancer was caused by cigarettes or the movie.

own instincts, no matter how shocking they might be. Over the course of his life, Hughes made a series of outlandish blunders that caused him to suffer injuries, illness, addiction, insanity, and, ultimately, death.

Hughes was brilliant but stunningly reckless. Like his father, who got rich by inventing a rotary drill bit for Texas oil fields, he was an inventor. He built his first radio transmitter at age eleven, motorized his bicycle at age twelve, and began taking flying lessons at age fourteen. By the time he was eighteen, both of his parents had died and he'd inherited 75 percent of his family's considerable fortune. Without parents around to tell him no, he dropped out of college and moved to Hollywood to become a hotshot moviemaker. His first movie turned out so badly that he destroyed the prints so it could never be released—but did that make him rethink his career choice? Heck no, he doubled down and launched his own production company. His next few films made money, one won an Academy Award, and *Hell's Angels*, released in 1930, was a genuine blockbuster—so, by the tender age of twenty-five, Hughes had achieved his ambition of hitting it big in Hollywood.

His other grand ambition was to become a hotshot aviator. (Wanting to be a "hotshot" was a recurring theme in his life.) He was determined to be more famous than aviation icon Charles Lindbergh, so designing and flying experimental airplanes became his passion—and, again, he succeeded. In 1935, he set the world speed record (352 miles per hour). In 1937, he broke the transcontinental speed record (LA to New York in 7 hours, 28 minutes). And in 1938, he broke the record for the fastest flight around the entire planet (3 days, 19 hours, 17 minutes).

But flying a metal tube through the air at ridiculously high speeds comes with a few unavoidable risks—and one of those is crashing. Hughes survived four plane crashes. He wasn't seriously injured in the first two, in 1930 and 1935. In the third crash, in 1943, two of his passengers were killed, and Hughes suffered a deep gash in his head. But it was the fourth crash that really messed him up. In 1946, he flew his prototype military reconnaissance plane, the XF-11, on its first test flight, and the plane failed spectacularly. It plummeted through the air and plowed through three houses in Beverly Hills before the fuel tanks exploded and the plane burst into flames. Doctors didn't expect him to survive the fiery crash: he had burns covering 78 percent of his body, 10 fractured ribs, a total of 54 broken bones, and 60 cuts to his face, shoulders, and hands; his skull was cleaved open, his left lung had collapsed, and his heart had shifted over to the wrong side of his chest.

But what had perhaps the most far-reaching consequences was the drug they used to treat him: codeine. Codeine is a naturally occurring opioid that is tremendously effective in soothing pain. But there's an important caveat: opioids shouldn't be used to treat long-term, chronic pain. Over time, the human body develops a higher tolerance for opioids as well as a stronger craving for them, meaning the patient will gradually take higher and higher doses while experiencing less and less relief. This is a biochemical trap that has ensnared countless souls. But Howard Hughes was the richest man in America, and no self-respecting doctor was going to let him experience pain if there was an easy way to make that pain go away—so they gave him codeine, and it wasn't long before he was hooked.

As a wealthy and powerful man, Hughes could go to extreme lengths to feed his addiction. He wanted more codeine than doctors could legally prescribe him, so he enlisted his personal physician to write prescriptions for Hughes's various aides and assistants—all of whom were perfectly healthy—and they simply handed over their pills to their boss. But soon, even swallowing codeine in pill form wasn't enough for him. He believed he could derive a stronger benefit by dissolving the pills in water and injecting the liquid codeine directly into his muscles. This became such a habitual practice that after Hughes died, an autopsy found five broken-off hypodermic needles embedded in his arms.

As if opioid addiction weren't bad enough on its own, the addiction amplified his preexisting mental illness. Hughes had long suffered from obsessive-compulsive disorder (OCD), which is often stereotyped in movies and TV as being odd but harmless, a sort of next-level anal retentive—I'm calling you out, Sheldon Cooper—but the reality is far more distressing. People with OCD tend to obsess over subjects that cause them severe anxiety, fear, and/or disgust, and they often feel compelled to take bizarre actions to cope with these obsessions.

For Hughes, it was germophobia. When he was a boy, his mother had been fanatical about disease. She'd scrub his naked body from head to toe as she sermonized about the many viruses and bacteria that could kill him. This dire fear of germs stuck with Hughes all his life. He was reluctant to shake hands or make physical contact with anyone, hated the idea of people touching his food, and washed his hands so obsessively that they were often cracked and bleeding. If someone around him got sick, he'd immediately burn all his clothes and order the house to be scoured and sanitized. As his codeine addiction got progressively worse, his OCD took over his life. He withdrew from everyone and everything around him and became a recluse.

At the same time, he was losing his mind due to syphilis. Despite his hang-ups about letting people touch him, Hughes had for many years made an exception for sex. As a big-time movie producer and wealthy business tycoon, he had the opportunity to engage in lots of coitus. In the thirties, forties, and fifties, he dated the most famous actresses in the world—Katharine Hepburn, Ava Gardner, Bette Davis, Ginger Rogers, Lana Turner, Rita Hayworth, even a young Marilyn Monroe—but this bevy of beautiful women wasn't enough for him. He scoured magazines looking for more large-breasted women he could turn into movie stars. At one point, he had 154 starlets under contract with his studio, and he had slept with most of them. But few ever appeared in his movies; they were essentially being housed and paid to be part of his private harem.

This creepy debauched behavior was bound to catch up with him. In the mid-1930s, he caught an STD from one of the scores of anonymous women he had slept with. If this had happened ten years later, he'd have gotten a shot of penicillin and everything would have been fine—but penicillin wasn't used to treat syphilis until 1943. Instead, Hughes got the so-called magic bullet treatment— his doctor injected low levels of mercury and arsenic into his bloodstream for several weeks in an attempt to kill the virus. Shockingly, this medically dubious approach did not succeed. His syphilis continued to fester and grow for the next forty years and blossomed into neurosyphilis, which causes psychosis, delirium, and—as in Hughes's case—irreversible insanity.

By 1957, Hughes's mental deterioration had become so glaringly obvious that he was terrified people around him were going to commit him to a mental institution. But a clever lawyer found a loophole: under California law, a married man couldn't be committed without his wife's consent, so Hughes quickly married actress Jean Peters, who swore she'd never have him institutionalized. But he was too terrified of germs to make physical contact with his blushing bride. They lived in separate parts of the house and communicated almost entirely by telephone. Of course, that didn't stop Hughes from having a team of private investigators follow her twenty-four hours a day and report to him on everything she did— because at this point in his life, controlling women was more important than sex. They stayed married for fourteen years, until Jean could no longer take it and filed for divorce.

Hughes ended up a crazy hermit, urinating in jars and wearing

Kleenex boxes on his feet. He'd sit naked in his private screening room, with a pink hotel napkin placed delicately over his genitals, watching the same movies over and over again, including *Ice Station Zebra* (because he liked Rock Hudson) and *The Conqueror* (to punish himself for making a movie that gave cancer to the cast and crew). For years at a time, he refused to leave his suite at the Desert Inn on the Las Vegas Strip. When hotel management insisted he vacate, he simply bought the hotel instead.

Even in his madness, Hughes knew what people were saying about him. He'd been world-famous for so long that it was inevitable people would gossip about him when he vanished from public view. But when he saw a newspaper story one day that referred to him as a "paranoid, deranged millionaire," he went ballistic. "Goddammit, I'm a *billionaire!*" he screamed.

# CHAPTER 25

# Judy Garland Was Drugged by Grown-ups

The entertainment industry is notorious for chewing up young performers and spitting them out. The tragic case of Judy Garland is an early and potent example. The combination of enforced drug use, body-shaming, sexual exploitation, and a grueling work schedule transformed a wonderfully talented child actor into a seriously troubled adult.

Her parents were vaudeville performers who thrust her into the spotlight almost as soon as she could walk. She was born on June 10, 1922, as Frances Gumm, and when she was only two years old, her parents plopped her onstage with her two older siblings, ages nine and seven, to perform as the Gumm Sisters. The tiny toddler was given her own solo number—she sang "Jingle Bells" to a packed house. The crowd roared with laughter and applause, and little Frances was so excited by the attention that she kept singing the song over and over, until her father finally had to walk onstage, pick her up, and carry her off.

Frances's domineering mother, Ethel, became her manager. Frustrated by the realization that she'd never be a star herself, Ethel sought to live out her fantasies through her daughter—a shy little girl with the rich, resonant voice of a grown-up woman. Ethel pinned all her hopes and dreams on Frances, and succeeded in infecting the child with her own fanatical overconfidence. Frances started telling everyone that she was going to be a movie star.

Frances was nine years old when her mom started drugging her. Ethel dragged young Frances to one audition after another, while also booking as many singing gigs for the Gumm Sisters as she could get. The pace was relentless, and Frances had trouble keeping up with her older sisters. Whenever her energy level flagged even a tiny bit, her loving mother would slip her a "pep pill." Soon, Ethel was feeding uppers to Frances when she wanted her to work and downers when she wanted her to sleep. When anyone dared to suggest that maybe Ethel was pushing the child too hard, Ethel's mantra was always the same: "I've got to keep these girls going!"

Despite Frances's amazing singing talent, movie studios kept rejecting her for acting roles. Why? Because the studio system was deeply misogynistic and incredibly limiting. Female roles fell into only two categories: you could be a cutesy little girl like Shirley Temple or a glamorous beauty queen like Lana Turner. But at ages ten through twelve, Frances Gumm didn't fall into either category. To paraphrase Britney Spears, she was no longer a girl but not yet a woman. She was too old for the saccharine cutesy roles played by small children but not old enough or sexy enough to play the stereotypical female object of desire in a big Hollywood movie.

Obviously, this was a ridiculous dichotomy. You'd think someone at the studios might have been smart enough to say, "Wow, maybe we should have a wider range of ideas about what an actress can be." But that didn't happen. Frances Gumm was punished for being a completely ordinary teenage girl, albeit one with a remarkable singing voice. She was treated as if she were flawed for not being able to magically transform herself to satisfy the mercurial whims of adult white male studio executives.

But making it in Hollywood often means changing who you are, starting with your name, and that's what happened with Frances. "The Gumm Sisters" was a drab, dreary name with no pizzazz. In fact, one time a theater mistakenly billed them as "the *Glum* Sisters"—a clear sign that it was time to rebrand. So, the trio borrowed the last name of a prominent New York theater critic, Robert Garland, and became the Garland Sisters, and twelve-year-old Frances dumped her dowdy old-fashioned first name in favor of a more marquee-friendly name. Voilà! Frances Gumm was reborn as "Judy Garland."

The rebranding worked. Hollywood might have roundly rejected Frances Gumm, but it quickly embraced Judy Garland. At the tender age of thirteen, Judy was summoned to the office of Louis B. Mayer, one of the most important men in Hollywood—the head of Metro-Goldwyn-Mayer. She sang two songs for Mayer, and the studio signed her to a seven-year contract that would pay her $100 a week at the beginning, escalating to $1,000 a week by the time she was twenty. In the 1930s, during the depths of the Great Depression, it was a staggering sum of money.

But it meant MGM owned her, body and soul. The studio now controlled every aspect of her life: she spent three hours every morning in a school classroom to satisfy the requirements of California law, then two hours with a vocal coach to hone her singing abilities, and then several more hours in beginner-level acting classes. The fickle Hollywood machine quickly decided she wasn't attractive enough to play a girl whom male movie characters would lust after, so they relegated her to the role of the quirky, sexless girl whom male characters would confide in about their crushes on other, prettier and more desirable girls. MGM repeatedly cast her as the "girl next door" in musical comedies, usually paired with Mickey Rooney, cranking out one film after another, with almost no time off for the young stars to rest. Judy appeared in five films in fifteen months—an average of one new movie every ninety days. It was exhausting work, but one thing was clear: audiences liked her.

Even though Judy was doing everything MGM asked, the studio was unwilling and unable to treat her respectfully. As a thirteen-year-old human being, she was experiencing puberty, and this basic biological fact was viewed by the studio as a huge inconvenience. She was short, less than five feet tall, with a roundish face, and now her chest was expanding, which made her appear chubby. Studio executives relentlessly body-shamed her and called her an "ugly duckling." The head of the studio referred to her as his "little hunchback." They took control over what she was allowed to eat. No matter what she ordered in the studio cafeteria, the kitchen staff was under strict orders to bring her nothing but chicken soup, coffee, and cigarettes.

Body image issues have long been a menace for women, especially those in the public eye, but Judy's case was exceptionally severe. She was systematically body-shamed and coerced into dangerous habits by her employer. A major movie studio was working around the clock to undermine a young girl's confidence and self-esteem, and not surprisingly, it succeeded. When Judy saw herself on-screen in her first film at age fourteen, she described herself as a "fat little frightening pig with pigtails." Later in life, she said: "Until MGM I had enjoyed being myself. I had been judged by my talent, but in the movies, beauty was the standard of judgment—and definitely I didn't have it. And so I began to dislike the me I saw reflected in my mirror, especially when I compared myself with the real beauties on the lot."

*The Wizard of Oz*, her biggest film ever, was a soul-crushing experience. MGM originally wanted Shirley Temple for the role of Dorothy, but she was under contract to Fox. So, they turned to Judy and told her point-blank: we need you to be prettier and thinner than you are. Judy was sixteen years old at this point, almost an adult, yet they forced her to her play a prepubescent little girl. They strapped down her breasts, bound her up in tight corsets to hide her figure, and costumed her in a kiddie-style dress and pigtails.

Hell-bent on extracting the maximum possible productivity from their "investment," MGM coerced Judy into routinely consuming drugs to lose weight and increase her energy level. They required her to work up to seventy-two hours in a row, a feat that wasn't possible without chemical assistance. Just like her mother had been doing since she was nine years old, the studio doctors fed her amphetamines when they wanted her to work, then barbiturates to put her to sleep for a few hours, and then more amphetamines to wake her up again. This vicious cycle was repeated every day. The drugs wreaked havoc on her body and on her mind. As Judy put it: "Half of the time we were hanging from the ceiling but it was a way of life for us." The studio treated her like an exploitable commodity, not a thinking and feeling human being. They preferred to get her addicted to drugs and ruin her life rather than give her a reasonable work schedule.

It wasn't just Judy who was railroaded into addiction. Hollywood in the 1930s was awash in drugs. Pretty much everyone in the movie biz was taking some kind of pill or another. The most widely abused pharmaceuticals were sedatives and amphetamines, glibly euphemized as "bolts and jolts." Amphetamines were the "jolts" that cranked you up, and sedatives were the "bolts" that knocked you out. Over the past several decades, people have learned the hard way about the nasty consequences of this sort of chemically induced behavior—but back in the thirties and forties, bolts and jolts were almost as common as aspirin.

No matter how much weight Judy lost, studio executives continued to tell her she didn't look good enough. But, of course, that didn't stop them from trying to have sex with her. From age sixteen to twenty, she was repeatedly propositioned by high-ranking MGM personnel, including Louis B. Mayer himself. She turned him down every time, but Mayer responded by groping and molesting her. He would stand extremely close to her and ostensibly compliment her singing, saying, "Nobody sings better than she does, and the reason is that she sings from the heart." Then, to show everyone where her heart was, he'd place his hand on top of her left breast. One day she stood up to him and told him never to do that again, and he broke down crying in front of her: "How can you say that to me, to me who loves you?"

*The Wizard of Oz* made Judy the movie star her mother had always dreamed she would be. Judy won an Oscar for her performance (although it was the Academy Juvenile Award, a shrunken, Mini-Me version of the regular-size Oscar statue given to grown-ups). She placed her hands and feet in wet cement in front of Grauman's Chinese Theatre in Hollywood, and she was undeniably rich. She signed a new contract with MGM that pushed her up the salary ladder early. Instead of having to wait until she was twenty to earn $1,000 per week, she would now earn $2,000 a week at age eighteen, increasing to $3,000 a week by the time she was twenty-three. And she bought her dream house in Bel Air, California. By age seventeen, Judy had attained the fame she'd been seeking since she was two years old—but it came at a terrible personal cost.

Beneath the surface, she was profoundly messed up. MGM's odious practice of overworking her, plying her with drugs, and shaming her for her appearance guaranteed her grown-up years would be filled with emotional and physical distress. They had turned Judy into a movie star but had demolished her confidence and sense of self in the process. The cruelty and negligence she received as a child actor imbued her with a crushing self-doubt that never went away and goaded her into a never-ending cycle of addiction: time and time again, she would clean herself up and make a triumphant comeback, only to fall off the wagon again soon after. Her romantic relationships were inevitably fraught with unhappiness; she was married five times in twenty-eight years. She tried to kill herself on more than twenty different occasions, including by slashing her wrists. She once asked, "If I am a legend, then why am I so lonely?" She ultimately passed away from an overdose of barbiturates in 1969, at the age of forty-seven.

Judy Garland was a talented, pretty young girl who was treated by the grown-ups in her life as if she was defective and inadequate. Her mother and the movie studio effectively stole her childhood from her. They forced her to use drugs and starve herself in an impossible pursuit of an idealized appearance. They controlled her with chemicals twenty-four hours a day, instead of just letting her rest, recover, and live.

The grim reality behind the scenes didn't stop her from becoming a cultural icon. She went on to give much-loved performances in *Meet Me in St. Louis* (1944), *Easter Parade* (1948), and *A Star Is Born* (1954). Her voice never lost its resonance and richness. Her biggest songs were "Over the Rainbow" and "You Made Me Love You," but she was a beloved singer of all sorts of standards. Her concert album, recorded live at Carnegie Hall in 1961, spent seventy-three weeks on the *Billboard* charts and won five Grammy awards. That's the kind of success and acceptance many aspiring performers can only dream of, but she actually lived it. It's a shame that because of how unjustly she was treated and how it harmed her psyche, she was never able to fully enjoy it.

# CHAPTER 26

# Andy Warhol Was Really Fond of Meth

In a double whammy of weirdness, Andy Warhol—the man famous for painting soup cans and hosting wild parties for his drugged-out bohemian friends—lived at home with his mother and went to church almost every day.

His childhood isn't what you'd expect: He was born in 1928 in the Slavic ghettos of Pittsburgh as Andrew Warhola, but he dropped the final "a" to avoid sounding "too ethnic." His immigrant father was a coal miner who died when Andy was thirteen. Andy was a sickly child who suffered from a rare disease called chorea (a.k.a. Saint Vitus' dance)—a rare neurological disorder that causes involuntary jerking movements of the hands and feet. He spent months confined to bed, and so to help him pass the time his mother taught him to draw (ooh, foreshadowing).

Andy's mother was a super-devout Catholic who attended mass multiple times a week, often daily. As Andy sat in church with his mother, he would stare for hours at the paintings on the walls—images of Jesus Christ, the saints, and the angels, all on gold-leaf backgrounds. The paintings were called "icons." Every day in church, young Andy was surrounded by these holy icons staring back at him from their monochromatic gold canvases.

When Andy became an artist, he painted icons of his own. But not the saints and angels from his church; instead, he painted "secular saints." He figured Americans didn't worship Jesus as much as they worshipped celebrities. Famous people were the new gods, so that's who he painted—icons like Marilyn Monroe, Elizabeth Taylor, Jackie Kennedy, Mick Jagger, and Elvis Presley. Instead of gold-leaf backgrounds, he used bright, bold, vibrant colors. He must have been right about what Americans worshipped, because his icons were a smash hit on the art scene. His image of Marilyn Monroe's face on a bright blue background would sell for $195 million in 2022—making it the most expensive piece of twentieth-century art ever sold.

His soup cans were also a tremendous success. He was fascinated by society's obsession with commercialism, so he created life-like reproductions of everyday products: Campbell's soup, Brillo scrubbing pads, Coke bottles—and don't forget money. Andy loved talking about money and painting pictures of it. For one of his early masterpieces, he drew an image of a dollar bill, duplicated it a ridiculous number of times, and called the resulting piece *200 One Dollar Bills*. It might sound simple, but it sold at auction for $43 million in 2009.

By elevating ordinary commercial goods to the status of fine art, he challenged the very notion of what constitutes "art." His groundbreaking work influenced countless other artists, including Keith Haring, Jean-Michel Basquiat, and Banksy, to name just a few. He's probably the most famous painter ever born in America, and he did it by painting soup cans—but also by cultivating a quirky, one-of-a-kind public persona.

Andy Warhol was the king of weird. He was famous for surrounding himself with an eclectic and hard-partying crowd, a fascinating assortment of cutting-edge counterculture artists and established public figures—Lou Reed, John Cale, Allen Ginsberg, William S. Burroughs, Judy Garland, Tennessee Williams, John Lennon, Mick Jagger, Rudolf Nureyev, and Jackie Kennedy. He hung out with all of them. Gossip rags reported breathlessly about the star-studded parties he threw at this New York City art studio.

His parties were legendary for their tales of wild, debauched excess. Endless drinking, drug-fueled orgies, filming of sexual acts between partygoers. An immensely talented twenty-eight-year-old dancer named Freddie Herko was a fixture at Andy's parties, until one night Freddie danced out of an open window at a friend's apartment while tripping on speed, LSD, and pot. Andy's parties were insane, reckless, and sometimes dangerous—but getting invited to them was everything. You could become famous just by being close to him. Andy Warhol was a kingmaker; he could make or break someone's career.

But there are consequences to having so much power. In 1968, a feminist playwright named Valerie Solanas shot Andy at point-blank range in the stomach and chest. When the police asked her why she did it, she said he "had too much control over [her] life." Andy was pronounced dead at the hospital—but once the doctors were told who he was, they resumed their efforts to resuscitate him, and it worked: they brought him back to life.

Andy claimed he didn't use drugs. Even though people all around him were snorting cocaine and tripping on acid, he insisted he didn't partake. But that wasn't exactly true. Bob Colacello, the former head of *Interview* magazine (which Andy founded), who spent years working side by side with him, says Andy absolutely flirted with cocaine but was sneaky about it. On multiple occasions, including one time at Mick Jagger's hotel suite, Bob saw Andy put cocaine up his nose or rub it on his gums—and yet, the very next second, Andy would flat-out deny it: "I did not, Bob. You're making it up." And everyone would laugh, including Andy.

Andy's drug of choice was meth. It came in the form of a diet pill called Obetrol. Andy didn't have a weight problem, but in the 1950s and '60s, diet pills were taken for all sorts of reasons. Obetrol was a powerful stimulant that combined methamphetamine with regular amphetamine; basically, it was pure medical-grade speed. At first, you could buy it over the counter at your local corner drugstore. By the midsixties, however, the FDA began to recognize meth was more dangerous than they'd originally thought, and changed the rules so you needed a prescription to get it. Of course, getting a prescription for diet pills wasn't hard to do, especially if you were rich and famous like Andy Warhol. In fact, Andy had just recently picked up his Obetrol from the drugstore when Valerie Solanas shot him at his studio.

Andy told people he only allowed himself to take a quarter of a pill each day—to give him "that wired, happy go-go-go feeling in your stomach that [makes] you want to work-work-work." But others who knew him well said he took four to eight times that much. He was popping diet pills like candy. Andy was, by nature, intense, passionate, and focused—and the meth hyperaccentuated those qualities. He was essentially using methamphetamine as a performance-enhancing drug. It probably explains how he was able to churn out such a prodigious amount of artwork. He produced (literally) thousands of pieces of art. The Warhol Museum in Pittsburgh contains more than nine hundred paintings, one thousand prints, four thousand photographs, sixty films, and four thousand videos.

How was it possible for one man to create so much art? Well, for one thing, he was more than one man. Andy realized he could produce more art (and make more money) if he involved more people in the process. So he hired assistants, gave them detailed instructions, and had them manufacture art for him. He functioned more like a fashion designer, expressing his vision to his underlings and allowing them to bring it to fruition. Also, he brought the industrial revolution to the fine art world by introducing mass production. He used silk-screening to duplicate the same image many times, making small tweaks in color or shading, producing multiple versions and variations in an extremely short period of time.

He named his art studio "the Factory," and that's pretty much what it was. He mass-produced fine art on a scale the world had never seen before. New art pieces emerged from the Factory at an astounding pace—sort of like that *I Love Lucy* episode where Lucy and Ethel are wrapping chocolates and can't keep up with the huge number of candies that go speeding by on the conveyor belt. Andy manufactured thousands of pieces of art at the Factory. He transformed the creation of "art" into a business—and it paid off big-time.

Despite his revolutionary approach to art and his wild bohemian parties, Andy was remarkably old-fashioned in some ways. Even as an adult, he continued to live with his mother and go to church almost every day (but typically not during mass because he was afraid of being recognized). He prayed with her in Old Slavonic each morning before he left the house. He wore a crucifix necklace, carried a string of rosary beads in his pocket, and kept a small prayer book at his bedside. He volunteered at homeless shelters and soup kitchens, especially around the holidays. He befriended the impoverished people he served there, and paid for his nephew to attend the seminary.

But he didn't like talking about his private life. As much as he craved fame, he was also painfully shy. When art critics asked him personal questions, he'd say: "If you want to know all about Andy Warhol, just look at the surface of my paintings and films and me, and there I am. There's nothing behind it." On those rare occasions when he did reveal something personal, such as the fact that he liked churches, he kept it simple. He claimed not to spend time thinking about God, but rather he went to churches because he thought they were pretty: "I like church. It's empty when I go. I walk around. There are so many beautiful Catholic churches in New York."

Andy coined the phrase "fifteen minutes of fame." It happened at an art exhibition in 1968, where he predicted that "in the future, everyone will be world-famous for fifteen minutes." But, clearly, he wasn't talking about himself—because more than sixty years have passed since he painted those Campbell's soup cans, and people are still talking about Andy Warhol.

Much like he did with the Empire State Building when he made the movie *Empire*, where he filmed the building for eight hours straight without ever moving the camera—quite possibly the result of one of his amphetamine-induced fixations—we just keep paying attention to him. We don't get bored and we don't avert our gaze.

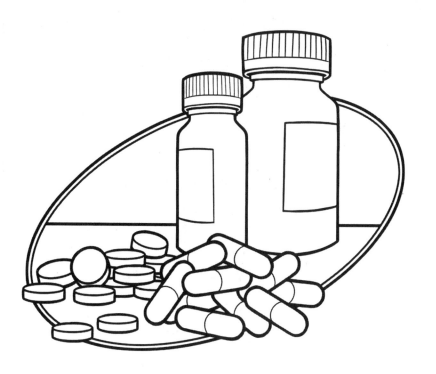

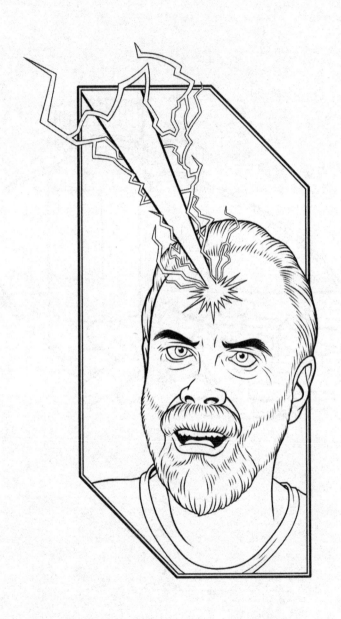

# CHAPTER 27

## Philip K. Dick Wrote Amphetamine-Fueled Science Fiction

---

Sometimes the same stuff that destabilizes a person's mind also provides them with brilliant inspiration for storytelling. Sci-fi legend Philip K. Dick consumed a colossal amount of amphetamines to temporarily boost his energy and focus so he could write story after story. At the same time, his incessant pill-popping weakened his already fragile mental state to the point where he sometimes couldn't distinguish reality from his fevered imagination. But Philip was such a unique talent that he was somehow able to channel the horrible side effects of amphetamine abuse into some of the most prescient science fiction that's ever been written.

He had the sort of profoundly discomfiting childhood that encourages a life of insecurity, mental illness, and drug abuse. Philip and his twin sister, Jane, were born in a poorly heated apartment in Chicago during the very cold winter of 1928. The babies were born six weeks prematurely, so they were very small: Philip weighed a little over four pounds, Jane only three and a half. Their mother, Dorothy, kept the babies in a shoebox, which she placed in the oven to keep them warm. Unfortunately, Dorothy didn't produce enough breast milk and didn't realize that her newborns were slowly starving to death. By sheer happenstance, a nurse stopped by the apartment for an entirely different reason and noticed the babies' desperate state, and they were rushed to the hospital. Philip just barely survived, but Jane died. For the rest of Philip's life, his mother blamed him for his sister's death. She said it was his fault because he was always clamoring for food, so she fed him more, and his poor sister died as a result of his greed.

Philip began taking amphetamines at age six; it was asthma medication that allowed him to breathe. While plenty of kids take amphetamine-based decongestants and don't end up hooked on speed, Philip's fraught relationship with his mother pretty much guaranteed she wasn't keeping an eye on him to make sure he was thinking about medicine in a healthy, productive way. Instead, Philip internalized the twisted lesson that he couldn't perform the basic functions of human life without chemical assistance. Basically, he started to believe that without amphetamines, he would die.

It wasn't long before he was taking way more amphetamines than the recommended dose. He was a shy loner at school, but amphetamines made him confident and fun to be around. Unfortunately, the same drug that made him more popular also gave him tachycardia (rapid heartbeat), which kept him out of school. Thus, by the time he was ten years old, amphetamines had already become a double-edged sword for Philip—temporarily solving one set of problems while creating a whole set of new ones.

Long-term amphetamine use can make a person hyped up and paranoid. Philip enrolled at UC Berkeley in 1949, eager to learn about philosophy, psychology, and history, but dropped out after only two months, overwhelmed by anxiety. Instead of learning from esteemed professors at a highly respected university, he was now sitting alone in his apartment, poring endlessly over a set of well-worn encyclopedias, focusing on the dark side of philosophy, reading about thinkers who believed nothing was real. He became increasingly convinced that the world as we know it is nothing more than an illusion. Then, needing to find a way to earn a living without a college degree, Philip decided to tap into his vivid and fearful imagination by writing pulp science fiction.

The problem with writing sci-fi was it paid next to nothing.[1] He had to crank out a ridiculous number of pages simply to keep his head above water. But Philip already knew a surefire way to maintain an insane level of productivity—speed. Lots of speed. He would sit down at his typewriter, swallow a handful of pills, and start pounding on the keys. His writing binges would last all night, up to twenty hours at a time. "The words come out of my hands, not my brain. I write with my hands," he said. He boasted that, cranked on amphetamines, he could write sixty-eight pages a day. He churned out entire novels in two or three weeks. During a five-year span in the 1950s, he wrote a staggering sixteen novels. But even then, he was living at or below the poverty line and sometimes had to resort to eating cat food.

Plenty of world-famous authors have used speed. W. H. Auden took a pill every morning to help him start writing. Graham Greene took two a day, one in the morning and another around midday so he wouldn't lose steam. And libertarian patron saint Ayn Rand started using amphetamines when she was rushing to finish *The Fountainhead*, and liked it so much that she kept using speed for the next thirty years.

But Philip K. Dick took more speed than all those writers combined. We're talking Caligula-like levels of excess. Remember when I told you how much Sartre liked drugs? That dude took maybe twenty pills a day. But Philip, after his fourth wife left him in 1970, was downing as many as a thousand pills *per week*. He literally stocked his refrigerator with jars containing a thousand pills

---

1. L. Ron Hubbard said at a sci-fi convention in 1948: "Writing for a penny a word is ridiculous. If a man wants to make a million dollars, the best way would be to start his own religion."

each, alongside a bunch of premade protein milkshakes so he wouldn't be ingesting all those drugs on an empty stomach (because, you know, that wouldn't be healthy). And that wasn't all. You know how on Halloween people pour candy into large bowls so trick-or-treaters can grab a handful? Philip did that with amphetamines. He kept a big bowl of uppers on his kitchen table and swallowed handfuls at a time like they were M&M's.

The effect this had on his brain and body was inconceivable. He'd go on manic writing binges, forgoing sleep entirely for several nights in a row, then not climbing out of bed for days. Half the time he didn't know if he was awake or asleep. Some of the most notorious side effects of amphetamine abuse are paranoia, delusions of persecution, visual and auditory hallucinations, and full-on psychosis. Philip claimed that he saw menacing figures hovering over his bed or lurking in the shadows. He developed a love/hate relationship with amphetamines, referring to them at various times as both his "happiness pills" and his "nightmare pills."

People who take too much speed often fear they are in imminent danger, that they are being deceived or lied to, and that sinister forces are conspiring against them. Philip experienced all that and more. In 1971, someone broke into his house—but the items they stole made no sense. His money and jewelry hadn't been touched, yet the thief had gone to the trouble of prying open his file cabinet, even though it wasn't locked. He became obsessed with figuring out who had done it, but his theories changed almost daily. At various times, he believed it was the CIA, the Black Panthers, Christian fundamentalists, or neo-Nazis. He ultimately became convinced the most likely culprit was himself—that he must have blacked out and broken into his own house in a fugue state, and now couldn't remember doing it. His connection to reality was like spotty wi-fi—it went in and out.

But his genius was such that he was able to take all these paranoid delusions and transform them into unforgettable storytelling. He wrote book after book about unhappy loners who know in their bones that something isn't right and ultimately discover, often after taking some kind of mysterious drug, that everything they know is a lie. In *Do Androids Dream of Electric Sheep?*[2] Rick Deckard (and pretty much every other human character in the book) worries, What if I'm a robot, but I don't know I'm a robot? In *We Can Remember It for You Wholesale*, Douglas Quail finds out his whole life is a fabricated memory that someone implanted in his head. In *A Scanner Darkly*, Bob Arctor is so whacked out by drugs that he doesn't realize the narcotics cop who has been surveilling him and feeding intel to the police is actually him—he's literally been spying on himself. Themes like this appear in Philip's works again and again.

However, there's a limit to how much speed you can take before something goes horribly wrong. For almost twenty-five years, Philip did an unbelievable job of turning paranoia into prose—but in February 1974, something happened that changed his life forever. He had two impacted wisdom teeth removed and was waiting for a delivery of pain medication. When the delivery lady arrived, she was wearing a fish-shaped necklace. He asked her what it meant, and she told him it was an early Christian symbol—the ichthys, popularly known as the "Jesus fish." That's when something incredible happened: according to Philip, the fish necklace shot out a brilliant pink laser beam that fired a cascade of magical visions into his brain and granted him psychic powers.

Was it a psychotic break or a religious experience? Philip was

---

2. Many of his stories have wonderfully intriguing titles that were simply too long to fit on a movie marquee—for example, *Do Androids Dream of Electric Sheep?* was replaced by the pithier title *Blade Runner*, and *We Can Remember It for You Wholesale* became *Total Recall*.

never entirely sure. He became obsessed with knowing the answer, devoting the rest of his life to trying to understand the magical pink laser beam. At times he believed that three-eyed aliens from outer space were transmitting information to him, an unplugged radio kept playing music (and sometimes insulted him), and the last two thousand years of recorded history were an illusion because in reality, it was still the year 70 CE. But he kept changing his mind: "On Thursdays and Saturdays I'd think it was God. On Tuesdays and Wednesdays I'd think it was extraterrestrials." He spent the next eight years, from 1974 to 1982, writing down more than a million words about his ever-shifting theories and conjectures; it formed an eight-thousand-page journal that Philip called his "exegesis."

While most people believe it was a psychotic episode brought on by a lifetime of amphetamine abuse, there are those who believe Philip genuinely developed precognition. As evidence, they point to the time he woke up from a nap screaming that his four-year-old son, Christopher, had a rare condition called an inguinal hernia and needed surgery right away. They rushed the boy to the hospital, where doctors confirmed the diagnosis—Christopher did indeed have an inguinal hernia and would have died without treatment. Proof of psychic powers, right? The problem with the story is that apparently, his wife, Tessa, had previously told Philip their son had a hernia, but he hadn't been listening, at least not consciously—until it bubbled up to the surface during his nap.

By 1977, he was suffering from irreversible pancreatic damage and regretted his years of over-the-top drug use. He knew the amphetamines made him aggressive and impossible to live with, resulting in five failed marriages. And even though his writing had earned him critical acclaim and a fanatical cult following, he was always running out of money because the drugs were so expensive—he was spending $300 a month on speed over half a century ago, which translates to roughly $1,700 a month today. But he also confessed he couldn't have accomplished all he had without the go-go-go pills. They were the high-test fuel he needed to pump out 44 novels and 121 stories in the span of only thirty years. "So I can't really say that for me amphetamines were a total negative thing," he said.

After spending his entire life on the brink of poverty, he finally hit pay dirt when Hollywood started turning his books into hit movies, such as *Blade Runner, Total Recall*, and *Minority Report*. But by then, drugs had wiped him out. He dropped dead of a stroke at age fifty-three before any of those movies opened.

Philip K. Dick was super messed up but a genius. His recurring themes—that something isn't right, that everything you believe is a lie, that shadowy forces are out to get you—resonate even more strongly today than they did when he wrote them. Unfortunately, the same stuff that imbued him with these dark thoughts—amphetamines—also ravaged his body and destroyed his mind. Thanks to ungodly amounts of amphetamines, Philip K. Dick didn't just write science fiction: he lived it.

# CHAPTER 28

# Johnny Cash Was Battling Demons

Johnny Cash was arrested for public drunkenness in a small Georgia town in 1967. He'd driven his Cadillac Eldorado off the side of the road and was banging on strangers' doors in the middle of the night, carrying a big bag of pills. When the cops showed up, he tried to bribe them with a fistful of hundred-dollar bills. They locked him in a jail cell overnight so he could sober up, and in the morning, the local sheriff had a long talk with Johnny. He said something to the effect of, "Son, I own every record you've put out, but you are throwing your life away, and if you don't cut it out, you're going to end up killing yourself." Johnny said that talk saved his life. Later, he returned to the small town to play a benefit concert at the local high school. They sold twelve thousand tickets—which was amazing given the town had only eighty-five hundred residents. He sold more tickets than they had people, and gave every penny back to the town.

That was Johnny Cash in a nutshell: Talented, but self-destructive. Bold and brash, but also humble and generous. A man who continually ran afoul of the law but remained a hero to the people. He was the iconic "Man in Black."

He was born to a poor family in Arkansas in 1932, during the Great Depression. Little Johnny was only five years old when he started picking cotton in the fields with the rest of his family, and they'd sing gospel hymns as they worked. Growing up like that meant he knew firsthand the struggles that people faced trying to make ends meet, and that hardscrabble experience inspired many of his songs.

Johnny suffered a devastating loss at an early age. His older brother Jack—his hero and best friend—died in a gruesome saw-mill accident at age fourteen. Child labor laws didn't exist back then, so Jack was working at the mill and got pulled into an unprotected table saw, which ripped into his stomach and practically cut him in half. Jack tried to stuff his intestines back into his torso and had to drag himself across the dirty shop floor to call for help. He stayed alive in horrible agony for a week before finally succumbing to his injuries. Twelve-year-old Johnny Cash had to dig his brother's grave.

He didn't stop believing in God when his brother died. If anything, the tragedy intensified his faith. Jack always planned to be a preacher, and Johnny wanted to honor his brother's path. He went to church three times a week with his family, and as an adult, he read the Bible almost every day. He recorded seven gospel albums, even though the record company begged him not to (because those albums didn't sell)—and he released a nineteen-hour spoken-word version of the New Testament that filled sixteen CDs.

But Johnny Cash was best known as an outlaw, and for good reason. He ran afoul of the law far too often. He was arrested no fewer than seven times, mostly due to his excessive drinking and drug use. But he never served more than a few nights in jail. He was famous, and that helped him escape more serious fallout.

He started swallowing amphetamines when he was twenty-five years old and his music career was just taking off. He mentioned to a fellow musician that he was so tired, he didn't know if he could perform. The guy reached into his pocket and gave Johnny a pill, and it was like magic: he was suddenly filled with energy. Soon, he was popping stimulants to stay awake as he drove from city to city to perform.

It spiraled out of control, of course. He was playing three hundred dates a year. He'd wolf down amphetamines to stay awake, then barbiturates to knock himself out. He quickly built up a tolerance, meaning he needed more and more pills to achieve the same effect. By the time he was twenty-eight, he was carrying around so many pills, they'd often spill out of his pockets. It reached the point where he was swallowing a hundred pills a day and washing them down with a case of beer. As he explained in an interview: "I was taking the pills for a while, and then the pills started taking me."

His fans had front-row seats to his addiction. His performances became erratic; he'd stumble around onstage and bump into sound equipment. Concert dates were missed because he didn't show up. An entire ten-day tour had to be canceled because no one knew where he was. One time, he overdosed before a show; his handlers found him passed out on the floor of his motor home, so they lifted him up, carried him onto the stage, and plopped him down in front of the microphone. Such was the life of a celebrity. People around him were all too willing to turn a blind eye to his addiction, as long as he could still perform.

His exploits became fodder for the tabloids. He was in and out of rehab multiple times. A show at Texas A&M had to be canceled at the last minute because he was arrested for smuggling pills across the Mexican border in his guitar case. He crashed a car into a telephone pole, and he drove a tractor into a lake. He instituted a policy that while touring, he needed to stay in a hotel suite large enough to have separate bedrooms for him and his wife, June Carter—that way, she couldn't search his bedroom to hide his pills.

In 1965, he accidentally started a forest fire. He was driving his truck camper named Jesse (after the outlaw Jesse James) through a national forest but was so dazed from pills and booze that he didn't know what he was doing. The truck overheated and sparked a blaze that destroyed five hundred acres, including a habitat for endangered condors. The federal government took him to court, but Johnny said, "I don't care about your damn yellow buzzards." He refused to admit drugs and alcohol played any role in the fire, insisting his camper had a defective exhaust system—which was impossible to disprove because the truck had been destroyed in the fire. When the judge asked him why he did it, Johnny said, "I didn't do it, my truck did and it's dead, so you can't question it."

In 1981, he famously fought an ostrich. (That's right, he ran afoul of a fowl.) He owned an exotic animal park filled with unusual creatures, including a llama, a buffalo, and an ostrich named Waldo. One day, he was walking through the park and saw Waldo blocking his path. The ornery ostrich hissed and spread his wings aggressively. Johnny decided it was time to show Waldo who was boss, so he picked up a large stick and swung it at the enormous bird. Bad idea. Waldo jumped on top of him, broke his ribs, and used its razor-sharp claws to rip open Johnny's stomach all the way down to his belt. The only reason Johnny didn't die (or get castrated) was because he was wearing a thick metal belt buckle—but recovering from the ostrich attack got him taking painkillers again, and he didn't stop when the pain went away. He kept taking the pills because he liked how they made him feel.

Johnny was never free from his addictions. He told an interviewer: "There is that beast there in me. And I got to keep him caged, or he'll eat me alive." He was a God-fearing Christian his whole life, but he was also hugely into alcohol and drugs. It's not a contradiction. People who have experienced adversity and loss often take solace in religion, but they also frequently seek relief from chemicals that make the pain go away, at least for a little while. It's like the hit song Johnny recorded titled "Sunday Morning

Coming Down," in which a man gets ready for church hungover from the night before, knowing he'll listen intently to the preacher and the choir but come out wishing he was still stoned.

Johnny wasn't a role model by any means. But he was an inspiration, not only for his talent, but for his honesty. He told *Rolling Stone*, "I'm the biggest sinner of them all." Instead of trying to hide his flaws, he bared them for all to see. That's what made his cover of the Nine Inch Nails song "Hurt" so powerful, because he sounded like he was speaking from the heart:

> And you could have it all
> My empire of dirt
> I will let you down
> I will make you hurt

Johnny didn't write the song. But the person who did, Trent Reznor, acknowledged Johnny's version had a naked sincerity that gave the song new meaning. It "wasn't my song anymore," Reznor said.

Johnny had many failings but always aspired to be better. He said once that when he saw the movie *Frankenstein*, he sympathized with the monster—because he was someone who was "made up of bad parts, but was trying to do good."

Johnny Cash was a country artist, but his popularity went far beyond that. He's one of the top-selling recording artists of all time, having sold more than ninety million albums worldwide. Why? Because he was authentic. He sang for the poor, the working class, and those who didn't have a voice. He performed in prisons and in churches. He was troubled and deeply flawed, yet he formed an emotional connection with his listeners because they knew as they listened to him that he was just like us.

# CHAPTER 29

## Elvis Presley Was a Narc

lvis Presley was a narc. He hated hippies and their free-wheeling attitude toward drug use. If he found out someone who worked for him had smoked marijuana, he would order them never to do it again. He despised recreational drug use so much that he asked for a face-to-face meeting with President Richard Nixon. There, he told Nixon that he was making it his personal mission to set the hippies straight and get them to stop using drugs. The ironic twist: Elvis was high as a kite during the meeting. How did this happen? Well, it's quite a story.

Today, everyone has heard of the opioid crisis. Millions of Americans have been prescribed these drugs for legitimate medical reasons, only to become addicted and watch their lives spiral out of control. Half a century ago, however, people did not understand it was possible to become addicted to prescription drugs. Medicine was supposed to help, not hurt. Before these dangers were under-stood, Elvis Presley fell victim to prescription drug abuse.

When Elvis burst onto the scene in 1954, he had it all: boyish good looks; a deep, resonant, soothingly masculine voice; and wild dance moves that made the girls scream and swoon. But perhaps the biggest force behind his fame was his style of music. In the 1940s, before Elvis rose to fame, the most popular acts for white audiences were big bands and slow sultry crooners. Elvis could croon, but—at the drop of a hat—he could also switch from slow and syrupy to fast and energetic. He played music that made audiences want to dance and shout, transforming the idea of what popular music could be. Basically, Elvis got white people into rock and roll.

The record producer who gave Elvis his first deal was specifically aiming for cultural appropriation when he took a chance on the young singer, telling people, "If I could find a white man who had the Negro sound and the Negro feel, I could make a billion dollars!" Unlike that producer, Elvis wasn't cynically attempting to rip off Black culture; his affection for the music was genuine and guileless. He was born in a shotgun shack lit by a single bulb. He brought his guitar to school and sang at recess, where he was teased by his classmates for being a white trash kid who played hillbilly music. He had no formal training, couldn't read music to save his life, and played everything by ear. But he fell in love with the musical traditions of his African-American neighbors, snuck into their churches to hear gospel singers, and violated segregation laws to attend Black-only concerts. His two great musical loves were country music, dominated by white people, and rhythm and blues, dominated by Black people. He decided to combine them.

Elvis's debut album was a smash hit. He made an even bigger splash when he sang on live TV in January 1956, swiveling his hips, gyrating his pelvis, and spinning around wildly onstage. Young people loved it; older people, not so much. Music critics denounced his suggestive moves as crass and talentless; local church dioceses phoned the FBI insisting he was a danger to the youth of America; and Ed Sullivan, host of the nation's most-watched variety show, declared him "unfit for family viewing." But his popularity couldn't be denied, and Sullivan eventually booked him onto his show—but had him filmed only from the waist up. At the end of the show, Sullivan stood beside Elvis and declared him "a real decent, fine boy."

Elvis's life changed forever when he was drafted into the US Army. It was 1957 and he was the biggest star in the world. Getting drafted meant putting his skyrocketing career on hold for several years, but he didn't fight it. He was a patriotic young man who believed in serving his country. In fact, when the army offered him a cushy job, saying he could perform concerts for the troops instead of going through basic training, he turned it down. He insisted on being treated like everyone else, saying: "The army can do anything it wants with me."

So, the army got him hooked on drugs. While Elvis was serving overseas in Germany in 1958, a sergeant told him amphetamines would make him stronger, faster, and an overall better soldier. (Sadly, this is not surprising—as mentioned in the chapter on Hitler, armies throughout history have used amphetamines as "go pills" to keep soldiers energized and alert.) Soon, Elvis was taking amphetamines on a daily basis and enthusiastically singing their praises to his fellow soldiers. He joined the army as a clean-cut kid but came back an addict.

He was still deployed in Germany when his mother became ill. He flew home on emergency leave, but his mother died shortly after he arrived. Her death hit him hard. He returned to Germany after the funeral, still reeling from the loss, feeling alone and unmoored. Amphetamines were there to dull the pain and keep him going.

His military service ended in 1960, but his amphetamine addiction did not. America had been pining for Elvis's return the entire time he served overseas. There was a huge pent-up demand for all things Elvis, and his manager, "Colonel" Tom Parker, was determined to squeeze every last dollar from it. He pushed Elvis to tour constantly, performing an average of one show every other night;

got him to sign a record contract requiring three albums a year; and booked him into a series of formulaic Hollywood movies that critics hated but the public loved, earning a fortune. Elvis Presley was box-office gold.

How did Elvis maintain this punishing schedule? By taking even more drugs. He took uppers when it was time to work and downers when it was time to sleep. Much like his time in the army, there were "go" pills when there was a job to do and "no-go" pills to make sure he rested when the mission was over.

Gradually, Elvis stopped enjoying the work. After a long line of lackluster films with subpar soundtracks, he became demoralized. He was still in his early thirties, but audiences were beginning to see him not as the bright shining star he'd once been but as a fading has-been. It damaged his self-esteem. He knew people considered him a sellout, and he had a hard time disagreeing. To compensate for his lack of engagement with his work, he began taking even more drugs.

His Las Vegas residency in 1969 was a chance to reestablish himself as the free-spirited rock-and-roller he had once been, and to distance himself from his new, schlocky persona. But in Vegas, his drug use only worsened. He popped amphetamines, trying to recapture his youthful energy, and took pain pills like crazy because he could no longer gyrate and swivel onstage without hurting his hips, back, and legs. His personal physician, Dr. George Nichopoulos (a.k.a. "Dr. Nick"), later testified that Elvis popped pills "from the time he woke up in the morning until the time he went to sleep at night" and took three suitcases full of prescription drugs when he went out on tour.

The drugs put a strain on his mental health. He became increasingly paranoid, convinced that people were trying to kill him. He purchased numerous guns and carried two or three with him at all times. Even when performing onstage, he had a derringer tucked in his boot and a .45-caliber pistol in his waistband. He was in constant physical and emotional pain, trying anything to feel better, including popping pills and stress-eating fatty fried foods, causing his weight to swell and his body to morph. Elvis was so heavily medicated that he struggled to support his own weight and could barely make it through shows, slurring his words, forgetting song lyrics, and stumbling around onstage. Audiences could tell something was wrong.

By age forty-two, Elvis could no longer hide his chemical dependency. Three of his bodyguards published a book in 1977 detailing his addiction to prescription drugs and the debilitating effects on his mental and physical health. Elvis was devastated. He regarded the book as an act of betrayal, yet almost everything the bodyguards wrote proved to be true. Two weeks after it was published, Elvis collapsed on his bathroom floor and died. The autopsy found fourteen different drugs in his system, ten of which were in significant amounts, including the opioids Demerol, Percodan, and codeine.

Why didn't anyone help him? Because he was surrounded by relentless enablers whose goal was to keep him performing rather than keep him healthy. Colonel Tom kept lining up the jobs, and Dr. Nick kept giving him drugs so he could do the jobs. The drugs masked the fact that he had overworked himself for years and never got the medical attention that could have solved his underlying issues.

After Elvis's death, the board of medical examiners held a hearing to determine whether Dr. Nick should be stripped of his medical license. Evidence showed that in the last twenty months of Elvis's life, Dr. Nick had given him more than twelve thousand prescription pills. The doctor testified he had no choice but to give Elvis drugs whenever he asked, reasoning that otherwise he would have gotten the drugs off the street, which would have been dangerous. Amazingly, the board accepted this defense. They concluded that by giving Elvis an endless supply of amphetamines and opioids, Dr. Nick had somehow been "acting in the best interests of the patient."

This brings us back to his infamous meeting with President Nixon. It was 1970, and Elvis's career was on the upswing thanks to the success of his Las Vegas residency. He arrived at the White House wearing a purple velvet suit with a matching cape and told the president he wanted to become an antidrug ambassador to the hippie youth of America, curing them of the disease of recreational drugs. All he asked for in return was an official badge from the Bureau of Narcotics to prove his bona fides. Nixon found the meeting incredibly awkward, but the request seemed harmless enough, so he instructed his aides to give Elvis a specially made tin shield. It was obviously a fake badge, but Elvis was ecstatic. He reached his arm around the president and hugged him.

To this day, the photo of Elvis shaking hands with Nixon in the Oval Office is the single most requested item from the National Archives, more frequently requested than copies of the Constitution or the Bill of Rights.

The story is both absurd and tragic. Elvis was a full-blown addict when he met the president and was almost certainly high during their meeting, yet he believed with all his heart that he could be an effective antidrug role model for America's youth because he wasn't taking illegal drugs, he was taking medicine prescribed by his doctor.

The takeaway here is not that drugs are bad. The types of pills that Elvis took have helped many people, but he was never educated about the dangers of taking too many—or of combining them with each other. The same drugs that can improve a person's health can also prove deadly if they are used improperly. Education is the key to ensuring better outcomes.

Elvis mistakenly believed his drug use couldn't be considered out of control if a doctor was willing to sign off on it. But doctors at the time didn't appreciate the full scope of the danger posed by prescription drugs. In the 1970s, when Percocet and Vicodin came on the scene, doctors knew addiction was possible, but most believed the risks could be easily managed and were outweighed by the drugs' remarkable efficacy in treating chronic pain.

Elvis began his career as a clean-cut, God-fearing young man with endless potential, but over time he became an addict whose life was controlled by his intense biochemical cravings. Even as his weight ballooned and his mind and body collapsed, Elvis believed that nothing his doctor gave him could ever truly hurt him.

# PART 7

# COUNTER-CULTURE MAYHEM

# CHAPTER 30

# Albert Hofmann Invented LSD by Accident

———————

Straitlaced laboratory chemist Albert Hofmann never imagined that while studying the medical applications of ergot fungus in 1943, he would accidentally stumble upon an unprecedented substance with the power to alter someone's perception of reality. For ten blissful years, his mind-warping creation was a huge boon to the field of psychotherapy and benefited patients greatly—until the CIA and hippies got involved and ruined everything.

It began innocently enough. Hofmann was working in his lab, combining small bits of ergot with a variety of organic molecules, trying to create something with a medical use. He tried twenty-five different combinations, but none of them did anything. A bunch of lab animals got weirdly excited when he dosed them with the twenty-fifth batch, but there didn't appear to be a pharmacological impact, so he shelved the experiment and moved on. But it nagged at him. Five years later, he tried the experiment again—and this time, a tiny bit of the twenty-fifth batch dripped onto his finger. He thought nothing of it at the time, just wiped off his finger and kept working. But it was too late—the mysterious substance had already been absorbed through his skin.

Forty minutes later, he felt woozy and disoriented, almost as if he were drunk. He went home and lay down on his couch, where he spent the next several hours in a pleasant dreamlike state, eyes closed, imagination running wild, experiencing an uninterrupted stream of fantastical images, extraordinary shapes, and a kaleidoscope of colors. When the effects finally wore off, he sat up sharply and asked himself, "What the hell was that?"

As a scientist, he knew further experimentation was required. But he also thought maybe he was imagining things, so he didn't tell anyone. Instead, he made plans to deliberately ingest a small amount of the mysterious substance that he'd abbreviated as "LSD-25." To ensure he was proceeding as safely as possible, he took precautions as if he were dealing with a deadly poison. He'd take a dose so ridiculously minuscule that even the most potent toxin known to man would have virtually no perceptible effect—only 250 *millionths* of a gram. Smart, right? Except it turns out LSD is even more potent than poison. Taking a dose the size of a grain of salt can totally rearrange your perception of reality—and Hofmann took 250 micrograms, which is the equivalent of dropping two and a half tabs of pure acid.

He knew immediately he was in trouble. He felt seriously unwell and told his lab assistant to take him home—except it was 1943, World War II was raging, and automobile usage was severely restricted. The only mode of transportation available was a bicycle. He was savvy enough to know there was no way he could safely operate a bike on his own, so he ordered his assistant to accompany him, and they rode away from the lab on their bikes, pedaling side by side.

What ensued was the ultimate bike *trip*. You know that famous painting of melting clocks—Salvador Dalí's *The Persistence of Memory*? Well, imagine a bewildered and megahallucinating Albert Hofmann riding his little bike through the surrealist landscape of that iconic masterpiece, because as he pedaled through the bustling streets of Basel, Switzerland, reality was melting away around him.

The sky was filled with geometric shapes and colors he'd never seen before, everyday objects assumed threatening forms and began to circle menacingly around him, and everything within his field of vision was wavering and shimmering as though distorted by a fun-house mirror. The entire world was unraveling.

It was the longest two and a half miles of his life. But now it's celebrated as "Bicycle Day." April 19, 1943: the first time anyone ever tripped on LSD. Dr. Albert Hofmann had just created the world's first synthetic psychedelic drug.

When he woke up the next morning, he felt incredible—he possessed a zest for life more vigorous and refreshing than anything he'd ever experienced. It was as if he'd formed a direct spiritual connection to Mother Nature herself. When he had begun his ergot experiments, he'd been hoping to create a new medicine for the human body, but he had inadvertently accomplished something much more profound—he had invented medicine for the soul.

The company he worked for was thrilled. Sandoz began selling his exciting new drug under the trade name Delysid. It was advertised as a powerful psychiatric tool that could help cure a wide variety of mental disorders, from alcoholism to schizophrenia. In small doses and under a doctor's watchful eye, the drug could prove transformative. Sandoz sent out free samples and encouraged psychiatrists to try the product themselves—it was a huge hit. For a brief shining moment in history, LSD was the treatment du jour in the field of psychoanalysis.

Until the US government came up with a few less altruistic, more sinister uses for the mind-altering power of LSD. In the early 1950s, the director of the CIA's top secret MK-Ultra program (you'll be hearing a lot more about this in chapters to come) paid $240,000 to buy up the entire world's existing stockpile of LSD. The CIA figured that since LSD was helping psychiatrists get their patients to open up during therapy, it could also be used as a way to interrogate prisoners—a sort of truth serum, a chemical crowbar to pry secrets out of anyone who refused to talk. This inspired the US military to speculate whether it could weaponize LSD and use it in combat. Instead of dosing one enemy combatant at a time, why not spray it as a "madness gas" on an entire enemy army?

Next came the hippies. In the early 1960s, LSD became the must-have pharmaceutical for every recreational drug user. These beatniks didn't have any medical need for the drug, they just wanted to break the shackles of conventional thinking and open their minds. LSD became the palpitating heart and psychedelic soul of the counterculture movement. People like Timothy Leary and Ken Kesey encouraged young people to "tune in, turn on, and drop out"—and LSD was the tuning fork they used to reach their perfect pitch.

It wasn't long before recreational use of LSD was far more widespread than legitimate psychiatric use. Freak-outs and bad trips grabbed all the headlines. Urban legends spread about how the drug could drive people insane—and that's when it got shut down. Governments all over the world started banning LSD. They didn't just make it illegal, they demonized it. The powers that be decided that Dr. Hofmann's creation, no matter how well-intentioned, was too dangerous to be allowed to exist.

Hofmann was heartbroken. He had inadvertently stumbled upon an extraordinary scientific breakthrough that had revolutionized the field of psychotherapy, yet now it was being dismissed and vilified as the province of foolish hippies and brain-addled stoners. He wrote a book called *LSD: My Problem Child*, reminding everyone that for more than a decade, LSD had been astonishingly successful in treating people and had made a genuinely positive impact on the world, until the counterculture movement hijacked it and pushed it underground. He detested the cavalier use of LSD as a drug for entertainment. Almost any drug is dangerous when used incorrectly.

That didn't mean LSD should be illegal; it meant it should be classified as a controlled substance, like morphine, that when used judiciously by trained medical professionals can be enormously beneficial.

He spent the rest of his life attempting to rehabilitate LSD's tattered public image in hopes of getting it reapproved for medical use. In 2007, a friend told him that tech billionaire Steve Jobs was a huge fan of LSD. Not only did Jobs publicly admit to using the drug, he even credited LSD with inspiring him to create the Apple computer. Hofmann was thrilled at the prospect of getting such an important man to support his cause. At the age of 101, he sent a handwritten letter to Steve Jobs that read:

Dear Mr. Steve Jobs,

Hello from Albert Hofmann. I understand from media accounts that you feel LSD helped you creatively in your development of Apple Computers and your personal spiritual quest. I'm interested in learning more about how LSD was useful to you.

I'm writing now, shortly after my 101st birthday, to request that you support Swiss psychiatrist Dr. Peter Gasser's proposed study of LSD-assisted psychotherapy in subjects with anxiety associated with life-threatening illness. This will become the first LSD-assisted psychotherapy study in over 35 years, and will be sponsored by MAPS.

I hope you will help in the transformation of my problem child into a wonder child.

Sincerely

Albert Hofmann

Unfortunately, it appears that Jobs never responded to Dr. Hofmann's letter. The medical study that Hofmann was desperately asking Jobs to support never got off the ground. And one year later, Hofmann died at age 102.

But his dream lives on. Microdosing LSD has gained a fervent following in Silicon Valley. Celebrities such as Steve Jobs, Michael Pollan, Paul McCartney, Anthony Bourdain, and A$AP Rocky have spoken openly about using the drug. Maybe one day Dr. Hofmann's "problem child" will gain scientific acceptance and finally get the chance to blossom into a well-adjusted and socially useful adult.

# CHAPTER 31

# Aldous Huxley's Shortcut to Enlightenment

S ome people experiment with psychedelic drugs when they're in college, but *Brave New World* author Aldous Huxley decided to wait until he was fifty-nine years old.

For almost his entire life, Huxley was bedeviled by the fact that everyone else could see more than he could. His vision problems began in 1911, when he was sixteen years old. He was struck blind by a disease called keratitis punctata. After eighteen long, painful months, he finally managed to recover some of his eyesight, but he remained partially blind for the rest of his life. His condition was severe enough that when he volunteered to join the British Army in 1916 to fight in World War I, the army rejected him because he was still half-blind in one eye. His awful eyesight also kept him from pursuing his life's ambition to be a laboratory scientist.

Huxley switched to academics because, apparently, wearing Coke-bottle glasses and using a magnifying glass to read were perfectly fitting for a professor. He briefly taught French at Eton College in 1917 and 1918, but keeping control of the classroom was hard work, and he sucked at it (at least according to George Orwell, who was one of his students). So, he switched gears and became a novelist, figuring it was easier to control the behavior of fictional characters than a bunch of unruly testosterone-fueled teenage boys. He soon became a darling of the literary world, publishing a string of novels satirizing modern society, leading up to *Brave New World* in 1932. Based on the book's smashing success, Huxley shipped out to Hollywood in 1937 and became a highly sought-after screenwriter. He wrote screenplays of cinematic classics such as *Pride and Prejudice* and *Jane Eyre*, and was soon earning the modern-day equivalent of $50,000 per week.

Sure, he was earning big bucks, but it still drove him crazy that he couldn't see as well as everybody else. In desperation, he tried something called the Bates Method, a controversial (and decidedly unscientific) treatment that theorized that vision problems were caused by too much stress on the eyes—and that wearing glasses only worsened the problem. The only true cure, according to this deeply dubious theory, was relaxation and natural sunlight. Not surprisingly, the Bates Method was eventually debunked, but for years Huxley insisted it was working. He published a book called *The Art of Seeing* in 1942, in which he sang its praises, claiming: "Within a couple of months, I was reading without spectacles, and what was better still, without strain or fatigue."

The truth was revealed in the most embarrassing way possible when Huxley was giving a speech at a Hollywood awards ceremony. Everyone was impressed that he wasn't wearing glasses yet seemed to be having no trouble at all reading from his notes. But in the middle of his speech, he fumbled his words and didn't know what to say next. It became agonizingly obvious to everyone in the room that he'd been reciting the entire speech from memory, except now he'd forgotten the words and couldn't see what was plainly written on the page in front of him. He pulled the notes closer and squinted as hard as he could, but he couldn't see a thing. Sadly, he had no choice but to abandon the masquerade and pull out his magnifying glass so he could finish his speech.

In desperation, he turned to Eastern mysticism. He was living in Los Angeles, which even back then was a hot spot for people seeking enlightenment in unusual ways. He studied with a swami, who showed him there were ways of seeing that didn't require good eyesight. Huxley was intrigued by the notion of gaining inner sight through exercises of the mind and spirit. Was it possible that he could "see" with his soul instead of his eyes? After looking into it extensively, he concluded it truly was possible. He could achieve spiritual enlightenment through dedication, discipline, and a herculean amount of meditation and study.

But, you know, all that would take a long time, and he was already pretty old. Lucky for him, he found a shortcut—a way to achieve enlightenment without all the muss and fuss. It was called mescaline.

He tried an experiment under controlled conditions. On May 5, 1953, he sat in his living room with a psychiatrist named Humphry Osmond, who was also his drug supplier and ad hoc tripsitter. He carefully dissolved four-tenths of a gram of mescaline into a glass of water and drank it. He was a fifty-nine-year-old man sipping a powerful psychoactive substance for the first time. It started out as pure intellectual curiosity. He had read scholarly write-ups about Indigenous peoples in America having mystical experiences while under the influence of peyote, and he simply wanted to know more.

But wow! He fell in love with mescaline right away. He felt suddenly transported, as if the drug had opened his eyes to a whole new world. In *Alice in Wonderland*, a young girl drinks a mysterious potion and enters a magical world where the rules of ordinary reality no longer apply. Huxley was having an analogous experience. He drank a mysterious potion and entered a world where, for the first time in his life, he could see *everything*.

He wrote an entire book extolling the virtues of mescaline. It was called *The Doors of Perception*.[1] He explained that the human brain is a valve that can be opened and closed. Most of the time, the valve is shut almost completely, allowing only a small trickle of information to the brain, which helps to keep people grounded, focused only on the things that are most essential to their survival—food, shelter, clothing, et cetera. But taking mescaline was like opening the valve all the way and letting the entire universe pour into your brain. He claimed it let him see and feel everything in the universe all at once: "Each person is at each moment capable of remembering all that has ever happened to him and of perceiving everything that is happening everywhere in the universe."

This was exactly what Huxley had been searching for his entire life. Thanks to mescaline, he didn't just see what other people saw; he actually saw more. He observed past, present, and future, at the same time. He was convinced such a drug could be incredibly beneficial in therapy. As he explained to one interviewer: "Many people get tremendous recalls of buried material. A process which may take six years of psychoanalysis happens in an hour—and considerably cheaper!"

From that moment on, Huxley was all in for psychedelics. He even helped Osmond coin the term "psychedelic." And he didn't stop at mescaline. He also became a huge fan of LSD, which he tried for the first time on Christmas Eve 1955 ('tis the season!) and declared as even more eye-opening than mescaline.

Interestingly, his real-world experience with psychedelics completely changed how he depicted drugs in his books. In *Brave New World*, the drug soma had been a tool used by the government to keep the populace comfortably numb; soma was a symbol of everything that was rotten in this dystopian society. But in

---

1. Jim Morrison's band the Doors took their name from the title of Huxley's book.

his final book, *Island*, he imagined a flourishing society that embraced psychopharmacology and handed out psychedelic pills called moksha, which Huxley described as "the reality revealer, the truth-and-beauty pill." In the span of thirty years, Huxley went from depicting drugs as chemical shackles that enslave humankind to portraying them as the key that unlocks human potential. He did a complete 180—going from dystopia to utopia—and all it took was a few tabs of acid.

Of course, in *Brave New World*, Huxley had mocked the idea that a drug could be used as a shortcut to improve people's lives: "In the past you could only accomplish these things by making a great effort and after years of hard moral training. Now, you swallow two or three half-gramme tablets, and there you are." But, ironically, this was precisely the shortcut Huxley took in his own life when he embraced mescaline and LSD as the path to enlightenment. He went from being someone who criticized "chemically induced happiness" to someone who genuinely believed in "better living through chemistry."

Being able to see meant everything to Huxley, but still he said there was no reason to overdo it. One of the great things about psychedelics, he believed, was that the drugs wore off, but the revelations stuck around. He said in an interview that he took mescaline only twice. He used LSD more often but was able to go for long stretches without using it at all.

Until the day he died—November 22, 1963. On his deathbed, unable to speak because of advanced throat cancer, he scribbled a note to his wife, asking her to let him take one last trip. He asked her to inject him with one hundred micrograms of LSD, so he could slip his mortal coil and become one with the universe. She unhesitatingly granted his request.

Of course, no one knows if it actually worked.

# CHAPTER 32

# How the CIA Accidentally Created the Unabomber

I t sounds like a supervillain origin story: in the 1950s and '60s, the CIA's top secret brainwashing program, MK-Ultra, inadvertently birthed one of the most notorious terrorists in American history. He was a shy seventeen-year-old kid who signed up for a psychology experiment at Harvard University—he had no clue it was actually a CIA operation. They dosed him with LSD without telling him, then verbally assaulted him and mocked his beliefs. They humiliated and degraded him on purpose, trying to see if LSD could be used to break someone. But getting unwittingly dosed with a psychedelic can make you think you're losing your mind—they only succeeded in traumatizing him. He became radicalized and vengeful, dropping out of society, living in the wilderness, and mailing homemade bombs to unsuspecting victims. His name was Ted Kaczynski, and he was the Unabomber.

Before MK-Ultra, he was a teenage whiz kid with enormous potential. He had an IQ of 167, and his classmates described him as "a walking brain." Harvard recognized immediately that he was a genius and accepted him at age fifteen, offering him a full scholarship. When he started in fall 1958, he was only sixteen years old and younger, smaller, and more naïve than his classmates. Harvard put him in the "egghead dorm," reserved for the most brilliant freshmen; it probably made it harder to bond with his classmates, but it didn't turn him into a psychopath. The doctor who performed his freshman intake exam said Kaczynski was "slightly shy and retiring but not to any abnormal extent." In other words, being quiet, awkward, and incredibly smart doesn't make you a terrorist—it makes you a typical Harvard freshman. The difference was that Kaczynski volunteered for a psych experiment during his sophomore year.

Here's what the description of the experiment told him to expect: write a brief essay about your personal philosophy and the guiding moral principles you live by, then another student will engage you in a collegial debate about the merits of your respective ideologies. This was intellectual catnip to a brilliant but isolated teen like Kaczynski—an opportunity to sit across a table from one of his peers and share a highbrow discussion of thoughts and ideas. It was like a dream come true.

But the reality was a nightmare—less *My Dinner with Andre*, more *A Clockwork Orange*. As soon as he stepped into the room, they strapped electrodes to his chest, shined a blinding spotlight in his eyes, and began attacking everything he'd written about in his essay. It was a complete bait and switch—it wasn't a friendly debate; it was a brutal interrogation. But instead of asking him questions, some government-sponsored asshole was belittling him and mocking his most cherished beliefs. The professor who designed the experiment said it was intended to be "vehement, sweeping, and personally abusive."

But it gets worse: they also dosed him with LSD. Remember, this poor kid was a "walking brain," a creature of pure intellect—except now his brain was being tampered with. He felt a formless yet growing terror that his mind was no longer his own. The purpose of the experiment was to find out if psychotropic drugs could be used to break someone, and screaming at a prisoner, insulting them, blinding them with bright lights—those are all great ways to destabilize someone you're interrogating. But if you really want to torment them, slip a tab of acid in their coffee without telling them. If you take LSD on purpose and something trippy happens, you think, *Of course that happened, I took LSD.* But drugging him without his knowledge would make the trip incomprehensible—it would undermine his sense of reality. As the world shifted and seethed around him, Kaczynski must have thought, as anyone would, that he was going insane. He'd lost control of his most prized possession—his mind.

Oh, I almost forgot, they filmed the whole thing. The CIA surreptitiously recorded him through a one-way mirror as a skilled interrogator ripped his essay to shreds and insulted his ideology. Then they forced Kaczynski to watch the tape. His lowest moments were played back over and over so he could see how stupid and pathetic he appeared, while his interrogator stood there, laughing and taunting him. They were highlighting his powerlessness by forcing him to relive the whole excruciating experience, so he could see how truly humiliating his intellectual beatdown had been. This seventeen-year-old genius, who prided himself on being self-possessed, articulate, and really goddamn smart, was required to watch himself behaving like a gibbering idiot. It was the ultimate degradation.

Believe it or not, I haven't told you the worst part yet: They didn't do this to him only once, and not only a handful of times. This utterly unethical experiment was repeated every week for the next three years—the entire remainder of his time at Harvard. Of course, they never said it was going to last three years. They just kept coming to see him—week in, week out, without fail. Kaczynski was tricked, cajoled, or coerced into continuing the ordeal until he finally graduated. It was like falling asleep, having night terrors, and being unable to wake up for three long years—if that's not torture, I'm not sure what is. Kaczynski described it as "the worst experience of [his] life."

Can you imagine what it did to him? I'm no apologist for the Unabomber, but you've got to admit the CIA stacked the deck against the guy. Of course the psych experiment caused his mind to crack. That was the whole point: to break him. But it sure looks like he didn't so much jump into evil as he was pushed. When you take a brilliant but fragile young man who's already sort of an odd-ball loner and you torture him psychologically for three years, you can't act too surprised when he turns into a horrifying monster. Kaczynski took a one-way trip from nobody to nightmare—but it was the CIA who bought him the ticket.

It wasn't obvious right away that he'd snapped. For a few years, it looked like he might be able to scrape together a normal life. He became an assistant math professor at UC Berkeley at age twenty-five—although, looking back now, it seems like he only took that job to build up a nest egg to fund his later terrorist activities. At age twenty-nine, he dropped off the grid and moved to a shack in the woods in Montana with no electricity or running water. He built package bombs and sent them through the mail for seventeen years, killing three people, wounding twenty-three more, and terrorizing an entire nation. He was finally captured in 1996, after the longest and most expensive manhunt in American history. Kaczynski ultimately died in a prison cell in 2023—the general consensus is that he hanged himself—at age eighty-one.

All this is documented: the hyperaggressive interrogation, belittling his beliefs, filming him through a mirror, repeating the experience every week. The only thing that isn't fully documented is the LSD. There are no official records still in existence that prove the CIA dosed him with LSD—and can you guess why? Because the CIA destroyed those records. They didn't want a bunch of incriminating evidence about their unhinged mind-control experiments being read out loud in some congressional hearing—so, in 1973, CIA director Richard Helms ordered the destruction of all

MK-Ultra files. That, too, is a documented fact. And don't forget: not even Kaczynski knew he'd been given LSD. That was absolutely crucial to the experiment—the CIA wanted to know if being dosed *unwittingly* made it easier to break someone. And it appears the answer was yes, because they certainly broke Ted Kaczynski.

But if Kaczynski didn't know he was being dosed, and if the CIA shredded the files that would have proved it, how do we know they actually gave him LSD? Well, lucky for us, the CIA was sloppy. Some of their files survived the purge, and those files have been made public under the Freedom of Information Act. While the recovered files don't say much about Kaczynski in particular, they do make one thing crystal clear: *MK-Ultra was obsessed with LSD.* The CIA was desperately afraid the United States was falling behind "the Commies" in the burgeoning field of trippy-ass mind-control technology. According to CIA director Helms: "There was a deep concern over the issue of brainwashing. We felt that it was our responsibility not to lag behind the Russians or the Chinese in this field, and the only way to find out what the risks were was to test things such as LSD and other drugs that could be used to control human behavior."

They tested the holy shit-snacks out of LSD. The man in charge of MK-Ultra was Sidney Gottlieb—a mad scientist who was having a love affair with LSD. By his own admission, he dropped acid more than two hundred times. He and other CIA employees used to fool around with it for fun—as a prank, they'd spike each other's drinks and put acid in each other's food. And you'll love this part: in the early fifties, he spent $240,000 of the CIA's money to buy up the entire world's supply of LSD so he could conduct all sorts of crazy experiments. One of his personal favorites was Operation Midnight Climax, in which prostitutes hired by the CIA dosed unsuspecting "johns" with LSD, while CIA agents hid creepily behind one-way mirrors to watch the johns freak out. Gottlieb was so thrilled with the results that he began doling out LSD for even more experiments. Altogether, there were more than 160 secret CIA-financed projects at eighty different universities, hospitals, and research foundations, mostly designed to test LSD (and other drugs) on unwitting victims. When Gottlieb was asked if he ever gave LSD to someone who wasn't "unwitting," he shrugged and said: "The very nature of that kind of interrogation is unwitting. So when you ask, 'Was there any administration . . . in interrogations other than unwitting?' that's kind of an oxymoron."

The guy who conducted the experiment at Harvard was Dr. Henry Murray—and he was cut from the same cloth as Gottlieb. Both of them used to work for the OSS (the precursor of the CIA), and both liked to drop acid while they worked. According to Harvard's student newspaper, the *Harvard Crimson*, the esteemed Dr. Murray once presented findings from a series of bizarre brainwashing experiments at an international conference in Copenhagen while actively tripping on LSD. Not surprisingly, when he returned to Harvard after leaving the OSS, he brought along his passion for LSD and whacked-out mind-control experiments. Pesky things like ethics and informed consent didn't bother him much—he was willing to be a total dick for science. At Harvard, he supervised not only the experiments on Kaczynski but also Timothy Leary's LSD experiments. Years later, when Kaczynski's lawyers were preparing his defense, they tried to get hold of Dr. Murray's files on Kaczynski, but Harvard was surprisingly unhelpful. Per the *Harvard Crimson*, the school has since permanently sealed all of Dr. Murray's records—not, of course, because they have anything to hide, but rather out of concern for patient confidentiality. That's the public explanation, anyway.

That's the story: the CIA dosed unwitting college students with LSD to avoid falling behind Russia and China in the agency's insidious inquiries into mind control. It was the Cold War—so while they plotted for the possibility of dropping bombs on people, they preferred to drop acid on them instead. If there's any moral to be gleaned from this twisted tale, it's that cruel and indefensible experiments like MK-Ultra are no-win scenarios—and they're very likely what set Kaczynski down the road to perdition and murderous derangement. The *New York Times* obituary summarized Kaczynski's tragic life by saying he went from "lonely boy genius to Harvard-trained star of pure mathematics, to rural recluse, to notorious murderer, to imprisoned extremist"—a very accurate summary, but they left out one important descriptor: CIA guinea pig.

# CHAPTER 33

# Ken Kesey and the Electric Kool-Aid Acid Test

olunteering for a psychology experiment is a roll of the dice. You have no idea what sort of holy hell they're going to put you through. Remember the Stanford Prison Experiment, where students assigned to play prison guards thoroughly brutalized other students who were randomly assigned to play prisoners?[1] Or the Milgram Experiment, where test subjects were ordered to inflict painful electric shocks on an unseen person just to find out how far they'd go to obey an authority figure? It's a real parade of horribles— a total crapshoot.

But when bright oddball Ken Kesey volunteered for a psych experiment, he hit the freaking jackpot. Doctors gave him LSD and told him to write down what it felt like when he was tripping. That was the whole experiment: drop acid and write a psychedelic dream diary. It was 1959, and the government really wanted to know what LSD was capable of, so they used volunteers like Kesey as guinea pigs. The experience changed the trajectory of Kesey's life. Trying LSD brought him fame, fortune, and happiness, at least for a little

---

1. There's been some recent scholarship indicating that the results of this experiment may have been exaggerated and/or falsified. All the same, it still seems to have been a bad time for all involved.

while—until, you know, the part where he faked his death and fled to Mexico to avoid being locked up in the slammer. But I'm getting ahead of myself.

Before the experiment, Kesey didn't do drugs. He grew up on a farm in Oregon, hunting, fishing, swimming, and doing chores. At school, he was a total jock—a football star, boxer, and championship wrestler; a handsome athlete with a thick neck and powerful forearms. As author Tom Wolfe put it in his iconic book *The Electric Kool-Aid Acid Test*: "He looks a little like Paul Newman, except he is more muscular." And he was actively training for the 1960 US Olympic team. But underneath the rock-hard, all-American farm boy exterior, he had a softer, more contemplative alter ego. He was a spiritual wanderer who'd read the Bible, the Bhagavad Gita, and the Daodejing, as well as modern philosophers. He was someone who liked to think about thinking. He was searching for universal truths and was hoping to write some universal truths of his own—which is why he landed in a graduate writing workshop at Stanford University. But until that fateful psych experiment, he had never tried drugs or gotten drunk on beer.

Ostensibly, the psych experiment was sponsored by the local VA hospital—but in reality, it was a front for the CIA. Their deranged MK-Ultra program was in full swing, and it was pretty much designed to explore whacked-out, bizarro ideas, like whether LSD could be used as a truth serum to force America's enemies to divulge their secrets, or be used to take control of someone's mind and turn them into a "Manchurian candidate" who'd assassinate a foreign leader of the agency's choosing (I'm talking about you, Fidel Castro). But the CIA didn't do anything nasty like that to Kesey. They only wanted him to report back on his LSD trips. (Remember the horrible things I told you they did to the Unabomber as part of MK-Ultra? Well, someone's gotta be in the control group, so Kesey lucked out big-time.) No brainwashing, no waterboarding, no programming him to kill—just take two tabs and call us in the morning.

Some of his buddies, like Beat poet Allen Ginsberg, told him it was a CIA plot, but Kesey didn't believe it: "I said aw, no, Allen, you're just paranoid. But he finally got all the darn records, and it did turn out the CIA was doing this. And it wasn't being done to try to cure insane people, which is what we thought. It was being done to try to make people insane—to weaken people, and to be able to put them under the control of interrogators. We didn't find this out for twenty years. And by that time the government had said OK, stop that experiment. All these guinea pigs that we've sent up there into outer space, bring them back down and don't ever let them go back in there again because we don't like the look in their eyes."

MK-Ultra was a living nightmare for many test subjects—but for Kesey, it was like a spiritual awakening. He loved how LSD made him feel. It reshaped his perspective, allowed him to see the bigger picture, and gave him empathy for everyone and everything. It even made him a better writer—or at least, a more successful one. Before trying LSD, he wrote a book that never got published. But after his psychedelic baptism, he took a job working the graveyard shift in the psych ward of the local VA hospital. There, pushing a wet mop down the corridor while tripping balls on LSD, he realized these mental patients were trapped in a health care system that wasn't making them any healthier. It wasn't clear if they were truly sick or if they were simply being punished for failing to conform to society's preconceived notions of what constituted normal behavior.

He wrote a new book: *One Flew over the Cuckoo's Nest*. He was only twenty-five years old. During a spectacular series of acid trips, he summed up his feelings on the whole messed-up mental health care establishment. Working super late at night, he pumped out page after page while under the influence of LSD and peyote. When he descended back to Earth the next day, he'd reread the stuff he had written and edit out the crappy, indecipherable parts.

The book was a huge success. It turned into a hit play starring Kirk Douglas, then, a few years later, an even bigger hit movie starring Jack Nicholson. It's one of the very few films to win Oscars in all five major categories—Best Picture, Best Actor, Best Actress, Best Director, and Best Screenplay—but Kesey never saw the movie. He got pissy because those stupid movie people wouldn't give final say over the script and casting to a guy who'd never made a movie before and was perpetually tripping on acid. The nerve of those guys!

So, what to do after writing a bestseller at age twenty-five? For his next act, Kesey became a traveling LSD dispensary. Not satisfied with sedentary tripping in the comfort of his own home, he hit the road to spread the gospel of psychedelics to as many people as humanly possible. He bought a twenty-five-year-old school bus and transformed it into a garish multicolored hippie mobile with an observation platform on the roof. He and his disciples, known as the Merry Pranksters, embarked on a wild transcontinental journey from California to New York, spreading good vibes, handing out free drug samples, and encouraging everyone they met to join their revolution, saying: "We won't blow up their buildings, we'll blow their minds."

This crazy road trip kicked off the entire 1960s counterculture movement. According to documentarian Alex Gibney, watching footage of the journey is "like watching a fuse being lit." Because this is where it all started: before Kesey and the Pranksters, you didn't see hippies with long hair, tie-dye clothing, and peace signs. The fifties and early sixties were the beatnik era—poets and intellectuals in berets, turtleneck sweaters, and black straight-leg cigarette pants. Even the Beatles were still wearing suits and ties in the early sixties. But Kesey's wild, unhinged journey across America in a school bus powered by LSD and imagination changed all that. He and his crew pioneered the iconic hippie look, replacing black and white stripes with a psychedelic explosion of color, wackiness, and individuality. Thanks to Kesey and the Amazing Technicolor Dream Bus, the sixties became about free expression, experimentation, and the search for enlightenment. Every single aspect of what we now think of as the sixties counterculture movement—hippies, drugs, love-ins, freak-outs—happened because the CIA asked Ken Kesey to take LSD.

When the road trip ended, Kesey found yet another way to spread LSD. He purchased a ranch in La Honda, California, and gave birth to the "acid tests." These were wild parties he threw at the ranch, where he dosed his guests with LSD (sometimes without their consent). He served them Kool-Aid laced with acid and dared them not to "freak out." But it was hard not to freak out because he blasted creepy music from hidden speakers, painted Day-Glo colors on the trees, turned on flickering strobe lights, and invited all sorts of weird and dangerous characters to attend the parties, including the Hells Angels motorcycle gang. Plus, there was live music at the acid tests, performed by the Grateful Dead, who were close friends with Kesey. In fact, it was at one of his acid test parties that they first performed under the name "the Grateful Dead" (they used to be called the Warlocks).

Kesey spent fifteen years giving away tons of LSD, which raises a question: Where did he get all that acid? At first, he nicked it from his workplace. That's why he got a job at the VA hospital to begin with. It was the same hospital where the LSD experiments were being conducted, and since he was a trusted employee, they gave him a key: "I found that my key opened a lot of the doors to the doctors' offices, where these drugs were being kept." He gave the drugs to his friends who were underground chemists, and they began manufacturing their own, homemade LSD in makeshift labs. "But it never was anywhere as good as that good government stuff," Kesey said. "The CIA always has the best stuff."

The US government wasn't happy. Kesey was corrupting the youth of America—never mind that it was the CIA who turned him on to drugs in the first place—and it was time to bring him to justice. Except for one small problem: LSD wasn't illegal yet. But the government figured a dirty no-good hippie like Kesey must be doing something against the law, and sure enough, they were right. He was smoking reefer, and that was all the excuse they needed to go after him. On April 23, 1965, a bevy of badges descended upon his home, including seventeen sheriff's deputies, an angry federal narcotics agent, and eight pot-sniffing dogs who started barking their heads off the second they got within sniffing distance. The boys in blue carted off Kesey and thirteen of his friends on marijuana charges.

Deeply unenthused by the prospect of jail, Kesey faked his death in 1966 and fled to Mexico. He lay low for a few months but missed his home and friends, so he snuck back into California. The FBI nabbed him and he spent five months in a prison work camp. Disillusioned, he made public statements denouncing LSD's supposedly miraculous powers as "temporary and delusional" and telling his followers they needed "to start doing it without the drugs"—but it was far too late to put the toothpaste back in the tube.

Kesey's days as an LSD guru had come to an ignominious end, but he had spread a powerful and enduring message. Like the Roman statesman Cincinnatus, he gave up his throne and returned to his plow. He spent his last thirty years living an ordinary life on the same Oregon family farm where he grew up, tending cattle and sheep, growing blueberries, teaching the occasional writing seminar, and coaching wrestling. He wrote a few more books, but nothing especially memorable. But every once in a while, when he was feeling nostalgic, Kesey would sneak out of the house to pay a visit to the old multicolored Pranksters school bus, which he kept hidden in the woods nearby—and he'd think back fondly to a time when he set the world afire and anything was possible.

TUNE IN
TURN ON
DROP OUT

# CHAPTER 34

# Timothy Leary Was the Most Dangerous Man in America

Timothy Leary was a tweedy college professor who tried mushrooms one time in 1960 and underwent a quasi-religious experience that turned him into a psychedelic evangelist who spent the rest of his life espousing the benefits of LSD and other drugs.

As a young man, he had a knack for mischief. He enrolled at the West Point military academy in 1940 because his disciplinarian father pressured him into it, but once there, he was always breaking the rules. He snuck out to go drinking, refused to report his fellow cadets for rule infractions, and was forced to exit the military school and transfer to the University of Alabama. Only a year later, the university kicked him out for spending a night in the women's dorms, so he lost his draft deferment and ended up in the army.

After the war, Leary seemed to straighten out. He met and married his first wife, earned a doctorate in clinical psychology, and lived the life of a conventional college professor (in his words, one of "several million middle-class, liberal, intellectual robots"), but it was utterly destroying him on the inside. His marriage was rocky, there was infidelity and heavy drinking on both sides—and it ended in tragedy when, on Leary's thirty-fifth birthday, he found his wife asphyxiated in the family car, sitting in the garage with the engine running. Leary was now a single parent of a six-year-old and an eight-year-old.

But his life changed when he tried mushrooms. He was hired by Harvard University in 1959, where a colleague told him about a psilocybin mushroom he had consumed on a recent trip to Mexico. Leary decided he needed to try these magic mushrooms for himself, so in 1960, he journeyed to Mexico on a "research expedition" and consumed hallucinogenic drugs. It was his first-ever psychedelic experience, and it was like a religious conversion for him. He rhapsodized that he learned more about the brain and its possibilities "in the five hours after taking these mushrooms than . . . in the preceding fifteen years of studying and doing research in psychology." His life was never the same after that.

When he got back to Harvard, he started the Harvard Psilocybin Project, in which grad students and faculty members would take controlled doses of mushrooms and write about their experiences. Skeptics questioned his scientific methods, with one describing it as "a bunch of guys standing around in a narrow hallway saying, 'Wow.'" Soon there were accusations of ethics violations: Leary giving psychedelics to undergrads and taking drugs himself alongside his study participants, and reports that grad students were feeling pressured to try psychedelics to avoid pissing off their psilocybin-loving professor. In 1963, Harvard fired Leary. Officially, it was for failing to show up for classes—but everyone knew the real reason was drugs.

Suddenly unencumbered by gainful employment, Leary formed a commune to promote psychedelics full-time. He turned a sixty-four-room mansion in Millbrook, New York, into a New Agey "space colony" for trippy intellectuals, offering lessons in yoga, meditation, and how to navigate the psychedelic realm. It was an intellectual bastion of glorious hippie-dippieness. Leary quickly became the high priest of the 1960s LSD movement. He helped organize a gathering of twenty thousand hippies at the "Human Be-In" in San Francisco's Golden Gate Park, where he coined his famous mantra: "Turn on. Tune in. Drop out." The Moody Blues wrote a song about him, he had an all-night psychedelic jam session with Jimi Hendrix, and he sat on a king-size hotel room bed beside John Lennon and Yoko Ono as they recorded "Give Peace a Chance."

But the times they were a-changin'. In the midsixties, Congress held hearings about the alleged dangers posed by psychedelics, and Leary was called as an expert witness. He beseeched the bureaucrats not to outlaw psychedelic drugs out of knee-jerk misunderstanding. When Senator Ted Kennedy asked if LSD was dangerous, Leary responded, "Sir, the motorcar is dangerous if used improperly.[1] . . . Human stupidity and ignorance is the only danger human beings face in this world." But he couldn't sway the powers that be. In 1966, California and Nevada passed laws outlawing LSD, and by 1968, it was banned nationwide.

Leary responded by founding a new religion called the League for Spiritual Discovery—or "LSD" for short. He claimed he could now use LSD legally, thanks to the "freedom of religion" clause of the Constitution. Not surprisingly, the feds didn't buy it. The FBI raided Leary's commune repeatedly, he was arrested by G. Gordon Liddy (who would later become notorious for orchestrating the Watergate break-in), and the constant government harassment drove him out of New York entirely. He relocated to California, the hotbed of the counterculture movement, but the drugs he loved so much were illegal there, too, so it didn't help. Thus began his era of repeated run-ins with the law.

Leary was arrested thirty-six times in the sixties and seventies. But it wasn't LSD that sent him to prison; it was good old-fashioned

---

1. Chappaquiddick hadn't happened yet, so Leary wasn't trolling Senator Kennedy by saying that.

marijuana. While laws against psychedelics were just starting to be enacted, anti-weed laws had been around since the "reefer madness" moral panic of 1937. The first time Leary was arrested for weed was 1965: he was crossing the Mexican border with his two kids and his girlfriend, and realized too late he'd forgotten to ditch a half ounce of pot before he crossed an international border. His eighteen-year-old daughter tried hiding the drugs in her underwear, but somehow the Feds found it (your tax dollars at work!). A local attorney advised him to take a plea bargain, but Leary said no, he wanted to prove a point. Unfortunately, the stern Texas jury missed his point and sentenced him to thirty years for smuggling drugs—but, amazingly, he beat the rap. Leary convinced the US Supreme Court in a unanimous ruling that being required to fill out a form saying whether or not you had drugs with you was a violation of his Fifth Amendment right against self-incrimination.

The next time, though, he wouldn't be so lucky. The day after Christmas in 1968, Leary got arrested again for weed, this time for an even tinier amount—two "roaches" (a.k.a. marijuana butts) found in his car. He was released pending trial, so—like anyone would—he decided to run for governor of California. He enlisted his pal John Lennon to write a campaign song for him. You might have heard of it—it was a little ditty called "Come Together." However, Leary's run for office came to a screeching halt when he was found guilty and sentenced to twenty years in prison. (Fortunately, the Beatles were able to find another use for the song.)

Leary was an inmate, but he was still a former Harvard professor with a genius-level IQ—so he outsmarted his jailers and escaped. New inmates were given a personality test to determine which job they were best suited for while serving time; it was called the Leary Interpersonal Behavior Inventory—he was literally the guy who designed the test. So he gave the answers that he knew would land him a job outdoors in the prison garden. One day while watering flowers, he hoisted himself up to a rooftop, climbed a utility pole, shinnied across a cable, and dropped to the ground on the other side of the cyclone fence. The Weathermen, the infamous ultra-left-wing underground radicals, were waiting there and smuggled him out of the country.

Leary was now an international fugitive. President Nixon called him "the most dangerous man in America." But even Leary couldn't run forever. The feds caught up to him at Kabul airport in Afghanistan. They sent him off to Folsom Prison, where he was put in solitary confinement in the cell next to murderous cult leader Charles Manson. The two men couldn't see each other, but they could hear each other, and they chatted about LSD. Manson only saw drugs as a way to control people. He seemed genuinely baffled by the notion that Leary would give LSD to someone without trying to control their life. (To Manson, this Timothy Leary guy was *crazy.*)

Leary secured an early release from prison in 1976 by narcing on the Weathermen. He tried assuring the radical group he wasn't giving the feds any useful information, but just in case they didn't buy it, he entered the witness protection program. In 1977, he moved to Los Angeles and lived out the rest of his life as a washed-up celebrity. He became a so-called stand-up philosopher who performed at nightclubs, and he toured the country with his former nemesis, G. Gordon Liddy, as two ex-cons debating the issues of the day from far-left and far-right perspectives.

When Leary was diagnosed with inoperable prostate cancer in 1995, he said he wanted to have his head cryogenically frozen so it could be thawed out and revived in the future. But three weeks before he died, he changed his mind. He said the cryogenics people were a humorless bunch with no sense of adventure: "I was worried

I would wake up in fifty years surrounded by people with clip-boards." He died peacefully in his sleep in 1996, and his last words were reportedly, "Why not?"

Timothy Leary always had an alternative streak. He was looking for something outside ordinary life that could infuse his existence with meaning and excitement but didn't find it until the fateful day in 1960 when he tried shrooms and had a religious conversion to the church of psychedelia. With evangelical fervor, he tried to get everyone in the world to try LSD—and millions actually did. As Leary was fond of saying: "I turned on five million people, and only five thousand ever thanked me."

It's easy to write off his attempt to form an LSD church as a gimmick to flout the law, but in Leary's case, it's likely his religious conviction was genuine. He was convinced humanity could attain a higher level of consciousness by using LSD. Admittedly, his scientific research methods were questionable given his obvious pro-drug bias, but if nothing else, the man was willing to go to prison because he believed with absolute certainty that the salvation of mankind could be found by tripping balls.

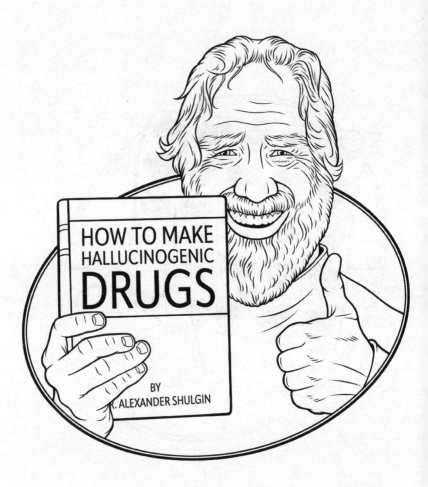

HOW TO MAKE HALLUCINOGENIC DRUGS

BY
R. ALEXANDER SHULGIN

# CHAPTER 35

# Alexander Shulgin, the DEA Employee Who Invented 230 Psychedelics

_____

I bet you didn't know there was a scientist who invented hundreds of psychedelic drugs in a makeshift laboratory at his farmhouse, while simultaneously working part-time for the DEA. He was the brilliant (and highly eccentric) chemist Alexander Shulgin—but his friends called him "Sasha."

Sasha got his start working for Dow Chemical, a large, stodgy multinational corporation. His job was to synthesize pesticides, which probably doesn't sound too exciting, but Sasha accomplished a minor miracle for the company in 1961 when he developed Zectran, the world's first biodegradable pesticide. It killed bugs without killing the environment. Dow Chemical earned accolades for its environmentalism and truckloads of cash for its stockholders.

Dow Chemical made so much money from Zectran, it told Sasha he could take his pick of any field of chemistry to work on next. Sasha had tried mescaline for the first time in 1960 and found it to be fascinating, so he chose the field of psychedelic drugs. Dow said sure, they liked the idea of owning some valuable drug patents. It wasn't long before their chemistry wunderkind created a powerful psychoactive stimulant called DOM that could send users tripping for up to forty-eight hours at a time.

But there was a problem: the superpowerful new hallucinogenic drug escaped into the wild. Sasha, it turns out, was a big-time believer in scientific transparency, so he freely shared his creation with friends, colleagues, and anyone else who might be interested. But one of his friends had motives that were less scholarly and more mercenary. He cashed in on Sasha's discovery by mixing up his own batch of DOM. Soon, the Hells Angels motorcycle club was selling counterfeit DOM to drug dealers all across the nation, from Haight-Ashbury to Manhattan, where one unfortunate user had a bad trip and ended up disemboweling himself with a samurai sword on Mother's Day.

Dow Chemical decided it was time to cut ties with Sasha. Having outlaw biker gangs selling drugs developed by Dow to zonked-out hippies wasn't good for the company's stock price. They gave Sasha his walking papers and told him not to let the door hit him on the way out. Sasha didn't mind. With no corporate overlords keeping tabs on him, he was free to do as he pleased. He constructed a makeshift laboratory in a cobweb-filled shed on his twenty-acre ranch in the hills east of Berkeley, California, and immediately started cooking up all sorts of new chemical concoctions.

Of course, you can't tell whether a drug is good or bad until you test it. Sasha tested all his creations, but not on lab animals—he tested them on himself. He'd start with a minuscule dose, so infinitesimally small that it couldn't possibly have a discernible effect, then cautiously ramp up the dosage until he began to feel it. If the drug passed muster, he'd share it with his "research group"—eight or so close friends, including a couple of psychologists and a chemist, all of whom shared his love for psychedelics. They'd get together on a weekend, dose themselves with Sasha's latest creation, then compare notes on their trippy experiences.

He quickly became the world's foremost expert on hallucinogens—"the godfather of psychedelics," they called him. He created more than 230 distinct psychoactive compounds over the course of his 88-year lifespan—including drugs that make you happy, drugs that make you sad, drugs that make you feel too much, drugs that make you feel nothing at all, drugs that speed up time, drugs that slow down time, and drugs that make you amorous at the drop of a hat. No one in the world knew more about psychoactive drugs than Sasha Shulgin.

That's why the DEA came knocking at his door. The agency was in awe of his unrivaled expertise in the area of controlled substances and wanted to learn from him. I wasn't there, but I like to think the conversation went something like this:

DEA: Please, sir, teach us what you know.
Sasha: What's in it for me?
DEA: You can cook up whatever drugs you want and we can't prosecute you.
Sasha: Put that in writing and you've got a deal.

The DEA granted him an extremely rare license to possess and synthesize Schedule I controlled substances at his home laboratory. For the next twenty years, Sasha essentially had a get-out-of-jail-free card from the DEA.

It was a sweet deal for the feds. Sasha held seminars to teach DEA agents about pharmacology, cooked up drug samples for their forensic teams, and testified as an expert witness against drug dealers. He even wrote the DEA's definitive handbook on controlled substances. Over the years, he became close friends with several top DEA agents—one of them officiated at Sasha's wedding in 1981, and a year later, a pair of DEA agents got married on Sasha's front lawn. The DEA heaped all sorts of awards on him, including a medal for his "significant personal efforts to help eliminate drug abuse."

But as much as he helped the DEA, he also did a bunch of stuff the agency absolutely hated. While he occasionally testified as an expert witness for the government in criminal drug trials, he also testified as an expert witness for the defense. And he was really fond of announcing to everyone he met that it was his deeply held belief that all drugs of every kind should be legal—which, in case you don't know, isn't exactly the DEA's motto.

Sasha believed in the free flow of information, and he didn't pick sides. He was happy to share his expertise with the DEA but just as happy to share it with drug users. He wasn't trying to entice anyone to use drugs, but he refused to support fearmongering to keep people away from them. For Sasha, it was all about education. He wanted to put all the information out there—"warts and all"—and let people decide for themselves. As he put it: "There's nothing wrong with making information available."

The DEA was willing to put up with his annoying libertarian streak to a certain extent, because the man was undeniably brilliant. But, Sasha being Sasha, he inevitably crossed the line. In 1991, he self-published a book titled *PiHKAL: A Chemical Love Story*. "PiH-KAL" was an acronym for "Phenethylamines I Have Known and Loved." The first half of the book was a memoir describing how he met and fell in love with his wife—the DEA was totally fine with that part. But the second half contained step-by-step instructions on how to make 179 different mind-bending compounds. A DEA spokesman said: "Those books are pretty much cookbooks on how to make illegal drugs."

Sasha's special relationship with the DEA came to a screeching halt. They raided his farmhouse, searched every nook and cranny of his lab, and fined him $25,000. They asked him to give up his drug-making license, which he agreed to because he refused to let the government try to impose any restrictions on his work. Once again, he was free to work independently. And how did he celebrate his newfound freedom? By self-publishing another book with even more recipes: *TiHKAL: The Continuation.*

The most famous drug that Sasha introduced to the world was MDMA, better known as "ecstasy" or "Molly." But he didn't actually invent MDMA—he brought it back from the dead. It was patented by the German drug company Merck way back in 1914, but Merck abandoned it because they couldn't find any legitimate medical use for it. Sixty-two years later, Sasha cooked up a batch for himself and published a research paper saying it was great for reducing anxiety. This led people to experiment with the drug, and it turned into a viral sensation on the underground club scene. The US government officially banned MDMA in 1985.

It's important to keep in mind that Sasha didn't create psychedelics to get people high. He genuinely believed these drugs could be used to improve people's lives—and maybe he was right. In 2004, the FDA authorized Harvard Medical School to study whether MDMA could be used to help terminal cancer patients deal with their fear and anxiety. More recently, there have been studies using the drug to treat people with autism and PTSD. Other drugs that Sasha created are currently being used to treat hypertension, senility, and nicotine cravings. But at the same time, because Sasha loved to share his research with the public, some of his creations have ended up becoming super-popular with recreational drug users.

Interestingly, the drugs that Sasha created weren't illegal—at least, not when he created them. That's because he was inventing drugs that had never existed before. But as soon as one of his concoctions became a fan favorite among drug enthusiasts, the DEA would step in and have it officially added to the list of prohibited Schedule I controlled substances. Then, in 1986, the federal government flipped the script on Sasha. They enacted the Controlled Substances Analogue Enforcement Act, a.k.a. the Designer Drug

Act, which said any new drug that got invented was automatically illegal if its chemical structure was "substantially similar" to that of an existing illegal drug. Now, instead of waiting for Sasha to create a new drug and then amending the law to make it illegal, his creations were deemed illegal from the moment he gave birth to them. Sasha absolutely despised the Designer Drug Act, calling it "one of the most freedom restricting things that has ever been put into the law."

But let me make this perfectly clear: while drug dealers have raked in billions of dollars by selling the compounds he invented, Sasha never made a dime from selling drugs. He earned his money from teaching, giving lectures, and writing books. He wasn't a drug dealer or a profiteer; he was a brilliant, fiercely independent scientist who believed in perpetually pushing the boundaries of human understanding—and, for better or worse, sharing his mind-altering discoveries with the world. Which is why he created more than 230 mind-bending concoctions, tested every one on himself, and then published the recipes for the world to see—all with the knowledge and (grudging) approval of the DEA.

# CHAPTER 36

# Sgt. Pothead's Loaded Hard-Drug Band (a.k.a. the Beatles)

The Beatles! One of the greatest bands of all time, right? Based on how trippy and psychedelic their music became, and the subtle (and not-so-subtle) references hidden in their lyrics, listeners might get the impression that maybe, just maybe, the Beatles dabbled with drugs. But the truth is far more intense: the Beatles were high on drugs nearly the entire time they topped the charts—and, like their music, their choice of pharmaceuticals evolved over time and became more untethered and experimental. The upshot was that drug use boosted their creativity and their productivity, but it also played a major role in why the band ultimately fell apart.

First came nicotine and alcohol. By the time John, Paul, George, and Ringo were old enough to smoke and drink legally, they had already been smoking and drinking for several years. Kids grew up quickly in hardscrabble Liverpool, a northern English port city that lacked the glamour and sophistication of London and was more of a transit point than a destination, but its residents often dreamed of going out into the world and doing something big. That's where fifteen-year-old Paul McCartney linked up with sixteen-year-old John Lennon and they started playing clubs as the Quarrymen, smoking and drinking like boozy chimneys.

Next came stimulants. Being up-and-coming musicians meant

endless toil. The band got a gig in Hamburg, Germany, playing ninety-two straight nights—seven hours a night during the week, and eight hours a night on the weekends. This punishing schedule practically screamed for chemical assistance. A friendly English rocker gave them pills called Preludin, saying: "Here's something to keep you awake." They were diet pills, technically, but users had noticed if you took enough of them, you'd be rewarded with super-human levels of energy and exuberance. Performing all those long nights was still hard work, but the "Prellies" were making the Beatles feel all right about it.

Prellies weren't always available, so the Beatles had to settle for a cheaper substitute: amphetamines. The band was starting to get famous, booking gigs they wouldn't have dreamed possible a few months earlier, but it meant they were busier than ever. Popping copious quantities of speed gave them the boost they needed for nonstop touring, recording sessions, press interviews, and public appearances. "I was the one who carried all the pills on tour," John said. "We just kept them in our pockets loose. In case of trouble." I guess it worked, because by 1963, the band had released their first sensational album and Beatlemania was sweeping America.

Now they needed a drug to chill them out. Their fateful meeting with Bob Dylan in 1964 turned the lads on to marijuana. Dylan was one of the most respected songwriters in the world, especially among the young and hip. Seeking to be good hosts, the Beatles offered him refreshments in the form of pills, but taking uppers wasn't Dylan's idea of relaxing, so he rolled joints for them instead. He wasn't good at it and spilled a fair amount of weed onto the table—but what was inside those unartfully crafted joints transported the Beatles to a new realm of imagination. It quickly became their favorite way to kick back and tune out the pressure of being the biggest band in the world. As Paul said later: "We were kind of proud to have been introduced to pot by Dylan."

Within months, the Beatles were full-time stoners. They were sky-high while writing *Help!* and filming the accompanying movie. "We were smoking marijuana for breakfast during that period," John said. "Nobody could communicate with us because it was all glazed eyes and giggling all the time." They began putting references to drugs in their lyrics. Stray mentions of "grass," being "high," "turning on," and "rolling up" were scattered throughout their songs, but it was done subtly, nothing too explicit. Each of the code words had a double meaning and could be interpreted as completely innocuous—but they were intended by the Beatles as winking references for those in the know.

The Beatles believed marijuana made them better musicians. They said cannabis helped to focus their attention on the details of their music in a way they never could before. It imbued them with deeper listening, allowing them to hear every individual sound more clearly. George said: "It mightn't have affected creativity for other people. I know it did for us, and it did for me."

John called *Rubber Soul* their "pot album" because its sound was more melancholy and self-reflective. The record was a love letter to cannabis, and each track was an individually wrapped marijuana valentine. The Beatles were so in love with marijuana that for *Revolver*, Paul wrote the song "Got to Get You into My Life," which he revealed later wasn't about a person—it was a love song about marijuana, or as he put it, "an ode to pot." He thought it was obvious but said "everyone missed it at the time."

Soon they added a new drug to the rotation: LSD. The first time they tried acid, it was by accident. John and George attended a dinner party hosted by a dentist acquaintance of theirs, but when it was time to go home, their host said, "You can't leave. You've had LSD." He'd snuck it into sugar cubes in their coffee. They were angry at first, but their fury melted away as John and George shared their first psychedelic experience—the room was shifting around them and elongating in surreal ways, they saw colors they'd never seen before, and they felt a deep, abiding love for everyone and everything. They came away from the experience thrilled and enlightened. It was like going from black-and-white movies to Technicolor.

It became their mission to preach the gospel of acid to their bandmates. George explained: "John and I decided that Paul and Ringo had to have acid, because we couldn't relate to them anymore . . . because acid had changed us so much." Laid-back Ringo was game to try it, but circumspect Paul was more hesitant: "I'm conservative. I feel I need to check things out. I was last to try pot and LSD and floral clothes." However, by the end of 1965, all four members of the Beatles had tried and thoroughly enjoyed acid.

*Sgt. Pepper* was their full-on acid album. The strain of being the Beatles had become so tremendous that they'd given up touring and come up with a trippy and whimsical idea—what if we were a different band? *Sgt. Pepper's Lonely Hearts Club Band* was a concept album in which the Fab Four adopted the alter ego of a wacky Edwardian performing group. Since they weren't going to perform it live, they could experiment to create bold new sounds that it wasn't possible to re-create outside a recording studio; their music could be more far-out and dreamy than ever before. Unlike their first album, which they'd recorded in a single day, this one took 400 hours over 129 days—and all the songs were inspired by LSD. The Beatles have long insisted the title of "Lucy in the Sky with Diamonds" wasn't an intentional LSD reference, but they freely admit the lyrics and imagery in the song were. Paul said, "When we were talking about 'cellophane flowers' and 'kaleidoscope eyes' and 'grow so incredibly high,' we were talking about drug experiences, no doubt about it." The album was a massive hit, and the Beatles became the trailblazers of psychedelic rock.

But it wasn't all sunshine and rainbows. John and George had been dropping way too much acid, using it practically every day. George told an interviewer: "That's the thing about LSD: you don't need it twice." The interviewer pushed back on the notion that he'd only taken acid once, and George corrected himself, laughing and saying: "Oh no, I took it lots of times. But I only *needed* it once." John told *Rolling Stone* he'd taken LSD literally a thousand times: "I used to eat it all the time." And now he was paying the price. He'd suffered through the horror of so many bad trips that he couldn't stand the idea of taking any more acid. Worse yet, LSD had destroyed his sense of self. He'd read a book calling "ego death" the first step toward "complete transcendence," and he'd taken it way too literally: "I destroyed my ego and I didn't believe I could do anything," John said. "I just was nothing. I was shit."

One Beatle who wasn't overdoing it on LSD was Paul—but he was busy having a love affair with cocaine. "I liked the paraphernalia," he said. "I was particularly amused by rolling up a pound note. There was a lot of symbolism in that: sniffing it through money!" Coke made him energetic, confident, and enthusiastic. It helped him step up and take over as the group's de facto leader, but it also made him rigid, controlling, and perfectionistic—which didn't endear him to his acid-soaked bandmates.

Then something quite unexpected happened: the Beatles suddenly gave up drugs. In August 1967, they held a press conference saying they were turning to Transcendental Meditation instead: "You cannot keep on taking drugs forever," Paul announced. "We were looking for something more natural. This is it." A few months later, they flew to India to study with a real-life maharishi. Since it was a religious retreat, drugs and alcohol were strictly off-limits. For one brief, shining moment in time, all four Beatles were drug-free.

But nothing gold can stay. They left India only a few weeks later, disillusioned after hearing rumors of sexual impropriety by the maharishi. Even before they left, John had found something new to intoxicate him—and her name was Yoko Ono. She'd been sending him daily letters, and he'd become obsessed with her. John had a long history of latching on to someone or something that he hoped would guide him down the path of personal growth, and Yoko was the one who really stuck. He had destroyed his ego with too much LSD and now didn't feel like he was a real artist, despite his tremendous commercial success. Yoko, on the other hand, was an art world sophisticate, and he became convinced she possessed the true artistic talent that he lacked—so he left India to follow her.

Yoko turned John on to heroin. She'd learned about heroin from her oddball art friends, and the couple took it up as a dangerous but thrilling hobby. Yoko called it "a celebration of ourselves as artists." As a precaution, though, they only sniffed heroin; they never injected it—which led them to believe it was a casual habit they could quit any time they wanted.

But fate intervened. There was a car accident in July 1969, in which John and Yoko were seriously injured. They upped their heroin use to cope with their pain. This was right when the Beatles were recording *Abbey Road*, so John had a hospital bed installed in the recording studio, with a microphone suspended above the bed, so everyone could hear Yoko's thoughts and suggestions about the recording sessions. It was as if there was suddenly a fifth member of the Beatles—except no one had bothered to ask the rest of the band if they actually wanted a fifth Beatle.

It became impossible to get anything done. John was seeking Yoko's input on everything; meanwhile, the others had to tiptoe around him to avoid triggering his fiery temper. It destroyed any sense of group cohesion. Heroin use made the already-prickly John even more difficult to work with and quashed his desire to collaborate or perform. He and Yoko would hang out, sniff dope, and nod off. There was no way to pry John away from the drugs, or from

Yoko. As John once said of himself, "I've always needed a drug to survive."

The Beatles' days as a band were numbered. Paul was trying his best to keep the group focused but was perceived as getting too bossy. John was in a world of his own with Yoko and high on opiates. George and Ringo were distressed by the constant tension and feeling a desire to strike out on their own. As soon as the *Abbey Road* recordings were completed, the Beatles went their separate ways.

For what it's worth, John tried to kick heroin. He made the gutsy decision to go cold turkey. He instructed Yoko to tie him to a chair for thirty-six hours, while he writhed in agony and delirium—and it worked; he stopped using heroin. Excited, he wrote a song about the experience and took it to the Beatles, even offering Paul a co-songwriting credit. But the band turned him down flat, another example of how their musical tastes were no longer in sync. John then took the song to his friend Bob Dylan—but, tragically, by the time he met with Dylan a few days later, he was already back to snorting heroin. He ended up recording "Cold Turkey" with the Plastic Ono Band.

The big question is this: Did the Beatles' fondness for drugs cause their fans to partake? Many scholars say the answer is yes. The Beatles achieved superstar status while unabashedly cranked up on speed, stoned on weed, and tripping on acid. An entire generation of youth patterned their lives after the Beatles—imitating the way they dressed, the way they wore their hair, and the way they got high. So, consciously or not, the Beatles were responsible for drug use among their fans.

But the Beatles themselves said, "not so fast." They never asked anyone to use drugs. Their only goal was to make great music and enjoy their lives. If fans chose to imitate their behavior, that was their choice. When reporters showed up on Paul's doorstep in 1967, asking him if he used drugs, Paul answered reluctantly: "You know what's going to happen here: I'm going to get the blame for telling everyone I take drugs. But you're the people who are going to distribute the news. I'll tell you. But if you've got any worries about the news having an effect on kids, then don't show it." John Lennon was more blunt, saying: "I don't ever feel responsible for turning [fans] on to acid. Because I don't think we did anything to kids; anything somebody does, they do to themselves."

Personally, I'm inclined to agree with the Beatles on this one. If simply publishing material that mentions drug use—and slyly alluding to the fact that maybe you have sampled certain substances yourself—merits moral condemnation, well, then, frankly, I'm in a lot of trouble.

PART **8**

# MODERN MYSTICS

# CHAPTER 37

# Carl Sagan Got Astronomically High

---

Carl Sagan brought science to the masses. Before Sagan, most people thought of scientists, if they thought of them at all, as nerdy guys with thick glasses and white lab coats who spent their days hunched over microscopes, slide rules, and calculators. They probably did stuff that was important to someone, but not to you and me, and certainly no one knew their names. But Sagan changed all that. He became famous by talking about how unbelievably awesome science was. He wrote books that sold millions of copies, created a hit TV show about astronomy, and produced a film about astrophysics that featured big-time movie stars. In our post-Sagan world, why does Bill Nye have 9.9 million TikTok followers? Why does Neil deGrasse Tyson have a podcast? Why did Stephen Hawking appear on *The Big Bang Theory*—heck, why is there a TV show called *The Big Bang Theory*? It's all because Carl Sagan made science cool.

He was the first-ever "celebrity scientist." Sure, there were a couple of eggheads like Albert Einstein and Robert Oppenheimer who were famous, meaning everyone knew their names. But those guys weren't celebrities. They didn't go on talk shows and do publicity tours. But Sagan did; he loved that stuff. He appeared on *The Tonight Show Starring Johnny Carson* twenty-six times, was hired by

Stanley Kubrick to consult on *2001: A Space Odyssey*, and turned his book *Contact*—about scientists who discover a way to communicate with extraterrestrials—into a big-budget movie starring Jodie Foster and Matthew McConaughey. He was such a huge celebrity that when he wrote, produced, and starred in the TV show *Cosmos* for PBS in 1980, it was watched by half a billion people—that's billion with a "B." Five hundred million people in sixty countries watched a show about science. He won two Emmys, three Hugo Awards, a Peabody Award, and a Pulitzer Prize.

Sagan absolutely loved attention. But that hurt him in the scientific community, because serious scientists weren't supposed to lower themselves to the level of common sci-fi. He made groundbreaking discoveries about the atmospheres of Venus, Mars, and other celestial bodies but was nonetheless rejected for membership in the National Academy of Sciences. And even though Harvard University recruited him and he taught there for five years, they denied him tenure, probably because his shameless publicity-seeking was considered a distraction (or possibly because it made other scientists jealous). But Cornell University had no such qualms. They snatched him up, gave him tenure, and used him as a magnet to attract students, big-money donations, and publicity for the next three decades. Everyone on campus was dying to catch a glimpse of the school's own personal celebrity wearing his trademark turtlenecks and blazers.

Oh, and speaking of "blazers"—Carl Sagan smoked a lot of pot.

Sagan started blazing around 1960, when he was in his midtwenties, and he never stopped. He remained a dedicated marijuana enthusiast for the rest of his life, smoking bales and bales of the stuff, but he tried to keep it on the down-low. Why? Because America looked up to Carl Sagan as its "gatekeeper of scientific credibility," and he didn't want to lose that. He knew if people found out he smoked pot, some of them would dismiss his work as the ramblings of a stoned guy. It's important to remember that marijuana was illegal the entire time he was alive, and the criminal penalties were incredibly severe. Back in the sixties, you could go to jail for thirty years for possessing a single joint. Even if the cops didn't bust him, schools like Harvard and Cornell could have fired him if they found out he was lighting up, and it's safe to say NASA would have chosen a different scientist to brief the astronauts before they flew their missions to the moon.

So, yes, Sagan tried to keep his love for marijuana a secret—but that doesn't mean no one knew. There were definite hints in his work that he was really into cannabis. In fact, if you treated it like a math problem and looked at all the different variables, you could probably figure it out—because when you think about it, the Venn diagram for "Carl Sagan's academic interests" and "things stoned people think are awesome" is pretty much just a circle.

First, Sagan had a passion for stargazing. He loved to look up at the night sky and ponder the vastness of the universe. That's textbook pothead behavior right there—and he succeeded in making an entire career out of it. Essentially, he got paid to stare up into space and say, "Whoa."

Second, Sagan was convinced that beings from outer space had already visited our planet. He did the math and concluded it was a "statistical likelihood" that an advanced extraterrestrial civilization had come to Earth and made direct contact with us at least once, probably during ancient times. He helped to organize a big UFO symposium, where everyone could tell their stories, and he co-founded a privately funded SETI (search for extraterrestrial intelligence) program. Several decades before *The X-Files* was even a glimmer in Chris Carter's eye, Carl Sagan believed "the truth is out there."

Third, he wanted to reach out and touch those supersmart space aliens. He convinced NASA to let him send a welcome message to them. He and his wife, Ann Druyan, led a team that produced two gold-plated records that were launched into outer space in 1977, as part of the *Voyager 1* and *Voyager 2* space missions. The gold records were intended to function like time capsules, imprinted with a wide array of sounds to give aliens a taste of what Earth was all about—everything from ambient nature sounds, to greetings in dozens of languages, to music ranging from ancient folk songs to Beethoven symphonies to Chuck Berry's rock and roll classic "Johnny B. Goode." Essentially, Sagan and his wife put together a mixtape of Earth's greatest hits to show aliens how cool we were. And with the launching of his "bottle into the cosmic ocean," Sagan transformed the idea of trying to talk to space aliens from a crank thing into a legitimate science thing.

But Sagan got so cheesed off by the fact that marijuana was illegal that he published an essay defending cannabis consumption. Of course, to protect his reputation, he had to come up with a super-clever pseudonym so people wouldn't know it was him—so he chose the pen name "Mr. X." His essay was included in a book published in 1971 called *Marihuana Reconsidered.* The book described Mr. X as "a professor at one of the top-ranking American universities"—but it wasn't until after Sagan's death in 1996 that the world finally discovered the truth that he was the mysterious Mr. X.

In his Mr. X essay, Sagan said smoking pot had a very positive impact on his life: "The cannabis experience has greatly improved my appreciation for art, a subject which I had never much appreciated before. . . . A very similar improvement in my appreciation of music has occurred with cannabis. . . . The enjoyment of food is amplified; tastes and aromas emerge that for some reason we ordinarily seem to be too busy to notice. I am able to give my full attention to the sensation." He also said it benefited his sex life. It helped to postpone his orgasm "by distracting [him] with the profusion of images passing before [his] eyes," and then prolonged his orgasm once it finally arrived—which he attributed to the "experience of time expansion which comes with cannabis smoking."

He also said marijuana helped him to recall childhood memories. He liked to sit back with a joint, reconstruct with incredible clarity the events from his past that were buried in his subconscious, and engage in some therapeutic self-analysis. Never a big fan of modesty, Sagan compared himself to Sigmund Freud:

> One night, high on cannabis, I was delving into my childhood, a little self-analysis, and making what seemed to me to be very good progress. I then paused and thought how extraordinary it was that Sigmund Freud, with no assistance from drugs, had been able to achieve his own remarkable self-analysis. But then it hit me like a thunderclap that this was wrong, that Freud had spent the decade before his self-analysis as an experimenter with and a proselytizer for cocaine; and it seemed to me very apparent that the genuine psychological insights that Freud brought to the world were at least in part derived from his drug experience.

Carl Sagan and Sigmund Freud—birds of a feather, right?

Now, here's the really interesting part about the Mr. X essay: while some people say marijuana saps your ambition and makes you dumber, Sagan believed smoking pot actually made him smarter. He said there was a commonly accepted "myth" that people who get high think they are experiencing profound insights, but once they sober up, they realize it was all gibberish. He said that wasn't true: "I am convinced that this is an error, and that the devastating insights achieved when high are real insights." The trick, he said, was getting these insights down on paper before the high wore off: "I can remember one occasion, taking a shower with my wife while high, in which I had an idea on the origins and invalidities of racism in terms of gaussian distribution curves. . . . I drew the curves in soap on the shower wall, and went to write the idea down. One idea led to another, and at the end of about an hour of extremely hard work I found I had written eleven short essays on a wide range of social, political, philosophical, and human biological topics."

Sagan concluded his essay by saying that he knew cannabis would eventually be legalized. He had no doubt whatsoever; it was inevitable—because, he said, cannabis wasn't physiologically addictive, was less harmful than alcohol and cigarettes, and could prove highly beneficial for many people. The final sentence of his essay states that "the illegality of cannabis is outrageous, an impediment to full utilization of a drug which helps produce the serenity and insight, sensitivity and fellowship so desperately needed in this increasingly mad and dangerous world." Basically, he took the position that prohibiting cannabis wasn't just bad public policy, it was bad science.

Was Carl Sagan a narcissist who craved attention? Sure, but at least he used his platform for good. He protested fiercely against the Vietnam War—in fact, he gave up his government security clearance, saying, "I certainly don't want to be a party to this crime." He insisted, decades before most other scientists, that climate change was man-made (his 1960 PhD thesis said the insane surface temperatures on Venus—as high as 864 degrees—were a direct result of greenhouse gases and if we didn't stop, Earth might end up the same way). But most of all, he inspired an entire generation of young people, including Bill Nye and Neil deGrasse Tyson (both of whom met and admired him), to choose careers in science. And it wasn't just science nerds who loved Sagan: Seth MacFarlane, the creator of *Family Guy*, gave the Library of Congress a large sum of money so it could purchase and preserve more than a thousand boxes of Sagan's personal documents.

Carl Sagan was a huge fan of cannabis who believed whole-heartedly that smoking pot enhanced his scientific work and granted him new insights. But there was at least one point where he was a bit too forgiving in his defense of the drug. In his Mr. X essay, Sagan took the position that driving while high was no big deal, saying: "I have on a few occasions been forced to drive in heavy traffic when high. I've negotiated it with no difficulty at all, though I did have some thoughts about the marvelous cherry-red color of traffic lights. . . . I don't advocate driving when high on cannabis, but I can tell you from personal experience that it certainly can be done."

Whoa, too far, Carl Sagan. Driving while impaired is deeply uncool, dude.

# CHAPTER 38

# Dock Ellis Pitched a No-Hitter While Tripping on Acid

---

**B**aseball is a weird sport. It tolerates an unexpectedly wide range of body types and fitness levels. Babe Ruth was a big dude with a prodigious belly but threw his weight into every swing. Tim Lincecum was a skinny kid with a stoner haircut but had an arm like a damn rocket. Joe Morgan was abnormally short for a ball player but was one of the best second basemen of all time. That's the cool thing about baseball—you don't have to be in peak physical condition to excel at it.

My favorite example is when Dock Ellis pitched a no-hitter while tripping on LSD. You don't have to be a baseball fan to appreciate that no-hitters are extraordinarily rare. There have only been 326 of them since 1876—that's an average of 2 per year, or roughly 1 in 700 games. But the number of people who have pitched a no-hitter while under the mind-warping influence of LSD—well, that's just one guy: Dock Ellis. I can't emphasize this enough—LSD is not a performance-enhancing drug. No one drops acid and says, "I took LSD and now my baseball skills are phenomenal." They're more likely to say, "I took LSD and now I can smell colors."

Dock didn't do it on purpose. He was twenty-five years old and loved walking on the wild side. His team, the Pittsburgh Pirates, was scheduled to play the San Diego Padres on Friday night, so on

Thursday, he headed north to Los Angeles to visit an old friend. They partied like rock stars—drinking screwdrivers, smoking pot, and dropping acid. At some point, Dock closed his eyes and slept for maybe an hour, but when he woke up, he was still pretty out of it and his awareness of time was skewed. He thought it was still Thursday, so he took a fresh dose of LSD and lay back down. His friend said, "Dock, you better get up. You gotta go pitch." Dock said not to worry, he didn't have to pitch until Friday, at which point his friend said—surprise!—it was already Friday. That's when Dock uttered his immortal words: "What happened to yesterday?"

The thing about LSD is once you ingest it, there's no option to stop the ride if you want to get off. Picture a roller coaster: once you've gone clickety-clack up to the top of the hill, it's too late to decide you don't want to go screaming downhill. There's no hand brake, no emergency exit; you are going to take that plunge. So, when planning a psychedelic trip, it's prudent to double-check your calendar and make sure you don't have anything else you're supposed to do that day, because—trust me, dude—you're not going to be able to accomplish much while you're tripping balls.

Dock had re-upped with a fresh dose of acid without realizing it was game day. There was zero chance the LSD was going to wear off in time—he took a hefty dose at twelve noon, and the game was starting at 6:05 p.m. So, while already tripping really hard, he somehow managed to navigate to the airport, catch a flight from LA to San Diego, hail a cab to the stadium, put on his Pirates uniform, and walk shakily out to the mound. It was June 12, 1970, and he was about to pitch the strangest game of his career.

Dock was no stranger to taking drugs before a game—but he typically chose drugs that would sharpen his skills, not make them worse. It's been a problem in professional sports for a long time that far too many athletes take performance-enhancing drugs to give themselves a competitive edge. Steroids, human growth hormone, stimulants, beta blockers, diuretics—the array of drugs is mind-bogglingly vast. Back in the seventies, when Dock was playing, amphetamines were super popular among baseball players because they were easy to get and the league didn't bother testing anyone to see if they were doping. The pills were known as "greenies," and Dock said over 90 percent of major leaguers were taking them. As ESPN put it: "Baseball and greenies go together like hot dogs and apple pie." Dock said he took greenies before every game—and he didn't just take one or two pills. He'd sometimes take as many as fifteen to seventeen. Why so many? Because he knew the other team was doping, too, so he devised a brilliant plan: "I would try to *out-milligram* any opponents."

But on that fateful Friday in 1970, Dock messed up. LSD was no PED. Just the opposite; it was a PUD: a performance-undermining drug. As soon as he got to the clubhouse, he tried swallowing a bunch of greenies, hoping to balance himself out and "knock that acid out of there"—but it didn't work.

Standing on the pitcher's mound with thousands of people watching him, he could feel that shit was getting profoundly bizarre. He said the baseball kept changing size, getting bigger and smaller. It no longer obeyed the laws of physics; it was some kind of *Alice in Wonderland* baseball with not only a mind of its own but also a personality. In the fourth inning, he got the crazy idea that Richard Nixon was the home-plate umpire, calling balls and strikes. He thought he saw Jimi Hendrix standing at the plate, swinging his guitar like it was a bat. And once the ball came rocketing at Dock so fast he had to dive out of the way—but it was just his imagination; the ball wasn't anywhere near him. In his drug-addled state, the wall between imagination and reality had disappeared. To quote Patrick Hruby's wonderfully evocative ESPN article, Dock was "throwing baseballs he couldn't always feel, in the general direction of batters he didn't always see, trying very, very hard not to fall over."

He made the record books—but he didn't pitch a "good" game. He walked eight players that day, and the bases were loaded several times. He hit at least one or two players with wild throws (he could never remember the exact number) and threw other pitches down into the dirt. The only reason the Padres didn't get a hit was because Dock's teammates saved the day with highlight-reel-worthy plays. Even Dock admitted he threw a lousy game, saying: "It was ugly, but it was still a no-no."

Some people say the story is bogus. If it happened in 1970, why did Dock wait until 1984 to tell the story? But the truth is he told the story to his biographer, Donald Hall, in 1976—but then ordered Hall to yank it out of the book because Dock was traded to the Yankees in 1976 and knew that owner George Steinbrenner would flip his lid. After Dock retired, the book was reprinted with the LSD story put back in—along with an apology saying the 1976 version was inaccurate "and on occasion mendacious."

Other people say the LSD story must be fake because Dock didn't "look high" when he was interviewed after the game. What a noob thing to say. The first thing you learn if you use drugs on a regular basis is how to wear a convincing mask of normalcy—even if your brain is bathing in a sea of chemical trippiness. It's called "hiding your power level"—a wonderful phrase coined by the writers of *Dragon Ball Z*. Dock knew as well as anyone how to hide his power level. This wasn't his first rodeo. But if you still need proof, even though Major League Baseball never released the full footage of the game, some partial footage was aired on HBO and shows Dock slipping and stumbling after throwing the ball—so there's your CSI physical evidence.

The LSD no-no wasn't Dock's only legendary story. He was a

flamboyant character who loved to get attention. In 1973, he started emerging from the locker room wearing big ol' curlers in his hair during the pregame warm-ups, which shocked his teammates and got the press snapping pictures left and right. The MLB commissioner threatened to suspend him if he ever did it again. A year later, in 1974, Dock got pissed off at the Cincinnati Reds for trash-talking his team, so he told his teammates he was going to bean every batter in the Cincinnati lineup. They foolishly assumed he was joking, but he most assuredly was not. He nailed each of the first three Cincinnati batters, hitting one in the side, one in the kidney, and one in the back. Now the bases were loaded, so everyone figured he'd have to stop. But not Dock—he threw directly at the fourth batter's head. The guy dodged four pitches and earned a walk to first base, meaning Dock had now walked in a run. The Pirates were losing 1–0 entirely because of Dock's crazy vendetta. When the fifth batter came up and Dock chucked the ball at his head twice in a row, the Pirates' coach said enough is enough and pulled Dock out of the game.

Dock advocated passionately for the rights of Black baseball players. Baseball was way too slow to integrate in the seventies, and he wasn't shy about saying so. In 1971, when the American League chose African-American Vida Blue as its starting pitcher for the All-Star Game, Dock slyly told reporters that it meant the National League would never choose him—because MLB wouldn't dare start "two brothers" in something as important as the All-Star Game. His remarks generated headlines all over the country and effectively pressured the National League to name Dock as the starting pitcher—which, of course, is exactly what he wanted. He received a thank-you letter from Jackie Robinson for his bold move saying: "In my opinion, progress for today's players will only come from this kind of dedication. . . . Sincerely, Jackie Robinson."

After Dock retired from baseball in 1980, his alcohol and drug addiction spiraled out of control. Thankfully, he checked himself into rehab and got sober. He became a substance abuse counselor, drawing on his own experiences to help others steer clear of drugs. For more than twenty-five years, he helped prison inmates, teenagers in juvenile detention centers, and even a few baseball players turn their lives around. In the end, though, all those years of drinking and drugs caught up with him; he died from cirrhosis of the liver at sixty-three.

Dock didn't want the "no-no" story to define him. He came to regret taking LSD because it "robbed him of his greatest professional memory." He was no longer the same guy who'd started using drugs as a teen in high school: "I went from liquor to marijuana, from marijuana to cocaine, and amphetamines, and everything else." Dock wanted his legacy to be the fact that he kicked drugs and spent decades guiding others down a better, healthier path.

I realize that by writing this chapter, I am perpetuating a story that Dock didn't want to define him. I am sorry about that, I truly am. But in fairness, this is a book about drugs—specifically, a book about people who achieved remarkable things while under the influence of drugs. I don't know how you can write a book like this and not mention the altogether true but wildly insane story of how Dock Ellis pitched a no-hitter while tripping on LSD.[1]

---

1. You can hear Dock tell the story in his own words, accompanied by some really fun animation, in a video on YouTube: https://www.youtube.com /watch?v=_vUhSYLRw14.

# CHAPTER 39

# John McAfee Was the World's Biggest Troll

Cybersecurity legend John McAfee is the poster boy for how drugs can mess you up. He looked out on the world and saw chaos. But instead of trying to bring order to the chaos, he chose to ride it like a surfer rides a monster wave. He leaned into the chaos, determined to out-crazy the craziness of the world around him.

He rose to fame in the 1980s, before the World Wide Web was born. Personal computers were a luxury item back then, owned mostly by tech geeks and rich folks who weren't worried about their computers being attacked—until they got hit by the "Brain" computer virus in 1986. The virus was created by two brothers in Pakistan who owned a computer store and wanted to see how far their homemade virus could propagate—so, in the code, they included their real names, phone number, and address. Suddenly, it didn't matter if you had any valuable secrets worth stealing; if you owned a personal computer, you were a target.

People started panicking, and McAfee saw a golden opportunity: a way to profit from the panic. The Brain virus reminded him of his turbulent childhood, with an alcoholic father who would lash out at him without warning. He'd been powerless to defend against his father's attacks—but a malicious computer virus was something he could fight back against because he was a technology wizard. He got to work devising an antivirus software program that could scan computers, seek out viruses, and remove them automatically. If his software worked, it would help ordinary people retain a sense of security and control over their lives—and hey, if it didn't work, he'd still get rich selling his stuff to millions of schmucks who didn't know any better. As a proud libertarian, McAfee was a firm believer in always looking out for number one.

Up to that point, McAfee hadn't been successful in life. He got bored easily and hated following rules. In an era when it was common for a skilled employee to stick with one company for their entire career, McAfee cycled through jobs like they were disposable wipes, repeatedly getting hired by prestigious organizations—NASA, UNIVAC, Xerox, Lockheed—only to get fired, lose interest, or leave in disgrace due to his wildly inappropriate behavior. He was tossed out of a PhD program for sleeping with one of his undergraduate students and fired by at least one of his employers for snorting lines of cocaine at his desk.

But with the creation of a first-of-its-kind antivirus software, McAfee finally achieved mainstream success. He started his own company (which, of course, he named after himself: McAfee Associates) in 1987, only four years after being fired for selling coke to his fellow employees. Soon, he was raking in $5 million a year. He was exactly the kind of weirdo who could thrive in the early Wild West days of home computing: he was driven, confident, and tech-savvy—but also erratic, unstable, self-important, and profoundly bizarre.

But you can't stay on top of the antivirus game by waiting around for people to start panicking about something. Sometimes, you have to instigate the panic yourself. So, when he heard rumblings about a new virus named Michelangelo in 1992, McAfee went into overdrive, contacting every newspaper and media outlet to portray this new virus as the single greatest threat to mankind, warning it would destroy over five million computers. His PR blitz did the trick—proving that one of McAfee's sharpest skills was his ability to infect others with his own intense brand of paranoia. Ultimately, the Michelangelo virus infected only a few thousand computers, leading people in the industry to ridicule him as an alarmist. But he didn't care. He'd already earned an astronomical amount of cash from all the antivirus software he sold to terrified consumers. People were pissed at him, but McAfee had money to blow—which would become a recurring theme in his life.

Ever the enemy of stability and the status quo, McAfee decided to cash out and retire only two years later, selling his stake in the company for $100 million. In retrospect, he would have been wiser to hold on to the stock a bit longer, because in 2010, Intel bought the company for $7 *billion*—but McAfee was never known for his patience. Then he proceeded to lose most of his fortune in the 2008 financial crisis. By the time the dust settled, only $4 million of the $100 million remained; the other $96 million had been wiped out.

That's when McAfee decided to become a full-time agent of chaos. He moved to a tiny island in Central America, fifteen miles off the coast of Belize, to become a professional narco-trafficker. He built his own drug fiefdom, complete with a secret laboratory, a private army of gun-toting thugs, a harem of scantily clad women of dubiously legal age who all claimed to be his girlfriend, and a pack of vicious off-the-leash guard dogs who barked endlessly and bit anyone who happened by.

He also doubled down on his drug consumption. The tech industry might have abandoned him, and his real estate investments might have gone bust—but getting insanely high? That was recession-proof. He once told a reporter from the *Wall Street Journal*: "My personality is such that I can't do something halfway."

Cocaine had been his go-to drug in the 1980s, but not anymore. Now he was obsessed with synthetic cathinones, better known by the street name "bath salts." They're called that because their white crumbly crystalline appearance somewhat resembles Epsom salts, but their effect is radically different. Unlike real bath salts, which dissolve in water and provide soothing stress relief, these synthetic "bath salts" operate like ecstasy, cocaine, and meth all rolled into one. They are a subtype of amphetamines known to induce intense feelings of euphoria. For a sex-obsessed egomaniac like McAfee, the prospect of being incredibly cranked up on drugs while his erotic experiences were vastly intensified seemed like a gateway to hedonistic bliss. That's why he called it his "super perv powder."

He posted literally hundreds of times on a website called Bluelight, an online forum for drug-use enthusiasts, raving about this supposed wonder drug. He explained in vivid detail that for optimum efficacy and maximum pleasure, one should "plug" the bath salts or "shelve" them—both of which were euphemisms for inserting the drugs into your butt. (Speaking of butts, McAfee also had a habit of injecting testosterone into his buttocks to increase his virility and help him feel younger.) Despite his repeated posts touting the wonders of bath salts, McAfee sometimes told reporters he hadn't personally used any drugs since 1983 and that his many posts were actually an elaborate prank designed to trick others into taking these dangerous compounds. (What a guy!) Then again, McAfee also put a gun to his head and pulled the trigger multiple times while being interviewed by a reporter from *Wired* in 2012—not because he wanted to kill himself but simply to prove a point. In other words, this was a man who loved to mess with people's minds.

Unfortunately, bath salts have other effects that are decidedly less sexy. They induce hallucinations, psychosis, and insane levels of paranoia. He was already a conspiracy-minded individual, and the bath salts pushed him over the edge into dark, delusional behavior. The more drugs he took, the more detached he got from reality. He became convinced a Mexican drug cartel was after him. He insisted to a reporter that this nefarious cartel had him under constant surveillance, and he could prove it—he dragged the reporter outside and pointed to an empty packet of cream cheese lying on the ground, screaming: "All they eat is cream cheese. I find cream cheese packets everywhere. If there's cream cheese, I know the cartel has been here."

Shortly after his Russian roulette interview with *Wired*, it all came unglued. One of McAfee's neighbors complained to the police about the incessantly barking guard dogs. When the police didn't act, the neighbor apparently decided to take matters into his own hands. Four of McAfee's dogs were poisoned, so badly that McAfee had to shoot them to put them out of their misery. Two days later, the neighbor himself turned up dead, shot execution-style in the back of the head. McAfee immediately went on the run, playing hide-and-seek with the local authorities. He taunted them by phone and online, claiming he was still living in his house and was avoiding detection by wearing silly disguises. While on the lam, he posted a video on YouTube titled "How to Uninstall McAfee Antivirus" in which he appears shirtless, surrounded by seven scantily clad women, his face caked in white powder, with a big container labeled "BATH SALTS" resting at his side.

Although he was never formally charged with murdering his neighbor, McAfee was actively pursued by jurisdictions all over the world for a wide variety of crimes, including drug trafficking, firearm violations, securities fraud, money laundering, and tax evasion. He was undeniably guilty of the last of these—he boasted frequently that he hadn't paid any taxes since 2010 because, in his view, taxes were "unconstitutional and illegal."

Guess what McAfee did in the midst of all his legal troubles: He ran for president. Twice. First in 2016, and again in 2020. He tried to shift the blame for his myriad legal woes, claiming he didn't do anything wrong, it was all "political persecution." Obviously, he didn't win, but can you imagine if he had—if we had a US president who did nothing but spout paranoid conspiracy theories and refuse to pay money he rightfully owed, and was only looking out for himself? I mean, seriously, *can you*?

The law finally caught up with him in 2020. McAfee was arrested in Barcelona as he was getting ready to board a flight to Istanbul with a British passport (no, he wasn't a British citizen). The Department of Justice asked Spain to extradite him so he could face trial in the United States for tax evasion, and McAfee didn't like that one bit.

But he continued to troll people until the bitter end. While languishing in a jail cell in Barcelona, waiting to see if his lawyers would be able to defeat the DOJ's efforts to extradite him, he posted on Twitter saying that prison life was awesome. He said in his tweet that he was perfectly happy living in a cell, he had plenty of friends, and the food was good. He ended his tweet by saying—quite explicitly—that if he was ever found hanging in his cell like Jeffrey Epstein (yes, he actually referenced Epstein), it was all a setup.

Then, only a few hours after the court ruled that McAfee would be extradited, he hung himself in his cell—knowing it would launch all sorts of paranoid postmortem conspiracy theories. Because John McAfee wanted to end his life in the same way he had lived—by giving everyone the double middle finger.

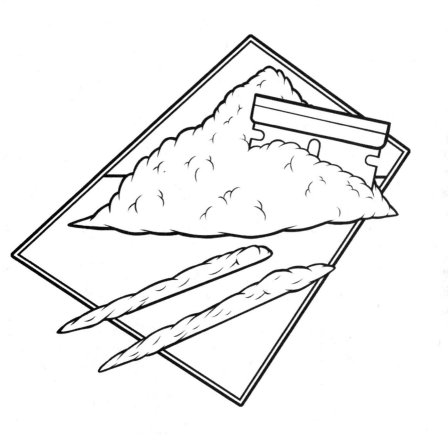

# CHAPTER 40

# Steve Jobs Loved LSD and Soaking His Feet in the Toilet

---

S teve Jobs said taking LSD was "one of the two or three most important things" he did in his life. While that sounds like something you'd be more likely to hear from a guy who owns a surf shop than the founder of one of the biggest technology companies in the world, you need to understand that Steve Jobs was an unconventional guy.

He started with absolutely nothing. As soon as he was born in 1955, his birth parents gave him up. He was adopted by a machinist and his wife, neither of whom had graduated high school, but they pledged to send him to college. They scraped together a small amount of money, enough to pay for a top-tier state school like UC Berkeley, but Jobs insisted on applying only to Reed College in Portland, Oregon, known for its free-spirited hippie aesthetic—and for being one of the most expensive colleges in the nation. His parents begged him to apply somewhere else, someplace they could afford, but Jobs said it was Reed or nothing. After one semester at Reed, he dropped out because he didn't like the idea of having to take "required courses"—and because he was starting to feel guilty about using up all of his parents' savings. He didn't have any money of his own, so, in his own words: "I slept on the floor in friends' rooms, I returned Coke bottles for the five-cent deposits to buy food with, and I would walk the seven miles across town every Sunday night to get one good meal a week at the Hare Krishna temple. I loved it."

Personal hygiene wasn't his strong suit. He walked around barefoot all the time, didn't take showers, and didn't bother to use deodorant. He was a strict vegetarian for most of his life, and sometimes that morphed into diets that were even more restrictive. For weeks at a time, he'd eat only apples and carrots, nothing else. He thought this meant there wasn't any mucus in his body, so it was impossible for him to have body odor—but his coworkers said he was very, very wrong. He smelled so bad that when, at age nineteen, he got a part-time gig working at Atari, the company was forced to put him on the night shift so no one else would have to smell him. And here's my favorite part—when he started his own company, if he was feeling particularly stressed out, Jobs would go into the company restroom and soak his feet in the toilet as a way to relax and unwind. (As you can imagine, it wasn't so relaxing for his employees, who were all too aware of his disgusting habit.)

Jobs quit the Atari job to make a spiritual pilgrimage to India. He wanted to find a guru to teach him more about enlightenment and Zen Buddhism. A friend who accompanied him said: "We were monk-wannabes." Jobs was already fond of LSD. He'd been dabbling with acid since his senior year in high school but was taking it even more frequently now because he viewed it as "yogi medicine." Jobs believed LSD was the pharmaceutical of choice for those seeking to become enlightened.

We know all this is true because he confessed it to the FBI. When Jobs was running Pixar, he applied for a top secret security clearance, which meant he had to disclose everything about his drug use. He told the FBI that he was fond of cannabis (which he started smoking at age fifteen) and hashish, but his favorite drug was LSD. He said he took it ten to fifteen times over a two-year period from 1972 to 1974 (between the ages of seventeen and nineteen). He wasn't ashamed at all; he was proud of it. He told the FBI, "I can say it was a positive life-changing experience for me and I am glad I went through that experience."

Why was he so inordinately fond of LSD, and why did he characterize it as one of the most important things he ever did? The answer is Jobs had a very specific goal when he started his company: "At Apple, we want to make computers that will change the world. We want to put a ding in the universe." And that's what he thought LSD did for him: expanded his mind, granted him insight, and enabled him to see the bigger picture.

Do you remember what computers looked like before Steve Jobs? They were ugly gray boxes with monochromatic black screens displaying line after line of boring green text. There were no icons, no pictures, and no aesthetic appeal. If you weren't a scientist or an engineer, you probably weren't going to like it. Jobs's LSD-infused brain told him he needed to change everything. At a time when computers were boxy, plain, and utilitarian, he wanted to design something sleek, modern, and beautiful—something that could be displayed in a home or office as a piece of art.

But how to do it? He wasn't a hardware engineer; he didn't have the technological know-how to design an entirely new sort of computer. He was a thinker, a visionary, the guy who brought geniuses together and pushed, prodded, and provoked them into doing their best work. He started Apple Computer Company[1] in his parents' garage in 1976, with a computer that his pal Steve Wozniak built by hand to show off to his friends. Woz's computer was amazing, but it didn't fundamentally change the idea of what a computer could be.

But in 1979, Jobs caught a glimpse of the future. He convinced some Xerox executives to let him sneak a peek at their experimental

---

1. He named the company Apple because that's all he was eating at the time.

computer called the Alto, in exchange for the chance to buy some Apple stock. The Alto had something Jobs had never seen before: little pictures on the computer screen called "icons"—they looked like documents and file folders. And you could use a small pointing device called a "mouse" to click on them. It was a visual metaphor for a desktop in a physical office space.

Jobs was blown away: "It was one of those sort of apocalyptic moments. I remember within ten minutes of seeing the graphical user interface stuff, just knowing that every computer would work this way someday. It was so obvious once you saw it. It didn't require tremendous intellect. It was so clear." Except it wasn't clear to Xerox. Their executives didn't seem to understand the enormity of what they had stumbled onto.

So, he stole their idea. Apple engineers immediately got to work on the Macintosh, which became the first computer to bring the graphical user interface to a mass audience. Instead of boring green text on a black computer screen, the Macintosh showed a desktop filled with icons that resembled everyday objects—trash cans, file folders, a paintbrush, even a bomb—and you interacted with these icons by pointing and clicking with a mouse. It was easy, intuitive, and fun. Some early reviewers dismissed it as a childish fad that would never last, but history proved that Jobs was right.

Today, every personal computer has a graphical user interface, and it's all because Jobs pirated the idea from Xerox. He didn't deny it; he freely admitted swiping their idea. His biographer, Walter Isaacson, said Jobs likened himself to Picasso: "Picasso had a saying—'good artists copy, great artists steal'—and we have always been shameless about stealing great ideas." Plus, you've got to love the irony of someone copying from Xerox—isn't copying what Xerox is all about? Jobs blamed Xerox for fumbling their big opportunity. They were sitting on a gold mine and "could have owned the computer industry," but they didn't see it, and Jobs did. It became one of the recurring themes in Jobs's life—taking credit for other people's ideas.

That's pretty much what the FBI concluded in their evaluation. They said Jobs was a genius but also kind of a dick. He would "twist the truth and distort reality in order to achieve his goals." Multiple employees said, "Jobs possesses integrity as long as he gets his way." When he didn't get his way, he'd throw tantrums like a spoiled child. He was a perfectionist, a narcissist, and a bully, all wrapped up in a black turtleneck sweater. He drove people around him crazy—he'd scream at them, tell them their ideas were worthless, then later take credit for those ideas if they worked. He'd park in handicapped spaces and honk angrily at cops who took too long to write him a ticket. And it took him years to finally admit the child that he conceived with his high school sweetheart was actually his daughter.

But you can't deny the man's genius. He revolutionized the world. Thanks to Jobs, computers aren't earmarked only for scientists and engineers; everybody has one. He wasn't selling a product so much as he was offering an entire digital lifestyle. He made computers an essential part of daily life. And he didn't stop with the personal computer. When he returned to Apple in 1997 after a twelve-year absence (he was fired in 1985 after losing a power struggle with the CEO), he oversaw the creation of one world-changing device after another—the iPod, the iPhone, and the iPad.

Jobs wanted people to fall in love with their computers, and they did—literally. Brain scans have shown that people react to their iPhones the same way they react to a best friend or a life partner. When they're away from their iPhones, they experience genuine separation anxiety; they don't feel whole. That's not an accident—that's precisely what Jobs was aiming for. As *Time* magazine put it, "Jobs knew how to inspire material lust."

When Jobs died of pancreatic cancer in 2011, a group of his

friends gathered at Stanford University for a memorial, where his daughter Eve summed up her father's life by reading the text of Apple's most famous commercial: "Here's to the crazy ones. . . . The ones who see things differently. . . . They push the human race forward. . . . Because the people who are crazy enough to think that they can change the world, are the ones who do."

That was Steve Jobs in a nutshell. He transformed a world of ugly utilitarian technology into something beautiful and deeply personal. He wasn't a perfect man by any means. He was selfish, he was overbearing, and he didn't shower nearly enough—but when he died, his net worth was over ten billion dollars, so go figure.

# EPILOGUE

So what have we learned?

These forty stories cover an extraordinary breadth of human experience, spanning thousands of years, but seeing them together, it hopefully becomes clear that drugs are fundamentally tools, not inherently forces of good or evil. It is true that numerous people ultimately came to grief from drugs, whether because they couldn't control themselves, didn't know enough to protect themselves, had drug use thrust upon them by outside forces, or, in some cases, were deliberately trying to destroy themselves. At the same time, however, it is undeniable that many of these individuals benefited pretty significantly from their drug use—or at least thought they did. Some treated medical problems that could otherwise have destroyed their lives, some tapped into previously unknown reservoirs of creative vitality, and some produced work of a quality (or, in some cases, quantity) they never would have achieved without pharmaceutical assistance.

Certain drugs tend to go badly more often than others. Opioids, for example, are great for treating acute short-term pain but terrible for treating chronic long-term conditions because they are so incredibly addictive. That's why the widespread availability of over-the-counter laudanum caused extensive tragedy and a raging addiction epidemic before its sale was rightly restricted. Amphetamines, too, have legitimate medical uses, but there's a reason you need a prescription to obtain them. The potential for misuse and abuse with the more habit-forming substances, like opioids and amphetamines, makes it much harder (though not impossible) to incorporate them as part of a healthy long-term lifestyle. As a point of comparison, plenty of people consume alcohol in moderation and are fine, but plenty of others fall into devastating addictions because they are either unable or unwilling to cut themselves off.

The future looks considerably brighter for cannabis and psychedelics. Attitudes toward drugs generally (and especially these drugs) have changed in recent years. The United States seems to have finally put the "Just Say No" era behind it. (Remember, the "War on Drugs" was a cynical political strategy instigated by President Nixon to vilify Black people and hippies.) Marijuana is legal for medical use in thirty-eight states, and adult recreational use is permitted in twenty-three states. Right now, the DEA is planning to reschedule cannabis from Schedule I (no accepted medical use) to Schedule III, a category containing drugs with legitimate medical uses, including codeine, ketamine, and anabolic steroids. Given that the federal government was historically one of the biggest opponents of legal marijuana, this is a fundamental paradigm shift. The massively increased social acceptance of cannabis seems to reflect that people have seen through the lies in the old propaganda campaigns against it. "Reefer madness" was a ridiculous myth. It turns out cannabis can help people in tons of ways—from relieving physical pain to suppressing seizures and soothing PTSD—but produces very little in the way of nasty side effects, addiction, or sociological disaster.

LSD and its psychedelic brethren have also made enormous strides. Public perception appears to be changing, as increasing numbers of people—including medical professionals—see them less as dangerous agents of chaos and more as paths to spiritual and personal discovery. In fact, in 2021, the Department of Veterans Affairs began clinical trials to determine whether psychedelics such as MDMA and psilocybin mushrooms could be used to treat returning soldiers suffering from PTSD—thus resurrecting the type of research that took place six decades ago, before LSD and other psychedelics were banned.

You'll remember that Albert Hofmann, LSD's creator, was emphatic that his creation had to be treated with respect and used responsibly. He understood the crucial lesson that drugs, like all tools, can be used for good or bad purposes. Ultimately, it's how we choose to employ these tools that determines whether they are an ally or an enemy. For ten years before it was banned, LSD was put to good use and helped thousands of people. Hofmann felt it was a tragedy that unethical experimentation and moral panic took it all away. He believed with all his heart that just because LSD could be misused, that did not negate its enormous potential. Maybe, at long last, the world is coming around to his way of thinking.

Consider the example of the internet: It can be used in horrifying ways to spread hate and lies. But at the same time, it also provides an unprecedented potential for connection, understanding, and sharing among people all over the world and from every walk of life. The capacity to use it for evil should not outweigh its immense capability for good. It's a question of installing safeguards, encouraging responsibility, cracking down on abuse, and avoiding excess.

People today seem more willing to embrace the notion that while all drugs have the potential for abuse, they also have the potential for good.

Much like the internet, you don't have to let drugs take over your life.

# ACKNOWLEDGMENTS

I want to begin by thanking my family for their enthusiastic support. My special and deepest gratitude goes to my dad, Kevin, who's been by my side every step of the way with his scrupulous fact-checking and in-house editing—thank you for making sure I always had the facts to back me up. My profound love and appreciation goes to my mom, Caroline, who has been my champion throughout this journey, offering me heaps of love, encouragement, and gentle prodding—thank you for keeping me driven. Profuse thank-yous to Rachel, Jacob, and my entire extended family for always expressing love and support, and never rolling their eyes when I told them I was writing a book about history and drugs.

Thank you to my awe-inspiring agent, Jeff Kleinman, who read a page-and-a-half book proposal way back in 2019 and said, hey, there's something here. He guided me through the process with patience and wisdom, and believed in me long before he had any reason to.

A huge and heartfelt thanks to everyone at Plume and Penguin Random House who helped transform this book from a dream into a reality. First and foremost, an enormous thank-you to the brilliant and generous Jill Schwartzman, VP and executive editor, for giving me the opportunity to write the book I have always pictured in my mind and for offering wonderful suggestions that helped to make the book better and smarter. Thank you to the fiercely intelligent Charlotte Peters for providing historical insights that were genuinely helpful and deeply appreciated. Thank you, John Parsley, vice president and publisher of Dutton, for taking a chance on a book with an unconventional and eyebrow-raising subject matter. And thank you to the rest of the phenomenal Plume team: Nicole Jarvis, Erika Semprun, Hannah Poole, Kaitlin Kall, Lorie Pagnozzi, Alice Dalrymple, and Patricia Clark, for working so tirelessly.

And thanks to my copy editor, Aja Pollock, and proofreaders, Kim Surridge and Rima Weinberg, for helping me fine-tune my work to make it the best it can be.

A very special thank-you to Paul Girard, illustrator extraordinaire. You are an immensely talented artist, and I deeply appreciate the way you helped to breathe life into these historical characters with your creativity, flair, and humor.

A shout-out to my followers on TikTok, who have watched my three-hundred-plus videos on bizarre historical topics, allowed me to share with them my unbridled enthusiasm for history, and hopefully have come to realize that history can be a whole lot of fun.

Finally, my everlasting thanks to all my history teachers and professors—from grade school through college—who sparked in me a deep and abiding love of history and inspired my lifelong passion for researching lots of really weird stuff. I hope I have done you proud.

# SELECTED BIBLIOGRAPHY

**Chapter 1: The Oracle of Delphi Was Huffing Fumes**

William J. Broad. *The Oracle: Ancient Delphi and the Science Behind Its Lost Secrets.* Penguin Books, 2006, 2–4, 12–13, 212–14, 238–40, 242–47.

William J. Broad. "For Delphic Oracle: Fumes and Visions." *New York Times,* March 19, 2002. https://www.nytimes.com/2002/03/19/science /for-delphic-oracle-fumes-and-visions.html.

John R. Hale et al. "Questioning the Delphic Oracle." *Scientific American* 289, no. 2 (2003): 66–73. https://www.scientificamerican.com/article /questioning-the-delphic-o-2003-08/.

Jelle Zeilinga de Boer and John R. Hale. "Was She Really Stoned: The Oracle of Delphi." *Archaeological Odyssey,* November/December 2002. https://www.biblicalarchaeology.org/daily/ancient-cultures/daily-life-and -practice/the-oracle-of-delphi-was-she-really-stoned/.

Haralampos V. Harissis, "A Bittersweet Story: The True Nature of the Laurel of the Oracle of Delphi." *Perspectives in Biology and Medicine* 57, no. 3 (2014): 351–60. https://www.academia.edu/7004301/A_bittersweet _story_the_true_nature_of_the_laurel_of_the_Oracle_of_Delphi.

Robin McKie. "Delphic Oracle Was Ancient Glue-Sniffer." *Guardian,* August 3, 2003. https://www.theguardian.com/world/2003/aug/03 /research.arts.

Heather Whipps. "New Theory on What Got the Oracle of Delphi High." *LiveScience,* October 31, 2006. https://www.livescience.com/4277 -theory-oracle-delphi-high.html.

**Chapter 2: Pharaoh Ramesses II Wanted Ganja**

Robert C. Clarke and Mark D. Merlin. *Cannabis: Evolution and Ethnobotany.* University of California Press, 2013, 127, 158, 245–46.

Arlette Leroi-Gourhan. *La Momie de Ramses II—Contribution Scientifique a l'Egyptologie.* Muséum National d'Histoire Naturelle, 1985, 162–65.

John Noble Wilford. "Tomb of Ramses II's Many Sons Is Found in Egypt." *New York Times,* May 16, 1995. https://www.nytimes.com/1995/05/16/us/tomb-of-ramses-ii-s-many-sons-is-found-in-egypt.html.

Christopher Parker. "Archaeologists Discover 2,000 Mummified Ram Skulls in Temple of Ramses II." *Smithsonian,* March 31, 2023. https://www.smithsonianmag.com/smart-news/archaeologists-discovered-2000-ram-skulls-temple-pharaoh-ramses-ii-180981911/.

Nicholas Brown. "Coffin of Ramesses II." American Research Center in Egypt. https://arce.org/coffin-ramesses-ii/.

Kristin Baird Rattini. "Who Was Ramses II?" *National Geographic,* May 13, 2019. https://www.nationalgeographic.com/culture/article/ramses-ii.

Joshua J. Mark. "Kadesh." *World History Encyclopedia,* September 2, 2009. https://www.worldhistory.org/Ramesses_II/.

Wu Mingren. "The Life and Death of Ramesses II, Ramesses the Great." Ancient Origins, July 5, 2020. https://www.ancient-origins.net/myths-legends-africa/ramesses-ii-001822.

Robert Brusco. "A Versatile Plant: What Were the Many Uses of Cannabis in Ancient Egypt?" Ancient Origins, September 4, 2021. https://www.ancient-origins.net/history-ancient-traditions/versatile-plant-what-were-many-uses-cannabis-ancient-egypt-007733.

Gina Heeb and Visual Capitalist. "Here's the 6,000 Year History of Medical Marijuana." *Business Insider,* June 21, 2018. https://www.businessinsider.com/heres-the-6000-year-history-of-medical-marijuana-2018-6.

Randa. "History of Cannabis—a Timeline." Home Grown Apothecary, February 7, 2023. https://homegrownapothecary.com/history-of-cannabis-timeline/?age-verified=abaf116679.

GDC. "Ancient Egypt and Cannabis." Dragon Cannabis, January 2, 2022. https://dragon-cannabis.com/en/2022/01/28/ancient-egypt-and-cannabis/.

"1800 BCE: Ancient Egyptian Magic Spells Require Cannabis." Hempshopper. https://hempshopper.com/hemp-history/1800-bce-ancient-egytian-spells-require-cannabis/.

## Chapter 3: Alexander the Great Was a Sloppy Drunk

John Maxwell O'Brien. *Alexander the Great: The Invisible Enemy.* Routledge, 1994, 1–4, 6–8, 56–59, 133–40, 210–16, 223–30.

Simon Denison. "Was Alexander a Great Alcoholic?" *Independent,* August 2, 1992. https://www.independent.co.uk/news/uk/was-alexander-a-great-alcoholic-1537664.html.

Owen Jarus. "Alexander the Great: Facts, Biography and Accomplishments." *LiveScience*, November 8, 2021. https://www .livescience.com/39997-alexander-the-great.html.

Sarah Pruitt. "Alexander the Great Died Mysteriously at 32. Now We May Know Why." History, January 23, 2019. https://www.history.com /news/alexander-the-great-death-cause-discovery.

F. J. Carod-Artal. "Psychoactive Plants in Ancient Greece." *Neurosciences and History* 1, no. 1 (2013): 28–38.

Lecia Bushak. "Civilization's Painkiller: A Brief History of Opioids." *Newsweek*, August 7, 2016. https://www.newsweek.com/civilization -painkiller-brief-history-opioid-486164.

"Alexander the Great." *Britannica*. https://www.britannica.com /biography/Alexander-the-Great.

## Chapter 4: Qin Shi Huangdi's Recipe for Immortality Backfired

Joseph Needham. "Elixir Poisoning in Medieval China." In *Clerks and Craftsmen in China and the West.* Cambridge University Press, 1970, 316–39.

Yan Liu. *Healing with Poisons: Potent Medicines in Medieval China.* University of Washington Press, 2021, 148–50. https://uw.manifoldapp.org/read /1abfa74f-92a6-4b5c-aec9-c2ab99bc1f74/section/46855186-01e9-48ef -ae54-4e201ab94c8e.

Yan Liu. "Poisons in the Premodern World." *Encyclopedia of the History of Science*, May 2021. https://doi.org/10.34758/yazp-kz74.

Brigit Katz. "2,000-Year-Old Texts Reveal the First Emperor of China's Quest for Eternal Life." *Smithsonian*, December 29, 2017. https://www .smithsonianmag.com/smart-news/2000-year-old-texts-reveal-first-emperor -chinas-quest-eternal-life-180967671/.

Megan Gannon. "China's First Emperor Ordered Official Search for Immortality Elixir." *LiveScience*, December 27, 2017. https://www .livescience.com/61286-first-chinese-emperor-sought-immortality.html.

Philip Ball. "Flowing Rivers of Mercury." *Chemistry World*, January 6, 2015. https://www.chemistryworld.com/features/flowing-rivers-of-mercury /8122.article.

Edward Burman. "The First Emperor's Pursuit of Immortality." *Lapham's Quarterly*, August 8, 2018. https://www.laphamsquarterly.org/roundtable /art-not-dying.

Jonathan Glancey. "The Army That Conquered the World." BBC, April 12, 2017. https://www.bbc.com/culture/article/20170411-the-army-that -conquered-the-world.

A. R. Williams. "Discoveries May Rewrite History of China's Terra-Cotta Warriors." *National Geographic*, October 11, 2016. https://www

.nationalgeographic.com/history/article/china-first-emperor-terra-cotta
-warriors-tomb?loggedin=true&rnd=1687386137012.

Lorraine Boissoneault. "Sticky Rice Mortar, the View from Space, and
More Fun Facts About China's Great Wall." *Smithsonian*, February 16, 2017.
https://www.smithsonianmag.com/history/sticky-rice-mortar-view-space
-and-more-fun-facts-about-chinas-great-wall-180962197/.

Helen O'Neill. "Quicksilver Can Cure, but It Can Also Kill Insidiously."
*Los Angeles Times*, September 14, 1997. https://www.latimes.com/archives
/la-xpm-1997-sep-14-mn-32062-story.html.

David F. Lloyd. "The Man Who Would Cheat Death and Rule the
Universe." *Vision*, Summer 2008. https://www.vision.org/qin-shi-huang
-quest-for-immortality-and-power-815.

Mark Oliver. "How the Search for Immortality Killed the First Emperor
of China." *Ancient Origins*, June 15, 2018. https://www.ancient-origins.net
/history-famous-people/search-immortality-killed-emperor-china
-0010207.

Sanj Atwal. "The Dark History Behind the Record-Breaking
Terracotta Army." *Guinness World Records*, March 11, 2022. https://www
.guinnessworldrecords.com/news/2022/3/the-dark-history-behind-the
-record-breaking-terracotta-army-694905.

"Qin Dynasty." History, December 21, 2017. https://www.history.com
/topics/ancient-china/qin-dynasty.

"Great Wall of China." History, August 24, 2010. https://www.history
.com/topics/ancient-china/great-wall-of-china.

### Chapter 5: St. John the Revelator Was Tripping on Shrooms

John M. Allegro. *The Sacred Mushroom and the Cross.* Gnostic Media, 2009,
132.

Jan Irvin and Andrew Rutajit. *Astrotheology & Shamanism: Christianity's
Pagan Roots.* Gnostic Media, 2009, 59, 144.

J. R. Irvin. *The Holy Mushroom: Evidence of Mushrooms in Judeo-Christianity.*
Gnostic Media, 2008, 1–7.

Richard J. Miller. "Religion as a Product of Psychotropic Drug Use."
*Atlantic*, December 27, 2013. https://www.theatlantic.com/health/archive
/2013/12/religion-as-a-product-of-psychotropic-drug-use/282484/.

Fergus M. Bordewich. "Patmos: Isle of the Apocalypse." *New York Times*,
April 14, 1985. https://www.nytimes.com/1985/04/14/travel/patmos-isle
-of-the-apocalypse.html.

Jason Hack. "Toxicology Q&A Answer: Yes, the Amanita Muscaria
Mushroom Is Toxic." *ACEP Now*, December 17, 2018. https://www.acepnow
.com/article/toxicology-qa-answer-yes-the-amanita-muscaria-mushroom
-is-toxic/.

Francesca Irene Rampolli et al. "The Deceptive Mushroom: Accidental Amanita Muscaria Poisoning." *European Journal of Case Reports in Internal Medicine* 8, no. 2 (2021). https://www.ejcrim.com/index.php/EJCRIM /article/view/2212.

Mateja Lampert and Samo Kreft. "Catching Flies with *Amanita Muscaria*: Traditional Recipes from Slovenia and Their Efficacy in the Extraction of Ibotenic Acid." *Journal of Ethnopharmacology* 187 (July 1, 2016). https://www .sciencedirect.com/science/article/abs/pii/S0378874116302008.

L. Michael White. "Understanding the Book of Revelation." *PBS Frontline*. https://www.pbs.org/wgbh/pages/frontline/shows/apocalypse /revelation/white.html.

"Religious Tolerance and Persecution in the Roman Empire." Teach Democracy. https://www.crf-usa.org/bill-of-rights-in-action/bria-13-4-b -religious-tolerance-and-persecution-in-the-roman-empire.

## Chapter 6: Marcus Aurelius's Sleepy-Time Medicine

Thomas W. Africa. "The Opium Addiction of Marcus Aurelius." *Journal of the History of Ideas* 22, no. 1 (1961). https://www.jstor.org/stable/2707876.

Pierre Hadot. *Philosophy as a Way of Life.* Blackwell Publishing, 1995, 180–81. https://ascetology.files.wordpress.com/2016/09/pierre-hadot -philosophy-as-a-way-of-life-spiritual-exercises-from-socrates-to-foucault -1.pdf.

Francois P. Retief. "Marcus Aurelius: Was He an Opium Addict?" *Sabinet African Journals*, January 1, 2007. https://www.journals.uchicago.edu/doi /abs/10.1086/364947?journalCode=cp.

Edward Charles Witke. "Marcus Aurelius and Mandragora." *Classical Philology* 60, no. 1 (1965). https://www.journals.uchicago.edu/doi/abs /10.1086/364947?journalCode=cp.

F. R. Jevons. "Was Plotinus Influenced by Opium?" Cambridge University Press. https://www.cambridge.org/core/services/aop-cambridge -core/content/view/91AF4316E07BCB35A7B9098358D959BC /S0025727300031021a.pdf/div-class-title-was-plotinus-influenced-by -opium-div.pdf.

Tim Brinkhof. "The High Life: Doing Drugs with Ancient Greeks and Romans." *Big Think*, July 9, 2022. https://bigthink.com/the-past/history -of-drugs-ancient-greece-rome/.

Kelsey Christine McConnell. "Worst Roman Emperors, from Incompetent to Insane." *Archive*, March 10, 2020. https://explorethearchive .com/worst-roman-emperors.

Jacob Bell. "Marcus Aurelius, Stoicism and Pain." *Classical Wisdom*, March 15, 2019. https://classicalwisdom.com/philosophy/stoicism/marcus-aurelius -stoicism-and-pain/.

Joshua J. Mark. "Marcus Aurelius." *World History Encyclopedia*, March 26, 2018. https://www.ancient.eu/Marcus_Aurelius/.

John Anthony Crook. "Marcus Aurelius, Emperor of Rome." *Britannica*, July 20, 1998. https://www.britannica.com/biography/Marcus-Aurelius -Roman-emperor.

"Marcus Aurelius." History, June 10, 2019. https://www.history.com /topics/ancient-history/marcus-aurelius.

Sarah Cunningham. "5 Myths of Current Christian Culture That Detract from Faith." *Huffington Post*, January 23, 2014. https://www.huffpost.com /entry/christian-myths_b_4026198.

## Chapter 7: The Hashashin, the Devout Killer Potheads

Mark Cartwright. "The Assassins." *World History Encyclopedia*, October 29, 2019. https://www.worldhistory.org/The_Assassins/.

Noah Tesch. "Who Were the Assassins?" *Britannica*. https://www .britannica.com/story/who-were-the-assassins.

James Gilmer. "Blood & Sand: The Rise and Fall of the Hashashin." *Medieval Warfare* 5, no. 3 (2015): 44–49. https://www.jstor.org/stable /48578456.

Carole Hillenbrand. "The Assassins in Fact and Fiction: The Old Man of the Mountain." *Medieval Warfare* 9, no. 2 (2019): 22–35. https://www.jstor .org/stable/8896c556-5259-31da-9fc4-b3bef9298213?read-now =1&seq=12.

Erin Blakemore. "Was the Medieval Order of Assassins a Real Thing?" *National Geographic*, June 1, 2020. https://www.nationalgeographic.com /history/article/medieval-order-assassins-islam?loggedin=true&rnd =1688303567438.

Paul Ratner. "History's First Terrorists." *Big Think*, July 23, 2016. https:// bigthink.com/the-past/historys-first-terrorists/.

Kallie Szczepanski. "Hashshashin: The Assassins of Persia." *ThoughtCo.*, September 19, 2019. https://www.thoughtco.com/history-of-the-assassins -hashshashin-195545.

Scott Cianciosi. "Fortress of the Assassins." *Damn Interesting*, October 2007. https://www.damninteresting.com/fortress-of-the-assassins/.

Jeff Hays. "Assassins (Hashshashin): Their History, Victims, and Hashish Training." *Facts and Details*, September 2018. https://factsanddetails.com /central-asia/Central_Asian_Topics/sub8_8b/entry-5874.html.

Hayden Chakra. "The Deadliest Medieval Order of Assassins: The Hashashins." *About History*, December 8, 2022. https://about-history.com /the-deadliest-medieval-order-of-assassins-the-hashashin/.

Wu Mingren. "The Notorious Hashshashins, the Original Assassins of Persia." *Ancient Origins*, July 22, 2022. https://www.ancient-origins.net /myths-legends-asia/hashshashins-001708.

**Chapter 8: William Shakespeare Was a Stoner**

Stephen Greenblatt. "General Introduction." In *The Norton Shakespeare.* W. W. Norton, 1997, 30–41.

Francis Thackeray. "Was William Shakespeare High When He Penned His Plays?" *Independent,* August 9, 2015. https://www.independent.co.uk /arts-entertainment/theatre-dance/features/william-shakespeare-high -cannabis-marijuana-stoned-plays-hamlet-macbeth-romeo-juliet-stratford -10446510.html.

Will Godfrey. "Shakespeare on Drugs: The Secret Narcotic History of the World's Greatest Playwright." *Salon,* April 23, 2014. https://www.salon .com/2014/04/23/shakespeare_on_drugs_the_secret_narcotic_history_of _the_worlds_greatest_playwright_partner/.

Mairi Mackay. "Was William Shakespeare a Stoner?" CNN, August 11, 2015. https://www.cnn.com/2015/08/10/europe/shakespeare-cannabis-pipe /index.html.

Charlotte Meredith. "New Study Suggests That Shakespeare Might Have Been a Stoner." *Vice,* August 10, 2015. https://www.vice.com/en/article /ev9n34/new-study-suggests-that-shakespeare-might-have-been-a-stoner.

Kristina Killgrove. "To Drug Test Shakespeare's Bones or Not to Drug Test Them? That Is the Question." *Forbes,* November 4, 2015. https://www .forbes.com/sites/kristinakillgrove/2015/11/04/pothead-willie-the-search -for-shakespeares-skull-and-the-truth-about-his-marijuana-use /#536c1ec28791.

Marco Werman and Nina Porzucki. "Did William Shakespeare Really Invent All Those Words?" *World,* August 19, 2013. https://www.pri.org /stories/2013-08-19/did-william-shakespeare-really-invent-all-those-words.

Jennifer Betts. "40 Common Words and Phrases Shakespeare Invented." *Your Dictionary,* June 18, 2021. https://grammar.yourdictionary.com/word -lists/list-of-words-and-phrases-shakespeare-invented.html.

"Shakespeare's Words." Shakespeare Birthplace Trust. https://www .shakespeare.org.uk/explore-shakespeare/shakespedia/shakespeares-words/.

**Chapter 9: George Washington's Terrible Teeth**

Jay Richardson. "Cherry Tree Myth." In *The Digital Encyclopedia of George Washington.* https://www.mountvernon.org/library/digitalhistory/digital -encyclopedia/article/cherry-tree-myth/.

William M. Etter. "Wooden Teeth Myth." In *The Digital Encyclopedia of George Washington.* https://www.mountvernon.org/library/digitalhistory /digital-encyclopedia/article/wooden-teeth-myth/.

William M. Etter. "False Teeth." In *The Digital Encyclopedia of George Washington.* https://www.mountvernon.org/library/digitalhistory/digital -encyclopedia/article/false-teeth/.

"The Trouble with Teeth." In *The Digital Encyclopedia of George Washington.*

https://www.mountvernon.org/george-washington/health/washingtons
-teeth/.

Jeanette Patrick. "George Washington's Health." In *The Digital Encyclopedia of George Washington*. https://www.mountvernon.org/george-washington
/health/.

Mary Thompson. "Madeira." In *The Digital Encyclopedia of George Washington*. https://www.mountvernon.org/library/digitalhistory/digital
-encyclopedia/article/madeira/.

"10 Facts About Washington & Slavery." In *The Digital Encyclopedia of George Washington*. https://www.mountvernon.org/george-washington
/slavery/ten-facts-about-washington-slavery/.

Stephanie Pappas. "What Were George Washington's Teeth Made Of? (It's Not Wood)." LiveScience, March 3, 2018. https://www.livescience.com
/61919-george-washington-teeth-not-wood.html.

Richard Norton Smith. "The Surprising George Washington." *Prologue* 26, no. 1 (1994). https://www.archives.gov/publications/prologue/1994
/spring/george-washington-1.html.

Rebecca Sutton. "Picture This! Gilbert Stuart's Famous Portrait of Our First President." National Endowment for the Arts, February 17, 2023.
https://www.arts.gov/stories/blog/2023/picture-gilbert-stuarts-famous
-portrait-our-first-president.

Stanton Peele. "George Washington: Boozehound." *Reason*, February 22, 2014. https://reason.com/2014/02/22/george-washington-boozehound/.

"The Founding Fathers on Drugs and Alcohol." Mountainside Treatment Center. https://mountainside.com/blog/alcohol/the-founding-fathers-on
-drugs-and-alcohol/.

"A Complete Guide to the US Presidents and Their Drug and Alcohol Use." Project Know, December 12, 2022. https://projectknow.com/blog
/a-complete-guide-to-the-us-presidents-and-their-drug-and-alcohol
-use/.

"George Washington Unanimously Elected First US President." History, February 1, 2022. https://www.history.com/this-day-in-history/first-u-s
-president-elected.

Erin Blakemore. "Did George Washington Really Free Mount Vernon's Enslaved Workers?" History, February 18, 2020. https://www.history.com
/news/did-george-washington-really-free-mount-vernons-slaves.

Olivia B. Waxman. "Bill Clinton Said He Didn't Inhale 25 Years Ago—but the History of US Presidents and Drugs Is Much Older." *Time*, March 29, 2017. https://finance.yahoo.com/news/bill-clinton-said-didn-t
-180844947.html.

## Chapter 10: Andrew Jackson Was a Mean, Crazy, Racist, Murderous Drunk

Jon Meacham. *American Lion*. Random House, 2008, 25–26, 37–40, 43–46, 48–49, 54–55, 61–62, 203–205.

Harry Watson. "Andrew Jackson, America's Original Anti-Establishment Candidate." *Smithsonian*, March 31, 2016. https://www.smithsonianmag.com/history/andrew-jackson-americas-original-anti-establishment-candidate-180958621/.

Lorraine Boissoneault. "The Attempted Assassination of Andrew Jackson." *Smithsonian*, March 14, 2017. https://www.smithsonianmag.com/history/attempted-assassination-andrew-jackson-180962526/.

C. Jarrett Dieterle and Kevin P. Kosar. "Why Can't Native Americans Make Whiskey?" *New York Times*, June 4, 2018. https://www.nytimes.com/2018/06/04/opinion/native-american-whiskey.html.

Jennifer Latson. "How Divine Providence—and a Heavy Stick—Saved a President's Life." *Time*, January 30, 2015. https://time.com/3676512/andrew-jackson-assassination-attempt/.

Ron Grossman. "How Andrew Jackson's Inauguration Day Went Off the Rails." *Chicago Tribune*, January 13, 2017. https://www.chicagotribune.com/opinion/commentary/ct-inaugurations-populists-president-flashback-perspec-0115-md-20170112-story.html.

Megan Garber. "The Worst Presidential Inaugurations, Ranked." *Atlantic*, January 20, 2017. https://www.theatlantic.com/entertainment/archive/2017/01/the-worst-presidential-inaugurations-ranked/513665/.

W. J. Rorabaugh. "Whiskey: An American Tradition." *Washington Post*, September 23, 1979. https://www.washingtonpost.com/archive/opinions/1979/09/23/whiskey-an-american-tradition/d7d8a767-5ee4-499c-9476-64e4a50c15c1/.

"Code Duello: The Rules of Dueling." PBS. https://www.pbs.org/wgbh/americanexperience/features/duel-code-duello-rules-dueling/.

Scott Bomboy. "When Presidential Inaugurations Go Very, Very Wrong." National Constitution Center, January 18, 2017. https://constitutioncenter.org/blog/when-presidential-inaugurations-go-very-very-wrong/.

"Indian Treaties and the Removal Act of 1830." Office of the Historian, US Department of State. https://history.state.gov/milestones/1830-1860/indian-treaties.

"3 Famous Duels Involving Andrew Jackson." *Owlcation*, July 19, 2022. https://owlcation.com/humanities/3-Famous-Duels-Involving-Andrew-Jackson.

"Remembering the Time Andrew Jackson Decided to Ignore the Supreme Court in the Name of Georgia's Right to Cherokee Land." SustainAtlanta. https://sustainatlanta.com/2015/04/02/remembering-the

-time-andrew-jackson-decided-to-ignore-the-supreme-court-in-the-name
-of-georgias-right-to-cherokee-land/.

Danny Sjursen. "American History for Truthdiggers: Andrew Jackson's
White Male World and the Start of Modern Politics." *TruthDig*, July 28,
2018. https://www.truthdig.com/articles/american-history-for
-truthdiggers-andrew-jacksons-white-male-world-and-the-start-of-modern
-politics/.

Jonathan L. Stolz. "Not All American Presidents Have Been Teetotalers,
One Was Known as 'Hero of Many Well-Fought Bottles.'" *Daily Press*,
November 26, 2021. https://www.dailypress.com/2021/11/26
/not-all-american-presidents-have-been-teetotalers-one-was-known-as
-hero-of-many-well-fought-bottles/.

Reeve Huston. "The Expansion of Democracy During the Jacksonian
Era." America in Class, 2011. https://americainclass.org/the-expansion-of
-democracy-during-the-jacksonian-era/.

Cameron Addis. "Jacksonian Democracy." *History Hub*, 2012. https://sites
.austincc.edu/caddis/jacksonian-democracy/.

Dave Roos. "How Andrew Jackson Rode a Populist Wave to Become
America's First 'Outsider' President." History, August 12, 2019. https://
www.history.com/news/andrew-jackson-populism.

"Andrew Jackson Holds 'Open House' at the White House." History,
March 3, 2020. https://www.history.com/this-day-in-history/jackson-holds
-open-house-at-the-white-house.

"Trail of Tears." History, April 20, 2023. https://www.history.com
/topics/native-american-history/trail-of-tears.

## Chapter 11: Andrew Johnson Was Blackout Drunk

Dorothy Meserve Kunhardt and Philip B. Kunhardt Jr. *Twenty Days: A
Narrative in Text and Pictures of the Assassination of Abraham Lincoln and
the Twenty Days and Nights That Followed.* Harper & Row, 1965, 66,
100–103, 108.

Megan Garber. "The Worst Presidential Inaugurations, Ranked." *Atlantic*,
January 20, 2017. https://www.theatlantic.com/entertainment/archive/2017
/01/the-worst-presidential-inaugurations-ranked/513665/.

"Andrew Johnson: 17th President." *Independent*, January 18, 2009. https://
www.independent.co.uk/news/presidents/andrew-johnson-1391124.html.

Joshua Zeitz. "When Congress Almost Ousted a Failing President."
*Politico*, May 20, 2017. https://www.politico.com/magazine/story/2017/05
/20/andrew-johnson-impeachment-donald-trump-215166.

Lillian Cunningham, host. *Presidential* podcast, episode 17, "Andrew
Johnson: Stitching Up a Torn Country." *Washington Post*, May 1, 2016.
https://www.washingtonpost.com/graphics/business/podcasts/presidential
/pdfs/andrew-johnson-transcript.pdf.

"Andrew Johnson's Inauguration." Senate.gov. https://www.senate.gov /about/officers-staff/vice-president/andrew-johnson-inauguration.htm.

Barbara Bogaev, host. *Shakespeare Unlimited* podcast, episode 114, "The Actor and the Assassin: Edwin and John Wilkes Booth." Folger Shakespeare Library, February 5, 2019. https://www.folger.edu/shakespeare-unlimited /edwin-john-wilkes-booth.

Sean Cunningham. "Lincoln's VP Andrew Johnson and His Drunk, Belligerent Inauguration Speech." *InsideHook*, January 20, 2017. https:// www.insidehook.com/article/news-opinion/andrew-johnson-drunk -inauguration-speech.

"Andrew Johnson." History, August 21, 2018. https://www.history.com /topics/us-presidents/andrew-johnson.

## Chapter 12: Samuel Taylor Coleridge's Trip Wore Off

Allison McNearney. "Did Opium Make Coleridge Forget the Rest of 'Kubla Khan'?" *Daily Beast*, April 14, 2018. https://www.thedailybeast.com /did-opium-make-coleridge-forget-the-rest-of-kubla-khan.

Sharon Ruston. "Representations of Drugs in Nineteenth-Century Literature." Victorian Web, December 9, 2022, https://victorianweb .org/science/addiction/drugs1.html.

Donald John Marotta. "Samuel Taylor Coleridge and Opium." *Electronic Theses and Dissertations*, East Tennessee State University, 2006. https://dc.etsu .edu/cgi/viewcontent.cgi?article=3545&context=etd.

Earl Leslie Griggs and Seymour Teulon Porter. "Samuel Taylor Coleridge and Opium." *Huntington Library Quarterly* 17, no. 4 (1954): 357–78. https:// www.jstor.org/stable/3816502.

Brian Hoey. "Hamlet and Opium: The Subtle Influence of Samuel Taylor Coleridge." *Blogis Librorum: A Blog About Books*, October 21, 2017. https:// blog.bookstellyouwhy.com/hamlet-and-opium-the-subtle-influence-of -samuel-taylor-coleridge.

Samuel Taylor Coleridge. "Lecture on Hamlet" (excerpt). Broadview Press. https://sites.broadviewpress.com/lessons/DramaAnthology /ColeridgeOnHamlet/ColeridgeOnHamlet_print.html.

"1834—Death of Coleridge." Keats-Shelley House. https://ksh.roma.it /romanticism/1834#:~:text=Coleridge%20died%20from%20heart %20failure,his%20life%20and%20poetic%20legacy.

Andrew Handley. "10 Literary Figures with Crippling Drug Addictions." *Listverse*, August 23, 2013. https://listverse.com/2013/08/23/10-literary -figures-with-crippling-drug-addictions/.

## Chapter 13: Queen Victoria Was the Biggest Drug Dealer of All Time

James Bradley. *The Imperial Cruise: A Secret History of Empire and War.* Back Bay Books, 2009, 271–76.

Stephen R. Platt. *Imperial Twilight: The Opium War and the End of China's Last Golden Age*. Vintage Books, 2019, 440–41.

Stephen R. Platt. "What Caused the First Opium War?" *History Extra*, September 1, 2019. https://www.historyextra.com/period/victorian/china -britain-opium-war/.

Tracy Borman. "Did This Beloved Queen of Britain Use Drugs?" *Smithsonian*, June 9, 2019. https://www.smithsonianmag.com/videos /category/history/did-this-beloved-queen-of-britain-use-drugs/.

Ellen Barry. "Chloroform in Childbirth? Yes, Please, the Queen Said." *New York Times*, May 6, 2019. https://www.nytimes.com/2019/05/06 /world/europe/uk-royal-births-labor.html.

Matt Schiavenza. "How Humiliation Drove Modern Chinese History." *Atlantic*, October 25, 2013. https://www.theatlantic.com/china/archive /2013/10/how-humiliation-drove-modern-chinese-history/280878/.

John Patrick Hayes. "The Opium Wars in China: Overview." Asia Pacific Curriculum. https://asiapacificcurriculum.ca/learning-module/opium-wars -china.

Steve Alexander, Ken Mackie, and Ruth Ross. "Themed Issue: Cannabinoids." *British Journal of Pharmacology* 160, no. 3 (2010): 421–22. https://www.ncbi.nlm.nih.gov/pmc/articles/PMC2931545/#.

"Queen Victoria." Biography, March 15, 2021. https://www.biography .com/royalty/queen-victoria.

Kenneth Pletcher. "Opium Wars." *Britannica*, April 17, 2015. https:// www.britannica.com/topic/Opium-Wars.

Thomas Grisaffi. "A Brief History of Coca: From Traditional Use to the Cocaine Economy." University of Reading working paper, 2021. https:// research.reading.ac.uk/coca-cocaine-bolivia-peru/wp-content/uploads/sites /127/2021/07/A-history-of-coca-Grisaffi-Website-V2.pdf.

"A Short History of Cocaine." Smart Drug Policy. https://smartdrugpolicy .org/a-short-history-of-cocaine/.

Tony McMahon. "Was Queen Victoria a Drug Addict?" *Beardy History*, April 11, 2017. https://beardyhistory.com/2017/04/11/queen-victoria-drug -addict/.

## Chapter 14: The Pope Who Loved Cocaine Wine

James Hamblin. "Why We Took Cocaine Out of Soda." *Atlantic*, January 31, 2013. https://www.theatlantic.com/health/archive/2013/01/why-we -took-cocaine-out-of-soda/272694/.

Paul Vallely. "Drug That Spans the Ages: The History of Cocaine." *Independent*, March 2, 2006. https://www.independent.co.uk/news/uk /this-britain/drug-that-spans-the-ages-the-history-of-cocaine-6107930 .html.

"Pope Leo XIII Passes Away." *New York Times*, July 20, 1903. https://

timesmachine.nytimes.com/timesmachine/1903/07/21/102014816.pdf?pdf
_redirect=true&ip=0.

Beccy Corkill. "The Cocaine Wine That Was Endorsed by the
Pope and Inspired Coca-Cola." *IFLScience*, March 22, 2023. https://www
.iflscience.com/the-cocaine-wine-that-was-endorsed-by-the-pope-and
-inspired-coca-cola-68097.

Wyatt Redd. "Vin Mariani—the Cocaine-Laced Wine Loved by Popes,
Thomas Edison, and Ulysses S. Grant." *All That's Interesting*, January 31,
2018. https://allthatsinteresting.com/vin-mariani.

Mike Vago. "This Cocaine-Infused Wine Was Endorsed by a 19th Century
Pope." *AV Club*, January 10, 2021. https://www.avclub.com/this-cocaine
-infused-wine-was-endorsed-by-a-19th-centur-1846013083.

"The Illustrious (& Outrageous) History of Vin Mariani." Proof Drinks,
March 14, 2017. http://proofdrinks.com/illustrious-outrageous-history-vin
-mariani/.

Giorgia Cannarella. "You Can Still Buy Alcohol Made with Coca Leaves."
*Vice*, May 18, 2021. https://www.vice.com/en/article/88n9db/coca-buton
-alcohol-coca-leaves.

Vicki Wielenga and Dawna Gilchrist. "From Gold-Medal Glory to
Prohibition: The Early Evolution of Cocaine in the United Kingdom and
United States." *Journal of the Royal Society of Medicine Short Reports* 4, no. 5
(2013). https://www.ncbi.nlm.nih.gov/pmc/articles/PMC3681233/.

David Masci. "A Look at Popes and Their Encyclicals." Pew Research
Center, June 9, 2015. https://www.pewresearch.org/short-reads/2015/06
/09/a-look-at-popes-and-their-encyclicals/.

John Hooper. "Pope's Encyclical on the Environment: Key Questions
Answered." *Guardian*, June 18, 2015. https://www.theguardian.com/world
/2015/jun/18/popes-encyclical-on-the-environment-key-questions
-answered.

Roger-Francois-Marie Aubert. "Leo XIII." *Britannica*, July 16, 2023.
https://www.britannica.com/biography/Leo-XIII.

Drew Kann. "Eight of the Worst Popes in Church History." CNN, April
15, 2018. https://www.cnn.com/2018/04/10/europe/catholic-church-most
-controversial-popes/index.html.

Ishaan Tharoor. "Seven Wicked Popes and the Terrible, Terrible Things
They Did." *Independent*, September 24, 2015. https://www.independent.co
.uk/news/people/7-wicked-popes-and-the-terrible-terrible-things-they
-did-a6666612.html.

Caroline Praderio. "The 11 Most Scandalous Popes in History." *Business
Insider*, January 13, 2017, https://www.insider.com/crazy-popes-in-history
-2017-1#alexander-vi-bought-his-way-into-the-papacy-and-had-a-rollicking
-sex-life-7.

Minhan. "St. Peter's Piazza." University of Washington Honors Program in Rome, September 22, 2005. https://depts.washington.edu/hrome/Authors /minhan/StPetersPiazza/243/pub_zbpage_view.html.

Melissa Sartore. "Details About Pope Alexander VI's Horrifyingly Over the Top Death." *Ranker*, September 23, 2021. https://www.ranker.com/list /pope-alexander-vi-last-days/melissa-sartore.

## Chapter 15: Friedrich Nietzsche Thought He Was Jesus

Water A. Kaufman. *Nietzsche: Philosopher, Psychologist, Antichrist*. Fourth edition. Princeton University Press, 2013, 46.

Christopher Middleton. *Selected Letters of Friedrich Nietzsche*. University of Chicago, 1969, 344–48.

R. Lanier Anderson. "Friedrich Nietzsche." In *Stanford Encyclopedia of Philosophy*, summer 2022 edition. https://plato.stanford.edu/entries/nietzsche/.

Sue Prideaux. "Far Right, Misogynist, Humorless? Why Nietzsche Is Misunderstood." *Guardian*, October 6, 2018. https://www.theguardian .com/books/2018/oct/06/exploding-nietzsche-myths-need-dynamiting.

Morten Hoi Jensen. "The Sufferings of Nietzsche." *Los Angeles Review of Books*, December 5, 2018. https://lareviewofbooks.org/article/the-sufferings -of-nietzsche/.

Parul Sehgal. "A Life of Nietzsche Turns the Spotlight on an Idol Long Misunderstood." *New York Times*, November 1, 2018. https://www.nytimes .com/2018/11/01/books/review-i-am-dynamite-life-of-nietzsche-sue -prideaux.html.

D. Hemelsoet, K. Hemelsoet, and D. Devreese. "The Neurological Illness of Friedrich Nietzsche." *Acta Neurologica Belgica* 108, no. 1 (2008): 9–16. https://www.actaneurologica.be/pdfs/2008-1/02-Hemelsoet%20et%20al .pdf.

Peter Sjöstedt-H. "Antichrist Psychonaut: Nietzsche and Psychedelics." *Psychedelic Press Journal* 12 (2015). https://philpapers.org/archive/SJSAPN.pdf.

"What Happened to Nietzsche? Madness and the Divine Mania." *Academy of Ideas*, June 17, 2021. https://academyofideas.com/2021/06/what-happened -to-nietzsche-madness-divine-mania/.

Scotty Hendricks. "5 Philosophers Who Took Drugs and What They Got Out of It." *Big Think*, July 23, 2018. https://bigthink.com/personal-growth /5-philosophers-who-took-drugs/.

Alma Gacanin. "Nietzsche's Letters of Insanity." Scribd, July 21, 2013. https://www.scribd.com/document/155192116/Nietzsche-s-Letters-of -Insanity#.

Martin Chalakoski. "The 'Letters of Insanity' and 'The Turin Horse': The Baffling Breakdown of Friedrich Nietzsche." *Vintage News*, September 1, 2017. https://www.thevintagenews.com/2017/09/01/the-letters-of-insanity -and-the-turin-horse-the-baffling-breakdown-of-friedrich-nietzsche/?Exc _D_LessThanPoint002_p1=1.

Brad Smithfield. "Friedrich Nietzsche Went Mad After Allegedly Seeing a Horse Being Whipped in the Italian City of Turin." *Vintage News*, February 5, 2017. https://www.thevintagenews.com/2017/02/05/friedrich-nietzsche -went-mad-after-allegedly-seeing-a-horse-being-whipped-in-the-italian -city-of-turin/.

Bernd Magnus. "Friedrich Nietzsche." *Britannica*, July 26, 1999. https:// www.britannica.com/biography/Friedrich-Nietzsche.

Paul B. Goodwin Jr. "Förster-Nietzsche, Elisabeth (1846–1935)." In *Women in World History: A Biographical Encyclopedia*, Encyclopedia.com, October 15, 2024. https://www.encyclopedia.com/women/encyclopedias -almanacs-transcripts-and-maps/forster-nietzsche-elisabeth-1846-1935.

## Chapter 16: Vincent van Gogh Ate Yellow Paint

Martin Bailey. *Starry Night: Van Gogh at the Asylum*. Francis Lincoln Publishing, 2022, 7, 9, 22–25, 77–85, 123–29, 170–71.

"Did Van Gogh Eat Yellow Paint Thinking That It Would Raise His Spirits?" Van Gogh Museum. https://www.vangoghmuseum.nl/en/art-and -stories/vincent-van-gogh-faq/did-van-gogh-eat-yellow-paint.

United Press International. "Why Van Gogh Ate Paint." *Washington Post*, November 24, 1988. https://www.washingtonpost.com/archive/lifestyle /1988/11/25/why-van-gogh-ate-paint/b8759a9e-6ab0-4fc9-8f86-9f7dcc 2663e5/.

Barbara Isenberg. "Did Absinthe Make Van Gogh's Mind Wander?" *Los Angeles Times*, November 30, 1988. https://www.latimes.com/archives/la -xpm-1988-11-30-ca-631-story.html.

Simon Cotton. "Vincent van Gogh, Chemistry and Absinthe." *Education in Chemistry*, April 30, 2011. https://edu.rsc.org/feature/vincent-van-gogh -chemistry-and-absinthe/2020272.article.

Chris Johnston. "Woman Who Received Van Gogh's Ear Named 130 Years After Artist Cut It Off." *Guardian*, July 20, 2016. https://www .theguardian.com/artanddesign/2016/jul/20/woman-who-received-van -goghs-ear-named-130-years-after-artist-cut-it-off.

Virgie Hoban. "What Actually Happened to Vincent van Gogh's Ear? Here Are Three Things You Should Know." Berkeley Library, November 26, 2019. https://www.lib.berkeley.edu/about/news/van-Gogh-ear.

Jesse Hicks. "The Devil in a Little Green Bottle: A History of Absinthe." *Distillations Magazine*, Science History Institute, October 5, 2010. https:// sciencehistory.org/stories/magazine/the-devil-in-a-little-green-bottle-a -history-of-absinthe/.

Kate Robertson. "Cannabis 101: What's the Deal with Terpenes?" Healthline, May 20, 2021. https://www.healthline.com/health/cannabis -terpenes.

Kathryn Harkup. "It Was All Yellow: Did Digitalis Affect the Way Van

Gogh Saw the World?" *Guardian*, August 10, 2017. https://www.theguardian.com/science/blog/2017/aug/10/it-was-all-yellow-did-digitalis-affect-the-way-van-gogh-saw-the-world.

### Chapter 17: Sigmund Freud Was Wrong About Cocaine

Howard Markel. *An Anatomy of Addiction*. Vintage Books, 2011, 6–7, 31, 46–47, 74–89, 170–74, 185–86.

Dominic Streatfeild. *Cocaine: An Unauthorized Biography*. Picador, 2001, 65–72.

Howard Markel and Ira Flatow, host. "A Tale of Two Addicts: Freud, Halsted and Cocaine." *Talk of the Nation*, NPR, November 25, 2011. https://www.npr.org/2011/11/25/142782875/a-tale-of-two-addicts-freud-halsted-and-cocaine.

Howard Markel and Betty Ann Bowser, host. "Cocaine: How 'Miracle Drug' Nearly Destroyed Sigmund Freud, William Halsted." *PBS News Hour*, October 17, 2011. https://www.pbs.org/newshour/show/cocaine-how-miracle-drug-nearly-destroyed-sigmund-freud-william-halsted.

Sherwin Nuland. "Sigmund Freud's Cocaine Years." *New York Times*, July 21, 2011. https://www.nytimes.com/2011/07/24/books/review/an-anatomy-of-addiction-by-howard-markel-book-review.html.

Jen Burd. "Sigmund Freud and Cocaine: A Love Story?" *Skeptoid*, May 16, 2013. https://skeptoid.com/blog/2013/05/16/sigmund-freud-and-cocaine-a-love-story/.

Scott Oliver. "How Cocaine Influenced the Work of Sigmund Freud." *Vice*, June 23, 2017. https://www.vice.com/en/article/how-cocaine-influenced-the-work-of-sigmund-freud/.

Nicholas Lord. "That Time Sigmund Freud Nearly Killed a Patient—and Then Got Hooked on Cocaine." *Narratively*, June 4, 2017. https://narratively.com/when-sigmund-freud-got-hooked-on-cocaine/.

"How Freud Shaped the 20th-Century Mind." *New York Times*, November 26, 1989. https://www.nytimes.com/1989/11/26/weekinreview/ideas-and-trends-how-freud-shaped-the-20th-century-mind.html.

Saul Mcleod. "Sigmund Freud: Biography, Theories and Contribution to Psychology." *Simply Psychology*, July 16, 2023. https://www.simplypsychology.org/sigmund-freud.html.

"Uber Coca, by Sigmund Freud." *Scicurious*, May 28, 2008. https://scicurious.wordpress.com/2008/05/28/uber-coca-by-sigmund-freud/.

### Chapter 18: Adolf Hitler Was Tweaked out of His Mind

Norman Ohler. *Blitzed: Drugs in the Third Reich*. Translated by Shaun Whiteside. Houghton Mifflin Harcourt, 2017, 12–13, 20–26, 112–14, 135–44, 153–62, 173–86, 215–24.

Norman Ohler and Terry Gross, host. "Author Says Hitler Was 'Blitzed' on Cocaine and Opiates During the War." *Fresh Air*, NPR, March 7, 2017.

https://www.npr.org/sections/health-shots/2017/03/07/518986612/author
-says-hitler-was-blitzed-on-cocaine-and-opiates-during-the-war.

Norman Ohler and Rachel Cooke (interview). "High Hitler: How Nazi Drug Abuse Steered the Course of History." *Guardian*, September 25, 2016. https://www.theguardian.com/books/2016/sep/25/blitzed-norman-ohler -adolf-hitler-nazi-drug-abuse-interview.

Norman Ohler and Elizabeth Nicholas (interview). "Hitler's Suicide and New Research on Nazi Drug Use." *Time*, April 28, 2017. https://time.com /4744584/hitler-drugs-blitzed/.

Peter Andreas. "How Methamphetamine Became a Key Part of Nazi Military Strategy." *Time*, January 7, 2020. https://time.com/5752114/nazi -military-drugs/.

John Cline. "Hitler, Meth, and the War: Sleepless on the Western Front." *Psychology Today*, September 29, 2019. https://www.psychologytoday .com/us/blog/sleepless-in-america/201909/hitler-meth-and-the-war -sleepless-the-western-front.

Ishaan Tharoor. "High Hitler: Nazi Leader Was a Meth Addict, Says New Documentary." *Washington Post*, October 14, 2014. https://www .washingtonpost.com/news/worldviews/wp/2014/10/14/high-hitler-nazi -leader-was-a-crystal-meth-addict-says-new-documentary/.

John Kuroski. "How Drugs Like Pervitin and Cocaine Fueled the Nazis' Rise and Fall." *All That's Interesting*, August 20, 2022. https:// allthatsinteresting.com/pervitin.

Lukasz Kamienski. "Combat High—How Armies Throughout History Used Drugs to Make Soldiers Fight." *Military History Now*, May 8, 2018. https://militaryhistorynow.com/2018/05/08/combat-high-a-sobering -history-of-drug-use-in-wartime/.

Eric Mankin. "War and Drugs: Together Since Forever." *Knowable Magazine*, August 6, 2019. https://www.knowablemagazine.org/article /society/2019/war-and-drugs-together-forever.

Charles Bracelen Flood. "Lance Corporal Adolf Hitler on the Western Front, 1914–1918." *Kentucky Review* 5, no. 3 (1985). https://uknowledge.uky .edu/cgi/viewcontent.cgi?article=1200&context=kentucky-review.

Peter Curry. "What Did Adolf Hitler Do in World War One?" History Hit, October 16, 2018. https://www.historyhit.com/what-did-adolf-hitler -do-in-world-war-one/.

"Adolf Hitler Wounded in British Gas Attack." History, October 13, 2020. https://www.history.com/this-day-in-history/adolf-hitler-wounded-in -british-gas-attack.

Philip Gavin. "The Rise of Adolf Hitler." History Place. https://www .historyplace.com/worldwar2/riseofhitler/warone.htm.

"Hitler Rocking in His Chair at the Olympics." Posted July 18, 2021, by Tiptup. YouTube. https://www.youtube.com/watch?v=KacXNs77R9Y.

**Chapter 19: Bill W. Took LSD to See God**

Don Lattin. *Distilled Spirits*. University of California Press, 2012, 55–57, 66–68, 190–200, 204–208, 239–42.

*"Pass It On": The Story of Bill Wilson and How the AA Message Reached the World*. Alcoholics Anonymous World Service, 1984, 42–56, 67–99, 120–21, 358–59, 368–77, 408.

Amelia Hill. "LSD Could Help Alcoholics Stop Drinking, AA Founder Believed." *Guardian*, August 23, 2012. https://www.theguardian.com /science/2012/aug/23/lsd-help-alcoholics-theory.

Howard Markel. "An Alcoholic's Savior: God, Belladonna or Both?" *New York Times*, April 19, 2010. https://www.nytimes.com/2010/04/20/health /20drunk.html.

Gabrielle Glaser. "The Irrationality of Alcoholics Anonymous." *Atlantic*, April 2015. https://www.theatlantic.com/magazine/archive/2015/04/the -irrationality-of-alcoholics-anonymous/386255/.

Aaron Frood. "LSD Helps to Treat Alcoholism." *Nature*, March 9, 2012. https://www.nature.com/news/lsd-helps-to-treat-alcoholism-1.10200.

Rebecca Tuhus-Dubrow. "Equipment for Living: Losing and Recovering Oneself in Drugs and Sobriety." *Nation*, June 5, 2018. https://www.thenation .com/article/archive/equipment-for-living/.

Ethan Trex. "5 Things You Didn't Know About Bill W." *Mental Floss*, July 9, 2010. https://www.mentalfloss.com/article/25150/5-things-you -didnt-know-about-bill-w.

John Springer. "Bill W's 1934 Towns Hospital Belladonna Treatment." *Medium*, April 15, 2020. https://medium.com/@johnspringer.architect/bill -ws-1934-towns-hospital-belladonna-treatment-5aafdc4252d.

Bob K. "Bill W., LSD, and AA Spirituality." AA Agnostica, November 18, 2018. https://aaagnostica.org/2018/11/18/bill-w-lsd-and-aa-spirituality/.

Roger R. "When 12 Step Programs Don't Work: AA Founder Bill W. on How LSD Can Help." *Psychedelic Times*, February 10, 2016. https:// psychedelictimes.com/when-12-step-programs-dont-work-aa-founder-bill -w-on-how-lsd-can-help/.

"Bill's Story." Stepping Stones: Historic Home of Bill & Lois Wilson. https://www.steppingstones.org/about/the-wilsons/bills-story/.

**Chapter 20: Jean-Paul Sartre's Really Long Bad Trip**

Annie Cohen-Solal. *Jean-Paul Sartre: A Life*. The New Press, 1985.

Mike Jay. "Sartre's Bad Trip." *Paris Review*, August 21, 2019. https://www .theparisreview.org/blog/2019/08/21/sartres-bad-trip/.

"When Sartre Talked to Crabs (It Was Mescaline)." *New York Times*, November 14, 2009. Excerpt from *Talking with Sartre: Conversations and Debates*, edited by John Gerassi. https://www.nytimes.com/2009/11/15 /weekinreview/15grist.html.

Henry Giniger. "Sartre Is Arrested at Last, but Briefly, for Role on a Maoist Weekly." *New York Times*, June 27, 1970. https://www.nytimes.com /1970/06/27/archives/sartre-is-arrested-at-last-but-briefly-for-role-on-a -maoist-weekly.html.

Stuart Jeffries. "Jean-Paul Sartre: More Relevant Now Than Ever." *Guardian*, October 22, 2014. https://www.theguardian.com/books/2014 /oct/22/jean-paul-sartre-refuses-nobel-prize-literature-50-years-books.

Sarah Bakewell. "Think Big, Be Free, Have Sex . . . 10 Reasons to Be an Existentialist." *Guardian*, March 4, 2016. https://www.theguardian.com /books/2016/mar/04/ten-reasons-to-be-an-existentialist.

William Rowlandson. "Fidel Meets Sartre: What Happened When the Cuban Leader Met Jean-Paul Sartre." *Salon*, November 28, 2016. https:// www.salon.com/2016/11/28/fidel-meets-sartre-what-happened-when-the -cuban-leader-met-jean-paul-sartre_partner/.

Jack Reynolds and Pierre-Jean Renaudie. "Jean-Paul Sartre." In *Stanford Encyclopedia of Philosophy*, March 26, 2022. https://plato.stanford.edu/entries /sartre/.

Benedict O'Donohoe. "Why Sartre Matters." *Philosophy Now* 53 (November/December 2005). https://philosophynow.org/issues/53/Why _Sartre_Matters.

Tarun Mittal. "To Be Is to Be: Jean-Paul Sartre on Existentialism and Freedom." *Your Story*, June 21, 2017. https://yourstory.com/2017/06/jean -paul-sartre-philosophy-existentialism-freedom.

John Gerassi and Tony Monchinsky. "The Second Death of Jean-Paul Sartre." In *Unrepentant Radical Educator: The Writings of John Gerassi*, edited by Tony Monchinsky. Brill, 2009. https://brill.com/display/book/edcoll /9789087908010/BP000012.xml.

Ian Birchall. "The Outrageous Optimism of Jean-Paul Sartre." *Wire*, April 20, 2020. https://thewire.in/books/the-outrageous-optimism-of-jean -paul-sartre.

"Fidel Castro Takes Blame for Persecution of Cuban Gays." BBC News, August 31, 2010. https://www.bbc.com/news/world-latin-america-11147157.

Jonathan Crow. "Photos of Jean-Paul Sartre and Simone de Beauvoir Hanging with Che Guevara in Cuba (1960)." *Open Culture*. https://www .openculture.com/2014/09/photos-of-jean-paul-sartre-simone-de-beauvoir -hanging-with-che-guevara-in-cuba-1960.html#google_vignette.

Josh Jones. "When Jean-Paul Sartre Had a Bad Mescaline Trip and Then Hallucinated That He Was Being Followed by Crabs." *Open Culture*, July 4, 2018. https://www.openculture.com/2018/07/jean-paul-sartre-bad -mescaline-trip-hallucinated-years-followed-crabs.html.

John Lanchester. "High Style: Writing Under the Influence." *New Yorker*, December 29, 2002. https://www.newyorker.com/magazine/2003/01/06 /high-style-3.

Domagoj Valjak. "Jean-Paul Sartre's Bad Mescaline Trip Led to the Philosopher Being Followed by Imaginary Crabs for Years." *Vintage News*, October 6, 2017. https://www.thevintagenews.com/2017/10/06/jean-paul -sartres-bad-mescaline-trip-led-to-the-philosopher-being-followed-by -imaginary-crabs-for-years/.

Thomas J. Riedlinger. "Sartre's Rite of Passage." *Journal of Transpersonal Psychology* 14, no. 2 (1982): 105–107. http://www.philosopher.eu/wp-content /uploads/2016/11/SartresRightofPassage-mescaline.pdf.

**Chapter 21: Richard Nixon Wanted to Nuke Everyone**

John A. Farrell. *Richard Nixon: The Life.* Doubleday, 2017, 4, 6, 28–41, 48–49, 58–59, 78, 347–70, 411–12, 445, 522–24, 680.

John A. Farrell. "The Year Nixon Fell Apart." *Politico*, March 26, 2017. https://www.politico.com/magazine/story/2017/03/john-farrell-nixon-book -excerpt-214954/.

Alden Whitman. "Nixon, Long a Master of Adversity, Was Overwhelmed by the Last of Many Crises." *New York Times*, August 9, 1974. https://www .nytimes.com/1974/08/09/archives/nixon-long-a-master-of-adversity-was -overwhelmed-by-the-last-of-man.html.

Emily Dufton. "The War on Drugs: How President Nixon Tied Addiction to Crime." *Atlantic*, March 26, 2012. https://www.theatlantic.com /health/archive/2012/03/the-war-on-drugs-how-president-nixon-tied -addiction-to-crime/254319/.

Merrill Fabry. "Now You Know: What Happens If the President Gets Drunk?" *Time*, June 2, 2016. https://time.com/4342019/drunk-president -history/.

Benjamin T. Smith. "New Documents Reveal the Bloody Origins of America's Long War on Drugs." *Time*, August 24, 2021. https://time.com /6090016/us-war-on-drugs-origins/.

Anthony Summers and Robbyn Swan. "Drunk in Charge (Part 2)." *Guardian*, September 2, 2000. https://www.theguardian.com/weekend /story/0,3605,362958,00.html.

Daniel Strauss. "The Politics of Racial Division: Trump Borrows Nixon's 'Southern Strategy.'" *Guardian*, September 5, 2020. https://www .theguardian.com/us-news/2020/sep/05/donald-trump-richard-nixon -southern-strategy.

Julia Campbell. "New Nixon Biography Gives Salacious Details." ABC News, August 29, 2000. https://abcnews.go.com/Politics/story?id=123021 &page=1.

Ben Wright. "Teetotal Trump and the Drinking Presidents." BBC News, January 19, 2017. https://www.bbc.com/news/world-us-canada-38651623.

Stephan Roget. "Nixon's Rampant Alcoholism Revealed His Disturbingly

Unstable Personality." *Ranker,* June 13, 2017. https://www.ranker.com/list
/drunk-richard-nixon-stories/stephanroget.

Jessica Lee. "Did Richard Nixon Order Nuclear Strike on North Korea
While Drunk?" Snopes, July 23, 2021. https://www.snopes.com/fact-check
/north-korea-richard-nixon-nuclear/.

Zachary Jonathan Jacobson. "The 'Madman Theory' Was Quintessential
Nixon." History News Network, March 26, 2023. https://
historynewsnetwork.org/article/185321.

"Public Enemy Number One: A Pragmatic Approach to America's Drug
Problem." Richard Nixon Foundation, June 29, 2016. https://www
.nixonfoundation.org/2016/06/26404/.

"Richard Nixon Timeline." Richard Nixon Foundation. https://www
.nixonfoundation.org/resources/richard-nixon-timeline/.

## Chapter 22: John F. Kennedy Was on All Sorts of Drugs

Robert Dallek. *An Unfinished Life: John F. Kennedy, 1917–1963.* Little
Brown, 2003.

Cari Beauchamp. "Two Sons, One Destiny." *Vanity Fair,* January 4, 2012.
https://www.vanityfair.com/news/2004/12/kennedy-200412.

Lawrence K. Altman and Todd S. Purdum. "In JFK File, Hidden Illness,
Pain and Pills." *New York Times,* November 17, 2002. https://www.nytimes
.com/2002/11/17/us/in-jfk-file-hidden-illness-pain-and-pills.html.

Boyce Rensberger. "Amphetamines Used by a Physician to Lift Moods of
Famous Patients." *New York Times,* December 4, 1972. https://www
.nytimes.com/1972/12/04/archives/amphetamines-used-by-a-physician-to
-lift-moods-of-famous-patients.html.

Peter Keating. "The Strange Saga of JFK and the Original 'Dr. Feelgood.'"
*Intelligencer,* November 22, 2013. https://nymag.com/intelligencer/2013/11
/strange-saga-of-jfk-and-dr-feelgood.html.

Oliver Burkeman. "Kennedy Lived on Cocktail of Drugs." *Guardian,*
November 18, 2002. https://www.theguardian.com/world/2002/nov/18
/artsandhumanities.research.

Wilfred Chan. "Cocaine in the White House: A Brief History." *Guardian,*
July 6, 2023. https://www.theguardian.com/us-news/2023/jul/06/cocaine
-in-the-white-house-a-brief-history.

Matt Noffs and Kieren Palmer. "JFK's Secret Meth Addiction." News
.com.au, June 13, 2018. https://www.news.com.au/lifestyle/health/health
-problems/jfks-secret-meth-addiction/news-story/7c00f3f851000e10d2
ea8745fbd46d42.

Thomas J. Cutler. "Courage and Tenacity: JFK, USN." *Naval History
Magazine,* June 2022. https://www.usni.org/magazines/naval-history
-magazine/2022/june/courage-and-tenacity-jfk-usn.

Josh Lee. "14 Facts About JFK You Need to Know." *GQ*, October 26, 2017. https://www.gq-magazine.co.uk/article/jfk-assassination.

Thomas Fleming. "John F. Kennedy's PT-109 Disaster." *Historynet.* https://www.historynet.com/john-f-kennedy/.

Dave Roos. "How Joseph Kennedy Made His Fortune (Hint: It Wasn't Bootlegging)." History, April 26, 2023. https://www.history.com/news /joseph-kennedy-wealth-alcohol-prohibition.

"Joseph P. Kennedy." John F. Kennedy Presidential Library and Museum. https://www.jfklibrary.org/learn/about-jfk/the-kennedy-family/joseph-p -kennedy.

## Chapter 23: Audie Murphy Was the Real-Life Captain America

David A. Smith. *The Price of Valor: The Life of Audie Murphy, America's Most Decorated Hero of World War II.* Regnery History, 2015.

"Audie Murphy, War Hero, Killed in Plane Crash." *New York Times*, June 1, 1971. https://www.nytimes.com/1971/06/01/archives/audie-murphy -war-hero-killed-in-plane-crash-audie-murphy-killed-in.html.

Jay Root. "Audie Murphy, a Texas Hero Still Missing One Medal." *New York Times*, June 20, 2013. https://www.nytimes.com/2013/06/21/us/audie -murphy-a-texas-hero-still-missing-one-medal.html.

Mandy Baker. "Audie Murphy: American War Hero, Actor, Advocate." *We Are the Mighty*, July 8, 2020. https://www.wearethemighty.com/mighty -trending/audie-murphy-hero-actor-advocate/.

Eric Milzarski. "5 Lesser-Known Facts About the Most Decorated Soldier in American History." *We Are the Mighty*, December 28, 2022. https://www.wearethemighty.com/history/audie-murphy-most-decorated -soldier.

Evan Andrews. "WWII Hero Audie Murphy: 'How Come I'm Not Dead?'" History, August 29, 2018. https://www.history.com/news/audie -murphys-world-war-ii-heroics-70-years-ago.

"Audie Murphy." Biography, April 14, 2021. https://www.biography.com /military-figure/audie-murphy.

"Audie Murphy." Arlington National Cemetery. https://www .arlingtoncemetery.mil/Explore/Notable-Graves/Medal-of-Honor -Recipients/World-War-II-MoH-recipients/Audie-Murphy.

"On Display at the Audie Murphy & Medal of Honor Museum." Audie Murphy and Medal of Honor Museum. https://audiemurphymuseum .com/items/#france.

"Ethchlorvynol." Bionity.com. https://www.bionity.com/en /encyclopedia/Ethchlorvynol.html.

David Morrell. *Rambo and Me*. MEI Books, 2012. https://davidmorrell .net/books/rambo-and-me/.

## Chapter 24: Howard Hughes, the Drug-Addled Billionaire

Peter Harry Brown and Pat H. Broeske. *Howard Hughes: The Untold Story.* Da Capo Press, 1996.

"Hughes's Death Laid to Massive Drug Use." *New York Times,* June 26, 1977. https://www.nytimes.com/1977/06/26/archives/hughess-death-laid -to-massive-drug-use-illegally-obtained-medicines.html.

Nicholas Barber. "Was This Billionaire Recluse Truly Mad?" BBC, December 6, 2016. https://www.bbc.com/culture/article/20161205-was -howard-hughes-really-insane.

M. Dittmann. "Hughes' Germ Phobia Revealed in Psychological Autopsy." *Monitor on Psychology* 36, no. 7 (2005): 102. https://www.apa.org/monitor /julaug05/hughes.

Jonathan Kirsch. "The Strange Saga of a Bizarre Billionaire: Howard Hughes: The Untold Story, by Peter Harry Brown and Pat H. Broeske." *Los Angeles Times,* June 5, 1996. https://www.latimes.com/archives/la-xpm -1996-06-05-ls-11777-story.html.

"Howard Hughes (1905–1976)." *PBS American Experience.* https://www .pbs.org/wgbh/americanexperience/features/lasvegas-hughes/.

Kelly McClure and William Fischer. "The Tragic Real-Life Story of Howard Hughes." *Grunge,* January 24, 2023. https://www.grunge.com /186106/the-tragic-real-life-story-of-howard-hughes/.

James Pasley. "Inside the Life of Eccentric Billionaire Howard Hughes, a Playboy Aviator Who Died a Germaphobic Recluse." *Insider,* March 2, 2023. https://www.insider.com/eccentric-billionaire-howard-hughes-playboy -aviator-germaphobic-recluse-2023-2.

Penelope Dening. "Dishing the Dirt on Howard Hughes." *Irish Times,* March 30, 1996. https://www.irishtimes.com/news/dishing-the-dirt-on -howard-hughes-1.37281.

Rory Carroll. "Hollywood and the Downwinders Still Grapple with Nuclear Fallout." *Guardian,* June 6, 2015. https://www.theguardian .com/film/2015/jun/06/downwinders-nuclear-fallout-hollywood-john -wayne.

"Conqueror Film Site Location, Utah." Center for Land Use Interpretation. https://clui.org/ludb/site/conqueror-film-location-site.

Jimmy Chang. "Howard Hughes' Lost Film: Uncovering 'Swell Hogan.'" UNLV University Libraries, August 2, 2021. https://www.library.unlv.edu /whats-new-special-collections/2021/2021-08/howard-hughes-lost-film -uncovering-swell-hogan-jimmy.

"Wild Welcome for Howard Hughes After World Record Flight— Archive, 1938." *Guardian,* July 15, 2020. https://www.theguardian.com /world/2020/jul/15/wild-welcome-for-howard-hughes-after-world-record -flight-1938.

"Chronic Pain: Medication Decisions." Mayo Clinic. https://www
.mayoclinic.org/chronic-pain-medication-decisions/art-20360371.

**Chapter 25: Judy Garland Was Drugged by Grown-ups**

Gerald Clarke. *Get Happy: The Life of Judy Garland*. Random House, 2000.

Dinitia Smith. "Finding New Cracks in an Exposed Life." *New York
Times*, March 30, 2000. https://www.nytimes.com/2000/03/30/books
/finding-new-cracks-in-an-exposed-life.html.

Mathew Brownstein. "The Rainbow That Judy Garland Never Got Over."
*New York Times*, June 22, 2016. https://www.nytimes.com/interactive
/projects/cp/obituaries/archives/judy-garland.

"Judy Garland, 47, Found Dead." *New York Times*, June 23, 1969. https://
archive.nytimes.com/www.nytimes.com/books/00/04/09/specials/garland
-obit.html.

Howard Markel. "The Day Judy Garland's Star Burned Out." *PBS News
Hour*, June 21, 2019. https://www.pbs.org/newshour/health/the-day-judy
-garlands-star-burned-out.

"The Star Who Fell to Earth." *Guardian*, June 18, 1999. https://www
.theguardian.com/books/1999/jun/19/books.guardianreview9.

Danny Leigh. "Drugs, Exploitation, 72-Hour Shifts: Can Hollywood
Take Care of Its Child Stars?" *Guardian*, August 30, 2019. https://www
.theguardian.com/film/2019/aug/30/drugs-exploitation-72-hour-shifts
-can-hollywood-take-care-of-its-child-stars.

Tracy McVeigh. "Garland's Ex-Husband in Oscar Sale Row." *Guardian*,
June 24, 2000. https://www.theguardian.com/world/2000/jun/25/filmnews
.film.

Suyin Haynes. "The True Story Behind the Movie 'Judy.'" *Time*,
September 26, 2019. https://time.com/5684673/judy-garland-movie-true
-story/.

Don Heckman. "E! Recounts the Unhappy Life of Judy Garland." *Los
Angeles Times*, January 13, 2001. https://www.latimes.com/archives/la-xpm
-2001-jan-13-ca-11765-story.html.

Julia Molony. "Judy Garland: The Diva, the Drugs and the Damage." *Irish
Independent*, May 31, 2015. https://www.independent.ie/entertainment
/movies/judy-garland-the-diva-the-drugs-and-the-damage/31264687.html.

Colin Bertram. "Judy Garland Was Put on a Strict Diet and Encouraged
to Take 'Pep Pills' While Filming 'The Wizard of Oz.'" Biography,
December 10, 2020. https://www.biography.com/actors/judy-garland-pills
-diet-wizard-of-oz.

Erin Blakemore. "Golden Age Hollywood Had a Dirty Little Secret:
Drugs." History, September 11, 2023. https://www.history.com/news/judy
-garland-barbiturates-hollywood-studio-drugs.

**Chapter 26: Andy Warhol Was Really Fond of Meth**

Andy Warhol and Pat Hackett. *POPism: The Warhol Sixties*. Houghton Mifflin Harcourt, 1980, 105–108, 126–31, 134–37, 198–204, 212–14, 226–28, 291, 342–44.

Bob Colacello. *Holy Terror: Andy Warhol Close Up*. HarperCollins, 1990, 50, 117–18, 346, 374–75.

Stephen Metcalf. "Warhol's Bleak Prophecy." *Atlantic*, January/February 2019. https://www.theatlantic.com/magazine/archive/2019/01/andy-warhol-pop-art-whitney/576412/.

Blake Gopnik. "Andy Warhol Inc.: How He Made Business His Art." *New York Times*, November 1, 2018. https://www.nytimes.com/2018/11/01/arts/design/andy-warhol-inc-how-he-made-business-his-art.html.

Isabelle Dufresne. "Ultra Violet on Viva." *New York Times*, March 5, 1989. https://www.nytimes.com/1989/03/05/books/l-ultra-violet-on-viva-768389.html.

Sean O'Hagan. "I Shot Andy Warhol: Photographer Billy Name on Drugs and Shooting at the Factory." *Guardian*, September 27, 2015. https://www.theguardian.com/artanddesign/2015/sep/27/billy-name-andy-warhol-factory-photographer-pop-art.

Glenn O'Brien. "Andy Warhol on Junk Food, Coca-Cola, Drugs, Painting, God and His Morning Routine." *Interview*, February 4, 2019. https://www.interviewmagazine.com/art/andy-warhol-glenn-obrien-1977-interview.

Jake Nevins. "Bob Colacello on the 'Secular Saints' of Andy Warhol's Portraits." *Interview*, September 15, 2023. https://www.interviewmagazine.com/art/these-are-secular-saints-bob-colacello-on-warhols-commissioned-portraits.

Bob Colacello. "Andy Warhol Takes Drugs." Warholstars.org, 1978. https://warholstars.org/warhol/warhol1/warhol1c/warhol1cl/warholdrugs2.html.

Stephanie Mansfield. "Warhol's Soiree Sidekick." *Washington Post*, September 18, 1990. https://www.washingtonpost.com/archive/lifestyle/1990/09/18/warhols-soiree-sidekick/a5551197-5ab7-48f6-9463-5c866b9ba6b8/.

Gary Comenas. "Art vs. Life vs. Pop: A Review of Andy Warhol (Icons of America Series) by Arthur C. Danto." Warholstars.org, 2009. https://warholstars.org/Warhol_Danto_1.html.

Linda Rosefsky. "The Sacred in the Profane: Understanding Andy Warhol's Relationship with the Visual Image." *Graduate Theses, Dissertations, and Problem Reports*, West Virginia University, 2011, 35–37, 39–42, 44–46. https://researchrepository.wvu.edu/cgi/viewcontent.cgi?article=1752&context=etd.

Barbara Klein. "A Pop Icon's Iconic Beginning." Carnegie Museums, Fall 2019. https://carnegiemuseums.org/carnegie-magazine/fall-2019/a-pop-icons-iconic-beginning/.

Charles Giuliano. "Gerard Malanga on Andy Warhol's Mother Julia." *Berkshire Fine Arts*, June 4, 2015. https://www.berkshirefinearts.com/06-04-2015_gerard-malanga-on-andy-warhol-s-mother-julia.htm.

Gilda Williams. "Andy Warhol's Mother." *Tate Etc.*, May 2007. https://www.tate.org.uk/art/artists/andy-warhol-2121/andy-warhols-mother.

"What Was Andy Warhol Thinking?" Tate. https://www.tate.org.uk/art/artists/andy-warhol-2121/what-was-andy-warhol-thinking.

Kathy Schiffer. "Andy Warhol's Image Belied His Life as a Faithful Catholic." *Aleteia*, November 5, 2014. https://aleteia.org/2014/11/05/andy-warhol-a-celibate-catholic/.

Hannah Doherty. "Andy Warhol and Byzantine Art: Warhol Expert Tells of Painter's Hidden Inspiration." *Lafayette*, April 14, 2017. https://www.lafayettestudentnews.com/blog/2017/04/14/andy-warhol-and-byzantine-art-warhol-expert-tells-of-warhols-hidden-inspiration/.

Matthew Israel. "10 Reasons Why Andy Warhol Matters." *Artsy*, June 25, 2013. https://www.artsy.net/article/matthew-10-reasons-why-andy-warhol-matters.

Emily Brown. "Andy Warhol and His Artistic Influence." *Culture Trip*, October 25, 2022. https://theculturetrip.com/north-america/usa/new-york/new-york-city/articles/andy-warhol-and-his-artistic-influence/.

"5 Ways Andy Warhol Changed the Art World." Catawiki. https://www.catawiki.com/stories/587-5-ways-andy-warhol-changed-the-art-world.

Rosie Lesso. "Who Shot Andy Warhol?" *Collector*, April 19, 2022. https://www.thecollector.com/who-shot-andy-warhol/.

Lisa A. Flowers. "Andy Warhol's 'Factory' Was the Weirdest Place on Earth for Two Decades." *Ranker*, September 6, 2019. https://www.ranker.com/list/andy-warhol-factory-stories/lisa-a-flowers.

Zoe Huxford. "Ozempic and the Dark History of Weight-Loss Drugs." *Dazed Digital*, April 4, 2023. https://www.dazeddigital.com/beauty/article/58533/1/brief-history-diet-pills-weight-loss-drugs-ozempic-obetrol-fenphen-benzedrine.

Tim Teeman. "Fred Herko: The Life and Dramatic Death of an Avant-Garde Hero." *Guardian*, October 23, 2014. https://www.theguardian.com/stage/2014/oct/23/fred-herko-life-and-dramatic-death-avant-garde-hero.

"Andy Warhol: Revelation." The Warhol. https://www.warhol.org/exhibition/andy-warhol-revelation/.

"Remembering Andy Warhol, Who Was No Stranger to Dallas." *Dallas Morning News*, May 15, 2015. https://www.dallasnews.com/arts-entertainment/architecture/2015/05/16/remembering-andy-warhol-who-was-no-stranger-to-dallas/.

Megan Cohen. "Historical Echoes: Andy Warhol and the Art of Money." Federal Reserve Bank of New York, July 12, 2013. https://libertystreeteconomics.newyorkfed.org/2013/07/historical-echoes-andy-warhol-and-the-art-of-money-.html.

Suzanne Raga. "12 Surprising Facts About Andy Warhol." *Mental Floss*, August 6, 2018. https://www.mentalfloss.com/article/84016/12-things-you-might-not-know-about-andy-warhol.

Stacy Conradt. "The Quick 10: 10 Famous People and Their Drug Habits." *Mental Floss*, October 9, 2008. https://www.mentalfloss.com/article/19817/quick-10-10-famous-people-and-their-drug-habits.

Renee Deveney. "5 World-Famous Artists and Their Drugs of Choice." Recovery Village. https://www.therecoveryvillage.com/drug-addiction/related-topics/artists-and-drugs/.

"Andy Warhol." Biography, March 11, 2022. https://www.biography.com/artist/andy-warhol.

Associated Press. "Warhol's Portrait of Marilyn Monroe Sells for $195 Million, Most for Any US Artist." PBS News, May 10, 2022. https://www.pbs.org/newshour/arts/warhols-portrait-of-marilyn-monroe-sells-for-195-million-most-for-any-u-s-artist.

## Chapter 27: Philip K. Dick Wrote Amphetamine-Fueled Science Fiction

Kyle Arnold. *The Divine Madness of Philip K. Dick*. Oxford University Press, 2016.

Simon Critchley. "Philip K. Dick, Sci-Fi Philosopher, Part 1." *New York Times*, May 20, 2012. https://archive.nytimes.com/opinionator.blogs.nytimes.com/2012/05/20/philip-k-dick-sci-fi-philosopher-part-1/.

Molly Young. "The Essential Philip K. Dick." *New York Times*, September 25, 2023. https://www.nytimes.com/2022/10/26/books/best-philip-k-dick-novels.html.

Charles Platt. "The Voices in Philip K. Dick's Head." *New York Times*, December 16, 2011. https://www.nytimes.com/2011/12/18/books/review/the-exegesis-of-philip-k-dick-edited-by-pamela-jackson-jonathan-lethem-and-erik-davis-book-review.html.

Charles McGrath. "A Prince of Pulp, Legit at Last." *New York Times*, May 6, 2007. https://www.nytimes.com/2007/05/06/books/06mcgr.html.

Lewis Beale. "Philip Dick: When Sci-Fi Becomes Real." *Los Angeles Times*, August 8, 1991. https://www.latimes.com/archives/la-xpm-1991-08-08-vw-97-story.html.

F. Kathleen Foley. "'Flow My Tears' Has Hallucinatory Style." *Los Angeles Times*, April 22, 1999. https://www.latimes.com/archives/la-xpm-1999-apr-22-ca-29736-story.html.

David L. Ulin. "Philip K. Dick Would Have Been 86 Today: Some

Thoughts on His Legacy." *Los Angeles Times*, December 16, 2014. https://www.latimes.com/books/jacketcopy/la-et-jc-philip-k-dick-at-86-some-thoughts-on-his-legacy-20141215-story.html.

Philip Purser-Hallard. "The Drugs Did Work." *Guardian*, August 11, 2016. https://www.theguardian.com/film/2006/aug/12/sciencefiction fantasyandhorror.philipkdick.

Mason Currey. "Auden, Sartre, Graham Greene, Ayn Rand: They Loved Amphetamines." *Slate*, April 22, 2013. https://slate.com/culture/2013/04/auden-sartre-graham-greene-ayn-rand-they-loved-amphetamines.html.

Eli Lee. "Collapsed Horizon: Philip K Dick's A Scanner Darkly, 40 Years On." *Quietus*, January 15, 2017. https://thequietus.com/articles/21571-philip-k-dick-a-scanner-darkly-anniversary-drugs-addiction-surveillance-grief.

Seamus O'Reilly. "Just Because You're Paranoid . . . Philip K. Dick's Troubled Life." *Irish Times*, October 7, 2017. https://www.irishtimes.com/culture/film/just-because-you-re-paranoid-philip-k-dick-s-troubled-life-1.3243976.

Kyle Arnold. "Was Philip K. Dick a Madman or a Mystic?" *Publishers Weekly*, July 8, 2016. https://www.publishersweekly.com/pw/by-topic/industry-news/tip-sheet/article/70857-was-philip-k-dick-a-madman-or-a-mystic.html.

Josh Ozersky. "The Need for Speed: Philip K. Dick, Adderall, and the Writing Life." *Medium*, December 9, 2013. https://medium.com/@ozerskytv/the-need-for-speed-6c135c3255db.

Uwe Anton and Werner Fuchs. "So I Don't Write About Heroes: An Interview with Philip K. Dick." *SF Eye* 14 (Spring 1996): 37–46. Reprinted by University of Massachusetts Boston. http://www.faculty.umb.edu/gary_zabel/Courses/Parallel%20Universes/Texts/So%20I%20Don%27t %20Write%20About%20Heroes%20An%20Interview%20with%20Philip %20K_%20Dick.htm.

## Chapter 28: Johnny Cash Was Battling Demons

Robert Hilburn. *Johnny Cash: The Life*. Little, Brown, 2013.

Julie Chadwick. *The Man Who Carried Cash*. Dundurn, 2017.

Robert Hilburn. "Johnny Cash's Dark California Days." *Los Angeles Times*, October 12, 2013. https://www.latimes.com/entertainment/music/posts/la-et-ms-johnny-cash-calif-story.html.

Adam Sweeting. "Obituary: Johnny Cash." *Guardian*, September 12, 2003. https://www.theguardian.com/news/2003/sep/13/guardianobituaries.artsobituaries.

Stephen Holden. "Johnny Cash, Country Music Bedrock, Dies at 71." *New York Times*, September 13, 2003. https://www.nytimes.com/2003/09/13/arts/johnny-cash-country-music-bedrock-dies-at-71.html.

Sharon Waxman. "The Secrets That Lie Beyond the Ring of Fire." *New York Times*, October 16, 2005. https://www.nytimes.com/2005/10/16 /movies/the-secrets-that-lie-beyond-the-ring-of-fire.html.

Tim Arango. "Behind Most Wildfires, a Person and a Spark: 'We Bring Fires with Us.'" *New York Times*, August 20, 2018. https://www.nytimes.com /2018/08/20/us/california-wildfires-human-causes-arson.html.

Alice Winkler. "I Walk the Line." NPR, December 23, 2000. https:// www.npr.org/2000/12/23/1115971/npr-100-i-walk-the-line.

Kory Grow. "Johnny Cash Talks God, Painkillers and Long Hair in Animated Interview." *Rolling Stone*, April 8, 2014. https://www.rollingstone .com/music/music-news/johnny-cash-talks-god-painkillers-and-long-hair -in-animated-interview-241355/.

James Sullivan. "10 Things You Didn't Know About Johnny Cash." *Rolling Stone*, October 31, 2013. https://www.rollingstone.com/feature /10-things-you-didnt-know-about-johnny-cash-78642/.

Dean Goodman. "Johnny Cash's Son Opens Up on Parents' Addictions." Reuters, May 31, 2007. https://www.reuters.com/article/us-cash/johnny -cashs-son-opens-up-on-parents-addictions-idUSN3046078520070531.

Frank Skinner. "Johnny Cash Started Me on the Rocky Road to Alcoholism." *Guardian*, April 24, 2018. https://www.theguardian.com /tv-and-radio/2018/apr/24/frank-skinner-johnny-cash-started-me-on-the -rocky-road-to-alcoholism-ostrich-attack.

Casey Cep. "Johnny Cash's Gospel." *New Yorker*, February 9, 2020. https://www.newyorker.com/books/page-turner/johnny-cashs-gospel.

Adam Crouch. "Johnny Cash, Eighties Man." *New Yorker*, March 31, 2014. https://www.newyorker.com/culture/culture-desk/johnny-cash-eighties -man.

Alice Stone. "Johnny Cash's Devastating Childhood Loss Morphed Him from Gregarious to Introspective." *Showbiz Cheatsheet*, January 27, 2021. https://www.cheatsheet.com/entertainment/johnny-cashs-devastating -childhood-loss-morphed-him-from-gregarious-to-introspective.html/.

A. J. Samuels. "The Good, the Bad, and the Real Johnny Cash." *Culture Trip*, December 2, 2016. https://theculturetrip.com/north-america/usa /arkansas/articles/the-good-the-bad-and-the-real-johnny-cash/.

Jack Whatley. "Johnny Cash Once Tried to Fight an Ostrich and, Predictably, Suffered a Heavy Defeat." *Far Out Magazine*, August 29, 2020. https://faroutmagazine.co.uk/johnny-cash-ostrich-fight-story/.

Joe McGasko. "Johnny Cash: 10 Things You Might Not Know About the Country Icon." Biography, December 10, 2020. https://www.biography.com /news/johnny-cash-10-interesting-facts.

"Johnny Cash: 10 Facts About the 'Man in Black.'" *Telegraph*, May 10, 2017. https://www.telegraph.co.uk/music/artists/johnny-cash-10-facts -about-the-man-in-black/.

"The Man in Black." *LaFayette Underground*, August 13, 2010. https://www.cityoflafayettega.com/2010/08/the-man-in-black/.

Vincent Lopez. "Trent Reznor: I Wasn't Prepared for What I Saw and It Really Wasn't My Song Anymore." *Society of Rock*, November 26, 2018. https://societyofrock.com/trent-reznor-i-wasnt-prepared-for-what-i-saw-and-it-really-then-wasnt-my-song-anymore/.

**Chapter 29: Elvis Presley Was a Narc**

Peter Guralnick. *Last Train to Memphis: The Rise of Elvis Presley*. Little, Brown, 1994.

Peter Guralnick. *Careless Love: The Unmaking of Elvis Presley*. Little, Brown, 1999.

Howard Markel. "Elvis' Addiction Was the Perfect Prescription for an Early Death." PBS News, August 16, 2018. https://www.pbs.org/newshour/health/elvis-addiction-was-the-perfect-prescription-for-an-early-death.

Travis M. Andrews. "Sixty Years Ago, Elvis Was Drafted into the Army. He Was Never the Same." *Washington Post*, March 22, 2018. https://www.washingtonpost.com/news/morning-mix/wp/2018/03/22/sixty-years-ago-elvis-presley-was-drafted-into-the-army-he-was-never-the-same/.

"Doctor Testifies About His Efforts to Control Presley's Use of Drugs." *New York Times*, October 31, 1981. https://www.nytimes.com/1981/10/31/us/doctor-testifies-about-his-efforts-to-control-presley-s-use-of-drugs.html.

Peter Guralnick. "How Did Elvis Get Turned into a Racist?" *New York Times*, August 11, 2007. https://www.nytimes.com/2007/08/11/opinion/11guralnick.html.

Dwight Garner. "Review: 'Sam Phillips: The Man Who Invented Rock 'n' Roll' by Peter Guralnick." *New York Times*, November 5, 2015. https://www.nytimes.com/2015/11/06/books/review-sam-phillips-the-man-who-invented-rock-n-roll-by-peter-guralnick.html.

Richard Zoglin. "Inside the Las Vegas Show That Turned Elvis' Career Around." *Time*, July 23, 2019. https://time.com/5628504/elvis-las-vegas-comeback-1969/.

Olivia B. Waxman. "The Story Behind That Famous Photo of Elvis Presley and Richard Nixon." *Time*, August 15, 2017. https://time.com/4894301/elvis-president-nixon-photo/.

Peter Carlson. "When Elvis Met Nixon." *Smithsonian*, December 2010. https://www.smithsonianmag.com/history/when-elvis-met-nixon-69892425/.

Rosa Cartagena. "Elvis Met Nixon 50 Years Ago Today in One of the Weirdest White House Meetings in History." *Washingtonian*, December 21, 2020. https://www.washingtonian.com/2020/12/21/elvis-met-nixon-50-years-ago-today-in-one-of-the-weirdest-white-house-meetings-in-history/.

Harold Jackson. "From the Archive, 3 December 1986: How Elvis Won His Anti-Drugs Badge from Nixon." *Guardian*, December 3, 2012. https://www.theguardian.com/theguardian/2012/dec/03/elvis-presley-nixon-drugs-1986.

"The Nixon-Presley Meeting, 21 December 1970." George Washington University National Security Archives. https://nsarchive2.gwu.edu/nsa/elvis/elnix.html.

Amanda Petrusich. "Going to Graceland." *New Yorker,* July 2, 2018. https://www.newyorker.com/culture/culture-desk/going-to-graceland.

Sean Coons. "Remembering Elvis with Memories of Friendship, the Beatles, and LSD." *Atlantic*, August 3, 2011. https://www.theatlantic.com/entertainment/archive/2011/08/remembering-elvis-with-memories-of-friendship-the-beatles-and-lsd/243031/.

Adrienne LaFrance. "The King, the Conspiracies, and the American Dream." *Atlantic*, January 8, 2015. https://www.theatlantic.com/entertainment/archive/2015/01/elvis-sightings-and-the-american-dream/384308/.

Sonia Moghe. "Opioid History: From 'Wonder Drug' to Abuse Epidemic." CNN, October 14, 2016. https://www.cnn.com/2016/05/12/health/opioid-addiction-history/index.html.

Lauren Hubbard. "Inside the Enduring Mysteries of Elvis Presley's Death." *Town & Country*, June 21, 2022. https://www.townandcountrymag.com/society/a26721749/elvis-presley-death-true-story/.

Kristina Robb-Dover. "The 10 Drugs That Were in Elvis Presley's System When He Overdosed—and Other Revelations." FHE Health, May 18, 2020. https://fherehab.com/learning/elvis-presley-drugs-led-to-overdose.

"RM 8-SU: Unintended Consequences: A Case Study of Elvis Presley." Manitoba Education. https://www.edu.gov.mb.ca/k12/cur/physhlth/frame_found_gr11/rm/8_su.pdf.

Robert Fontenot. "What Was Elvis Presley's Relationship with Drugs?" *LiveAbout*, January 20, 2019. https://www.liveabout.com/elvis-presleys-relationship-with-drugs-2522425.

Mike Sager. "The Inside Story of How Vegas Changed Elvis Presley: Drugs, Debauchery & Superstition." *Billboard*, March 13, 2015. https://www.billboard.com/articles/news/6495222/elvis-presley-las-vegas-history.

Eric Meisfjord. "The Dark Reason Elvis Would Bring His Guns on Stage." *Grunge*, July 21, 2020. https://www.grunge.com/228582/the-dark-reason-elvis-would-bring-his-guns-on-stage/.

Maureen Lee Lenker and Joshua Rothkopf. "Fact or Fiction: 5 Scenes from *Elvis* and the Real-Life Stories Behind Them." *Entertainment Weekly*, June 26, 2022. https://ew.com/movies/fact-or-fiction-5-scenes-from-elvis-real-life-stories-behind-them/.

Eddie Deezen. "The Night Elvis Was Shown from the Waist Up." *Today I*

*Found Out*, April 9, 2013. http://www.todayifoundout.com/index.php /2013/04/the-night-elvis-was-shown-from-the-waist-up/.

Ayun Halliday. "Elvis' Three Appearances on *The Ed Sullivan Show*: Watch History in the Making and from the Waist Up (1956)." Open Culture, October 25, 2021. https://www.openculture.com/2021/10/elvis -three-appearances-on-the-ed-sullivan-shows.html.

Rachel Chang. "Elvis in the Army: 'People Were Expecting Me to Mess Up.'" Biography, September 8, 2020. https://www.biography.com/musicians /elvis-army-career-draft.

Ruthe Stein. "Girls! Girls! Girls! From Small-Town Women to Movie Stars, Elvis Loved Often but Never True." *SFGate*, August 3, 1997. https:// www.sfgate.com/entertainment/article/Girls-Girls-Girls-From-small-town -women-to-2814423.php.

Meagan Paese. "Elvis Presley 40th Anniversary Tribute, Pt 3." History of Rock and Roll. https://thehistoryofrockandroll.net/elvis-presley-40th -anniversary-tribute-pt-3/.

"Elvis Presley: 1956." PBS Culture Shock. https://www.pbs.org/wgbh /cultureshock/flashpoints/music/elvis.html.

## Chapter 30: Albert Hofmann Invented LSD by Accident

Albert Hofmann. *LSD: My Problem Child*. Fourth edition. Multidisciplinary Association for Psychedelic Studies, 2009.

Craig S. Smith. "Nearly 100, LSD's Father Ponders His 'Problem Child.'" *New York Times*, January 7, 2006. https://www.nytimes.com/2006/01/07 /pageoneplus/world/the-saturday-profile-nearly-100-lsds-father-ponders -his.html.

Craig S. Smith. "Albert Hofmann, the Father of LSD, Dies at 102." *New York Times*, April 30, 2008. https://www.nytimes.com/2008/04/30/world /europe/30hofmann.html.

Benedict Carey. "A Psychedelic 'Problem Child' Comes Full Circle." *New York Times*, May 4, 2008. https://www.nytimes.com/2008/05/04 /weekinreview/04carey.html.

Ernesto Londoño. "After Six-Decade Hiatus, Experimental Psychedelic Therapy Returns to the VA." *New York Times*, June 24, 2022. https://www .nytimes.com/2022/06/24/us/politics/psychedelic-therapy-veterans.html.

Tom Shroder. "'Apparently Useless': The Accidental Discovery of LSD." *Atlantic*, September 9, 2014. https://www.theatlantic.com/health/archive /2014/09/the-accidental-discovery-of-lsd/379564/.

Rebecca Greenfield. "The Inventor of LSD Asked Steve Jobs for PR Help." *Atlantic*, November 14, 2011. https://www.theatlantic.com/technology /archive/2011/11/inventor-lsd-asked-steve-jobs-pr-help/335512/.

"Steve Jobs Tried LSD." *Daily Beast*, April 24, 2017. https://www .thedailybeast.com/cheats/2011/10/07/steve-jobs-tried-lsd.

Terry Gross, host. "The CIA's Secret Quest for Mind Control: Torture, LSD, and a Poisoner in Chief." *Fresh Air*, NPR, November 20, 2020. https://www.npr.org/2020/11/20/937009453/the-cias-secret-quest-for-mind-control-torture-lsd-and-a-poisoner-in-chief.

David Biello. "Albert Hofmann, Inventor of LSD, Embarks on Final Trip." *Scientific American*, April 30, 2008. https://www.scientificamerican.com/article/inventor-of-lsd-embarks-on-final-trip/.

Christopher Reed. "Obituary: Dr. Albert Hofmann." *Guardian*, April 30, 2008. https://www.theguardian.com/science/2008/apr/30/drugs.chemistry.

Trina Calderon. "Flashback: LSD Creator Albert Hofmann Drops Acid for the First Time." *Rolling Stone*, April 19, 2018. https://www.rollingstone.com/culture/culture-news/flashback-lsd-creator-albert-hofmann-drops-acid-for-the-first-time-629085/.

Stacy Mosel. "History of LSD." Recovery.org, November 15, 2022. https://www.recovery.org/lsd-addiction/history/.

### Chapter 31: Aldous Huxley's Shortcut to Enlightenment

Aldous Huxley. *The Doors of Perception*. Harper Perennial, 1954, 9–10, 22–24, 65–79.

Sam Jordison. "The Doors of Perception: What Did Huxley See in Mescaline?" *Guardian*, January 26, 2012. https://www.theguardian.com/books/2012/jan/26/doors-perception-huxley-mescaline-reading-group.

Robert Bennett. "Aldous Huxley Foresaw America's Pill-Popping Addiction with Eerie Accuracy." *Literary Hub*, March 21, 2019. https://lithub.com/aldous-huxley-foresaw-americas-pill-popping-addiction-with-eerie-accuracy/.

Peter Bebergal. "Getting There Too Quickly: Aldous Huxley and Mescaline." *Revealer*, January 2, 2012. https://therevealer.org/getting-there-too-quickly-aldous-huxley-and-mescaline/.

Douglas Martin. "Humphry Osmond, 86, Who Sought Medicinal Value in Psychedelic Drugs, Dies." *New York Times*, February 22, 2004. https://www.nytimes.com/2004/02/22/us/humphry-osmond-86-who-sought-medicinal-value-in-psychedelic-drugs-dies.html.

Mo Costandi. "A Brief History of Psychedelic Psychiatry." *Guardian*, September 2, 2014. https://www.theguardian.com/science/neurophilosophy/2014/sep/02/psychedelic-psychiatry.

Michael Horowitz and Cynthia Palmer. "Huxley on Drugs and Creativity." In *Moksha: Aldous Huxley's Classic Writings on Psychedelics and the Visionary Experience*, edited by Michael Horowitz and Cynthia Palmer. Park Street Press, 1999. https://maps.org/news-letters/v10n3/10317hux.html.

Edward Rothstein. "A Mind-Altering Drug Altered a Culture as Well." *New York Times*, May 5, 2008. https://www.nytimes.com/2008/05/05/arts/05conn.html.

Domagoj Valjak. "Aldous Huxley Was George Orwell's French Teacher at Eton College." *Vintage News*, January 30, 2017. https://www.thevintagenews .com/2017/01/30/aldous-huxley-was-george-orwells-french-teacher-at -eton-college/.

Nikola Davis. "From Aldous Huxley to the Beatles: How LSD Has Inspired Art." *Guardian*, April 2, 2020. https://www.theguardian.com /science/2020/apr/02/from-aldous-huxley-to-the-beatles-how-lsd-has -inspired-art.

"Aldous Huxley (1894–1963)." Eton College. https://findoes.etoncollege .com/aldous-huxley/.

"Aldous Huxley." *New World Encyclopedia*. https://www.newworld encyclopedia.org/entry/Aldous_Huxley.

## Chapter 32: How the CIA Accidentally Created the Unabomber

Michael Mello. *The United States of America Versus Theodore John Kaczynski*. Context Books, 1999, 37–38.

Jonathan D. Moreno. *Mind Wars: Brain Science and the Military in the 21st Century*. Bellevue Literary Press, 2012, 85–89.

Stephen Kinzer. *Poisoner in Chief: Sidney Gottlieb and the CIA Search for Mind Control*. St. Martin's Griffin, 2019, 54, 60, 100–101, 106, 132–33, 194–95, 244–45.

Alston Chase. "Harvard and the Making of the Unabomber." *Atlantic*, June 2000. https://www.theatlantic.com/magazine/archive/2000/06 /harvard-and-the-making-of-the-unabomber/378239/.

Alex Traub. "Ted Kaczynski, 'Unabomber' Who Attacked Modern Life, Dies at 81." *New York Times*, June 11, 2023. https://www.nytimes.com /2023/06/10/us/ted-kaczynski-dead.html.

Sharon Weinberger. "Poisoner in Chief: Sidney Gottlieb and the CIA Search for Mind Control." *New York Times*, September 10, 2019. https:// www.nytimes.com/2019/09/10/books/review/poisoner-in-chief-stephen -kinzer.html.

Mark Jacobson. "The CIA Can Do Mind Control." *New York Magazine*, November 25, 2013. https://nymag.com/news/features/conspiracy-theories /cia-mind-control/.

Bryan Pietsch. "Before He Was the Unabomber, Ted Kaczynski Was a Mind-Control Test Subject." *Washington Post*, June 11, 2023. https://www .washingtonpost.com/history/2023/06/11/unabomber-ted-kaczynski -harvard-experiment/.

Alexander Cockburn. "We're Reaping Tragic Legacy from Drugs." *Los Angeles Times*, July 6, 1999. https://www.latimes.com/archives/la-xpm-1999 -jul-06-me-53482-story.html.

Jonathan D. Moreno. "Harvard's Experiment on the Unabomber, Class of '62." *Psychology Today*, May 25, 2012. https://www.psychologytoday

.com/us/blog/impromptu-man/201205/harvards-experiment-the
-unabomber-class-62.

Robert D. Mather. "US Government Mind Control Experiment:
Hypnosis, LSD, and the Unabomber." *Psychology Today*, April 26, 2020.
https://www.psychologytoday.com/us/blog/the-conservative-social
-psychologist/202004/us-government-mind-control-experiments.

Karl Eschner. "What We Know About the CIA's Midcentury Mind-
Control Project." *Smithsonian*, April 13, 2017. https://www.smithsonianmag
.com/smart-news/what-we-know-about-cias-midcentury-mind-control
-project-180962836/.

Kim Zetter. "April 13, 1953: CIA OKs MK-Ultra Mind-Control Tests."
*Wired*, April 13, 2010. https://www.wired.com/2010/04/0413mk-ultra
-authorized/.

Katie Serena. "What Was MK-Ultra, the CIA's Top-Secret Cold War
Research Program." *All That's Interesting*, September 9, 2022. https://
allthatsinteresting.com/mk-ultra.

Kirsten G. Studlien. "Murray Center Seals Kaczynski Data." *Harvard
Crimson*, July 14, 2000. https://www.thecrimson.com/article/2000/7/14
/murray-center-seals-kaczynski-data-plondon-buried/.

Aaron Feis. "Ted Kaczynski's Connection to MK-Ultra Explained."
*Messenger*, June 10, 2023. https://themessenger.com/news/ted-kaczynskis
-connection-to-mkultra-explained.

Brian Dunleavy. "What Happened to Ted Kaczynski at Harvard?" History,
June 12, 2023. https://www.history.com/news/what-happened-to-the
-unabomber-at-harvard.

Brianna Nofil. "The CIA's Appalling Human Experiments with Mind
Control." History. https://www.history.com/mkultra-operation-midnight
-climax-cia-lsd-experiments.

"Project MK-Ultra." Freedom of Information Act Electronic Reading
Room, CIA.gov. https://www.cia.gov/readingroom/document/06760269.

## Chapter 33: Ken Kesey and the Electric Kool-Aid Acid Test

Tom Wolfe. *The Electric Kool-Aid Acid Test*. Picador, 1968.

David Bianculli, host. "Ken Kesey on Misconceptions of Counterculture."
*Fresh Air*, NPR, August 12, 2011. https://www.npr.org/transcripts
/139259106.

Tom Vitale. "Kesey's 'Cuckoo's Nest' Still Flying at 50." *All Things
Considered*, NPR, February 1, 2012. https://www.npr.org/2012/02/01
/146210681/keseys-cuckoos-nest-still-flying-at-50.

Terry Gross, host. "The CIA's Secret Quest for Mind Control: Torture,
LSD, and a Poisoner in Chief." *Fresh Air*, NPR, November 20, 2020. https://
www.npr.org/2020/11/20/937009453/the-cias-secret-quest-for-mind
-control-torture-lsd-and-a-poisoner-in-chief.

Christopher Lehmann-Haupt. "Ken Kesey, Author of 'Cuckoo's Nest,' Who Defined the Psychedelic Era, Dies at 66." *New York Times*, November 11, 2001. https://www.nytimes.com/2001/11/11/nyregion/ken-kesey-author -of-cuckoo-s-nest-who-defined-the-psychedelic-era-dies-at-66.html.

Edward Helmore. "How Ken Kesey's LSD-Fuelled Bus Trip Created the Psychedelic 60s." *Guardian*, August 6, 2011. https://www.theguardian.com /film/2011/aug/06/lsd-ken-kesey-pranksters-film.

Bill Van Niekerken. "Ken Kesey vs. the Cops: Looking Back at Author's 1965 Pot Bust." *San Francisco Chronicle*, December 15, 2015. https://www .sfchronicle.com/thetake/article/Ken-Kesey-vs-the-cops-Looking-back-at -6700243.php.

Mark Oliver. "The Electric Kool-Aid Acid Test: How the Author of 'One Flew Over the Cuckoo's Nest' Spread LSD Across America." *All That's Interesting*, December 1, 2017. https://allthatsinteresting.com/acid-tests.

John Daniel. "The Prankster-in-Chief Moves On." *Open Spaces*, December 2001. https://open-spaces.com/articles/the-prankster-in-chief-moves-on/.

"The Psychedelic '60s." University of Virginia Library. https://explore.lib .virginia.edu/exhibits/show/sixties/walkthrough/kenkesey.

## Chapter 34: Timothy Leary Was the Most Dangerous Man in America

Don Lattin. *The Harvard Psychedelic Club*. Harper One, 2010.

David Colker. "'60s Drug Guru Timothy Leary Dies at 75." *Los Angeles Times*, June 1, 1996. https://www.latimes.com/archives/la-xpm-1996-06 -01-mn-10774-story.html.

Bart Barnes. "LSD Advocate, '60s Icon Timothy Leary Dies at 75." *Washington Post*, June 1, 1996. https://www.washingtonpost.com/archive /local/1996/06/01/lsd-advocate-60s-icon-timothy-leary-dies-at-75 /d853cd36-5bf3-4fbd-8e14-20f9cd3e01e4/.

Laura Mansnerus. "Timothy Leary, Pied Piper of Psychedelic '60s, Dies at 75." *New York Times*, June 1, 1996. https://www.nytimes.com/1996/06/01 /us/timothy-leary-pied-piper-of-psychedelic-60-s-dies-at-75.html.

Greg Miller. "Timothy Leary's Transformation from Scientist to Psychedelic Celebrity." *Wired*, October 1, 2013. https://www.wired.com /2013/10/timothy-leary-archives/.

Edward Kosner. "Review: Timothy Leary, 'The Most Dangerous Man in America.'" *Wall Street Journal*, January 18, 2018. https://www.wsj.com /articles/review-timothy-leary-the-most-dangerous-man-in-america -1516320277.

Ed Prideaux. "Timothy Leary Turns 100: America's LSD Messiah, Remembered by Those Who Knew Him." *Vice*, October 23, 2020. https:// www.vice.com/en/article/epdg3k/timothy-leary-lsd-acid-history.

Emily Witt. "The Science of the Psychedelic Renaissance." *New Yorker*,

May 29, 2018. https://www.newyorker.com/books/under-review/the
-science-of-the-psychedelic-renaissance.

Bob Boilen. "Old Music Tuesday: 40 Years of Giving Peace a Chance."
*All Songs Considered*, NPR, June 30, 2009. https://www.npr.org/sections
/allsongs/2009/06/old_music_tuesday_40_years_of_2.html.

Kirstin Butler. "When the 'Summer of Love' Took Over San Francisco."
*PBS American Experience*, August 3, 2021. https://www.pbs.org/wgbh
/americanexperience/features/when-summer-love-took-over-san-francisco/.

"Timothy Leary Was FBI Narc." CBS News, June 30, 1999. https://www
.cbsnews.com/news/timothy-leary-was-fbi-narc/.

Sam Kemp. "Listen to Jimi Hendrix and Timothy Leary Share a
Psychedelic Jam Session." *Far Out*, November 5, 2022. https://faroutmagazine
.co.uk/jimi-hendrix-timothy-leary-psychedelic-jam-session/.

Stephen D. Lerner. "Leary Gets 30 Years on Marijuana Charge." *Harvard
Crimson*, March 12, 1966. https://www.thecrimson.com/article/1966/3/12
/leary-gets-30-years-on-marijuana/.

Io Y. Gilman and Kendall I. Shields. "At Harvard, Psychedelic Drugs'
Tentative Renaissance." *Harvard Crimson*, February 19, 2022. https://www
.thecrimson.com/article/2022/2/19/psychedelics-tentative-renaissance/.

"Inside the Strange Journey of Tim Leary, from Harvard Professor to the
'High Priest of LSD.'" *All That's Interesting*, July 16, 2022. https://
allthatsinteresting.com/timothy-leary.

Matthew Burke. "Experimental Facts About Timothy Leary, the Father of
Psychedelics." Factinate, September 4, 2020. https://www.factinate.com
/people/facts-timothy-leary/.

"Top 10 Things You Didn't Know About the Beatles." *Time.* https://
content.time.com/time/specials/packages/article/0,28804,1921062_1921061
_1921088,00.html.

## Chapter 35: Alexander Shulgin, the DEA Employee Who Invented 230 Psychedelics

Alexander Shulgin. *The Nature of Drugs: History, Pharmacology, and Social
Impact.* Volume 1. Transform Press, 2021, xvii–xxiii, xxv, 88, 92, 106.

Drake Bennett. "Dr. Ecstasy." *New York Times Magazine*, January 30,
2005. https://www.nytimes.com/2005/01/30/magazine/dr-ecstasy.html.

Bruce Weber. "Alexander Shulgin, Psychedelia Researcher, Dies at 88."
*New York Times*, June 7, 2014. https://www.nytimes.com/2014/06/08/us
/alexander-shulgin-psychedelia-researcher-dies-at-88.html.

Alexis Petridis. "How Did Alexander Shulgin Become Known as the
Godfather of Ecstasy?" *Guardian*, June 3, 2014. https://www.theguardian
.com/science/shortcuts/2014/jun/03/alexander-shulgin-man-did-not
-invent-ecstasy-dead.

Ros Davidson. "Archive, 1997: Interview with Alexander Shulgin, 'the

Godfather of Ecstasy.'" *Guardian*, June 3, 2014. https://www.theguardian
.com/science/from-the-archive-blog/2014/jun/03/shulgin-alexander
-drugs-ecstasy-mdma.

Mike Power. "Alexander Shulgin Obituary." *Guardian*, June 3, 2014.
https://www.theguardian.com/science/2014/jun/03/alexander-shulgin.

Dennis Romero. "Sasha Shulgin Has Worked Just This Side of the Law
Inventing Mind-Altering Drugs. Should They Be Legal? He Thinks It's . . .
High Time." *Los Angeles Times*, September 5, 1995. https://www.latimes
.com/archives/la-xpm-1995-09-05-ls-42435-story.html.

David Colker. "Alexander Shulgin, Chemist Behind MDMA, Dies at 88."
*Los Angeles Times*, June 4, 2014. https://www.latimes.com/local/obituaries
/la-me-alexander-shulgin-20140605-story.html.

Brian Vastag. "Chemist Alexander Shulgin, Popularizer of the Drug
Ecstasy, Dies at 88." *Washington Post*, June 3, 2014. https://www
.washingtonpost.com/national/health-science/chemist-alexander-shulgin
-popularizer-of-the-drug-ecstasy-dies-at-88/2014/06/03/19fd9580-eb34
-11e3-b98c-72cef4a00499_story.html.

Ethan Brown. "Professor X." *Wired*, September 1, 2002. https://www
.wired.com/2002/09/professorx/.

Hamilton Morris. "The Last Interview with Alexander Shulgin." *Vice*,
May 1, 2010. https://www.vice.com/en/article/avjewz/the-last-interview
-with-alexander-shulgin-423-v17n5.

"'Shulgins I Have Known and Loved'—Alexander Shulgin Interview."
Posted September 29, 2020, by Psychedelic History of Texas, YouTube.
https://www.youtube.com/watch?v=JYlAuf-3t0g.

David Gems. "Book Review: *PIHKAL—A Chemical Love Story*;
*TIHKAL—The Continuation*." University College London. https://www.ucl
.ac.uk/~ucbtdag/bioethics/writings/shulgin.html#:~:text=Two%20DEA
%20agents%20even%20got,4%2C5%2Dtrimethoxyphenethylamine).

## Chapter 36: Sgt. Pothead's Loaded Hard-Drug Band (a.k.a. the Beatles)

Joe Goodden. *Riding So High: The Beatles and Drugs*. Pepper & Pearl, 2017.

Steven Nelson. "Drug Use Belied Beatles' Squeaky-Clean Image." *US
News & World Report*, January 22, 2014. https://www.usnews.com/news
/special-reports/articles/2014/01/22/drug-use-belied-beatles-squeaky
-clean-image.

Jeff Greenfield. "They Changed Rock, Which Changed the Culture,
Which Changed Us." *New York Times*, February 16, 1975. https://www
.nytimes.com/1975/02/16/archives/they-changed-rock-which-changed
-the-culture-which-changed-us.html.

Allan Kozinn. "Meditation on the Man Who Saved the Beatles." *New*

*York Times*, February 7, 2008. https://www.nytimes.com/2008/02/07/arts /music/07yogi.html.

Jann S. Wenner. "John Lennon: The Rolling Stone Interview, Part 1." *Rolling Stone*, January 21, 1971. https://www.rollingstone.com/music/music -news/john-lennon-the-rolling-stone-interview-part-one-160194/.

"How the Beatles Took America: Inside the Biggest Explosion in Rock & Roll History." *Rolling Stone*, January 1, 2014. https://www.rollingstone .com/music/music-features/how-the-beatles-took-america-inside-the -biggest-explosion-in-rock-roll-history-244557/.

Mikal Gilmore. "Beatles' Acid Test: How LSD Opened the Door to 'Revolver.'" *Rolling Stone*, August 25, 2016. https://www.rollingstone.com /feature/beatles-acid-test-how-lsd-opened-the-door-to-revolver-251417/.

Jordan Runtagh. "Beatles' 'Sgt. Pepper' at 50: Remembering the Real 'Lucy in the Sky with Diamonds.'" *Rolling Stone*, May 18, 2017. https:// www.rollingstone.com/music/music-features/beatles-sgt-pepper-at-50 -remembering-the-real-lucy-in-the-sky-with-diamonds-121628/.

Douglas Wolk. "'Magical Mystery Tour': Inside Beatles' Psychedelic Album Odyssey." *Rolling Stone*, November 27, 2017. https://www.rollingstone .com/music/music-features/magical-mystery-tour-inside-beatles-psychedelic -album-odyssey-118466/.

David Chiu. "The Beatles in India: 16 Things You Didn't Know." *Rolling Stone*, February 14, 2021. https://www.rollingstone.com/feature/the-beatles -in-india-16-things-you-didnt-know-203601/.

Dan McQuade. "The Drug That Helped Turn the Beatles into the World's Greatest Band." *Village Voice*, August 14, 2014. https://www.villagevoice.com /the-drug-that-helped-turn-the-beatles-into-the-worlds-greatest-band/.

Mark Beaumont. "'We Were Smoking Marijuana for Breakfast': The Beatles and the Making of 'Help!'" *Independent*, February 22, 2020. https:// www.independent.co.uk/arts-entertainment/films/features/the-beatles -help-album-anniversary-john-lennon-marijuana-a9344936.html.

Kenneth Womack. "In 1969 the Fifth Beatle Was Heroin: John Lennon's Addiction Took Its Toll on the Band." *Salon*, February 15, 2019. https:// www.salon.com/2019/02/15/in-1969-the-fifth-beatle-was-heroin-john -lennons-addiction-took-its-toll-on-the-band/.

"Every Song the Beatles Wrote About Drugs." *Far Out*, February 10, 2021. https://faroutmagazine.co.uk/beatles-songs-about-drugs-lennon -mccartney-harrison-starr/.

## Chapter 37: Carl Sagan Got Astronomically High

Keay Davidson. *Carl Sagan: A Life.* John Wiley & Sons, 1999.

Carl Sagan. "Mr. X." In *Marihuana Reconsidered*, by Lester Grinspoon. Harvard University Press, 1971, 109, 112–14, 116.

Carl Sagan. "Direct Contact Among Galactic Civilizations by Relativistic Interstellar Spaceflight." *Planetary and Space Science* 11, no. 5 (1963): 485–98. Reprinted by Science Direct. https://www.sciencedirect.com/science /article/abs/pii/0032063363900722.

David A. Hollinger. "Star Power." *New York Times*, November 28, 1999. https://archive.nytimes.com/www.nytimes.com/books/99/11/28/reviews /991128.28holingt.html.

Glenn Collins. "The Sagans: Fact and Fiction Back to Back." *New York Times*, September 30, 1985. https://www.nytimes.com/1985/09/30/style /the-sagans-fiction-and-fact-back-to-back.html.

Timothy Ferris. "How the Voyager Golden Record Was Made." *New Yorker*, August 20, 2017. https://www.newyorker.com/tech/annals-of -technology/voyager-golden-record-40th-anniversary-timothy-ferris.

Joel Achenbach. "Why Carl Sagan Is Truly Irreplaceable." *Smithsonian*, March 2014. https://www.smithsonianmag.com/science-nature/why-carl -sagan-truly-irreplaceable-180949818/.

Leslie Mullen. "Carl Sagan (1934–1996)." NASA Science. https://science .nasa.gov/people/carl-sagan/.

"Carl Sagan Drew Inspiration from Getting High." *Guardian*, August 24, 1999. https://www.theguardian.com/science/1999/aug/24/spaceexploration.

Nick Wing. "Carl Sagan, Marijuana Advocate, Explains What It's Like to Be High While Carl Sagan." *HuffPost*, December 6, 2017. https://www .huffpost.com/entry/carl-sagan-marijuana_n_3367112.

Scotty Hendricks. "Carl Sagan on Why He Liked Smoking Marijuana." *Big Think*, October 16, 2018. https://bigthink.com/health/carl-sagan-on -smoking-marijuana/.

German Lopez. "Read Carl Sagan's Newly Revealed Letters About the War on Drugs." *Vox*, October 9, 2014. https://www.vox.com/xpress/2014 /10/9/6946659/carl-sagan-marijuana-legalization-war-on-drugs.

Shaunacy Ferro. "12 Out-of-This-World Facts About Carl Sagan." *Mental Floss*, October 10, 2017. https://www.mentalfloss.com/article/64954/11-out -world-facts-about-carl-sagan.

Laurie L. Dove. "10 Cool Things About Carl Sagan." *HowStuffWorks*, November 9, 2021. https://science.howstuffworks.com/dictionary/famous -scientists/10-cool-things-carl-sagan.htm.

Amanda Sedlak-Hevener. "Fascinating Facts About Carl Sagan." *Ranker*, August 24, 2020. https://www.ranker.com/list/facts-about-carl-sagan /amandasedlakhevener.

**Chapter 38: Dock Ellis Pitched a No-Hitter While Tripping on Acid**

Donald Hall with Dock Ellis. *Dock Ellis in the Country of Baseball*. Simon & Schuster, 1989.

Billy Witz. "For Ellis, a Long, Strange Trip to a No-Hitter." *New York Times*, September 4, 2010. https://www.nytimes.com/2010/09/05/sports/baseball/05nohitter.html.

Jon Taylor. "Today Is the 47th Anniversary of Dock Ellis' Acid-Fueled No-Hitter." *Sports Illustrated*, June 12, 2017. https://www.si.com/mlb/2017/06/12/dock-ellis-acid-no-hitter-pittsburgh-pirates-anniversary.

Britni de la Cretaz. "How Dock Ellis, Player Who Pitched a No-Hitter on LSD, Is Misremembered." *Rolling Stone*, December 19, 2017. https://www.rollingstone.com/culture/culture-sports/how-dock-ellis-player-who-pitched-a-no-hitter-on-lsd-is-misremembered-199528/.

Patrick Hruby. "The Long, Strange Trip of Dock Ellis." ESPN, August 24, 2012. https://www.espn.com/espn/eticket/story?page=Dock-Ellis&redirected=true.

Mark Kreidler. "Baseball Finally Brings Amphetamines into Light of Day." ESPN, November 15, 2005. https://www.espn.com/mlb/columns/story?columnist=kreidler_mark&id=2225013.

Craig Calcaterra. "Today in Baseball History: Dock Ellis Tossed His LSD-Fueled No Hitter." NBC Sports, June 12, 2020. https://www.nbcsports.com/mlb/news/today-in-baseball-history-dock-ellis-tosses-his-lsd-fueled-no-hitter.

Marlow Stern. "'No No,' a Documentary on MLB Pitcher Dock Ellis, Who Pitched a No-Hitter While Tripping on Acid." *Daily Beast*, February 5, 2014. https://www.thedailybeast.com/no-no-a-documentary-on-mlb-pitcher-dock-ellis-who-pitched-a-no-hitter-while-tripping-on-acid.

Josh Peter. "50 Years After Dock Ellis' No-Hitter, His Story Resonates During Time of Protest." *USA Today*, June 12, 2020. https://www.usatoday.com/story/sports/mlb/pirates/2020/06/12/pittsburgh-pirates-dock-ellis-no-hitter-50-years-ago/3170865001/.

David Mikkelson. "Did Dock Ellis Pitch a No-Hitter on LSD?" *Snopes*, June 9, 2003. https://www.snopes.com/fact-check/dock-ellis-lsd-nohitter/.

Bruce Markusen. "Dock Ellis' Journey Helped Him Shine a Light for Others." National Baseball Hall of Fame. https://baseballhall.org/discover/dock-ellis-journey-helped-shine-a-light-for-others.

Kat Eschner. "Why Was Babe Ruth So Good at Hitting Home Runs?" *Smithsonian*, February 6, 2017. https://www.smithsonianmag.com/smart-news/why-was-babe-ruth-so-good-hitting-home-runs-180961998/.

Jessica DeLine. "Getting to Know Tim 'the Freak' Lincecum." SB Nation Halos Heaven, May 16, 2016. https://www.halosheaven.com/2016/5/16/11686608/getting-to-know-tim-the-freak-lincecum-angels.

Chad Dotson. "Why Joe Morgan Was the Best Reds Player of All Time." *Cincinnati Magazine*, August 10, 2021. https://www.cincinnatimagazine.com/article/why-joe-morgan-was-the-best-cincinnati-reds-player-of-all-time/.

## Chapter 39: John McAfee Was the World's Biggest Troll

Joshua Davis. "John McAfee Fled to Belize, but He Couldn't Escape Himself." *Wired*, December 24, 2012. https://www.wired.com/2012/12/ff-john-mcafees-last-stand/.

William P. Davis, Mary Williams Walsh, and Coral Murphy Marcos. "John McAfee, Software Pioneer Turned Fugitive, Dies in Spanish Prison." *New York Times*, June 23, 2021. https://www.nytimes.com/2021/06/23/business/john-mcafee-dead.html.

David Segal. "John McAfee Plays Hide-and-Seek in Belize." *New York Times*, December 1, 2012. https://www.nytimes.com/2012/12/02/business/john-mcafee-plays-hide-and-seek-in-belize.html.

James R. Hagerty and Robert McMillan. "John McAfee, the Silicon Valley Entrepreneur Who Died in a Spanish Jail Cell." *Wall Street Journal*, June 25, 2021. https://www.wsj.com/articles/john-mcafee-the-silicon-valley-entrepreneur-who-died-in-a-spanish-jail-11624643268.

Danny Yadron. "John McAfee at Def-Con: Don't Use Smartphones." *Wall Street Journal*, August 8, 2014. https://www.wsj.com/articles/BL-DGB-37022.

Glenn Rifkin. "John McAfee, Software Entrepreneur with Outlaw Persona, Dies in Prison at 75." *Washington Post*, June 23, 2021. https://www.washingtonpost.com/local/obituaries/john-mcafee-dead/2021/06/23/912f66ce-9ac8-11eb-9d05-ae06f4529ece_story.html.

Sam Jones. "John McAfee, Antivirus Software Pioneer, Arrested in Spain." *Guardian*, October 6, 2020. https://www.theguardian.com/us-news/2020/oct/06/john-mcafee-antivirus-software-pioneer-charged-with-tax-evasion-in-us.

Rebecca Greenfield. "John McAfee's Alter Ego Becomes Self-Aware." *Atlantic*, June 19, 2013. https://www.theatlantic.com/technology/archive/2013/06/john-mcafees-alter-ego-becomes-self-aware/314110/.

Rebecca Greenfield. "John McAfee Unleashes the Full Crazy." *Atlantic*, December 14, 2012. https://www.theatlantic.com/technology/archive/2012/12/john-mcafee-cnbc-interview/320486/.

Jeff Wise. "The Obscure, Legal Drug That Fuels John McAfee." *Intelligencer*, September 30, 2016. https://nymag.com/intelligencer/2016/09/the-obscure-legal-drug-that-fuels-john-mcafee.html.

Dan Mangan. "John McAfee Dead of Apparent Suicide in Spanish Jail After Court Approves His Extradition to US on Tax Charges." CNBC, June 27, 2021. https://www.cnbc.com/2021/06/23/john-mcafee-found-dead-after-spanish-court-oks-extradition-for-tax-crimes-.html.

Martin Savidge. "A Bizarre Visit to John McAfee's Pleasure Palace in Belize." CNN, November 20, 2012. https://www.cnn.com/2012/11/18/world/americas/belize-mcafee-enclave/index.html.

Gavin Haynes. "Bath Salts, Orgies, Murder, and Anti-Virus Software."

*Vice*, November 20, 2012. https://www.vice.com/en_us/article/kwn5yy
/john-mcafee-bath-salts-belize-murder-fugitive-gregory-faull.

Michael Zelenko. "How an Award-Winning Documentarian Unearthed a
Damning New Case Against John McAfee." *Verge*, September 14, 2016.
https://www.theverge.com/2016/9/14/12904402/john-mcafee-rape-murder
-accusations-gringo-documentary-tiff-interview.

Agence France-Presse. "Fugitive Millionaire Antivirus Guru John
McAfee Plans US Presidential Run . . . from Yacht in Cuba." *South China
Morning Post*, July 7, 2019. https://www.scmp.com/news/world/united
-states-canada/article/3017562/fugitive-millionaire-antivirus-guru-john
-mcafee.

Julia Naftulin and Katie Canales. "Inside the Wild Life of the Late Former
Fugitive and Eccentric Cybersecurity Legend John McAfee, Who Claimed
to Have 47 Children and a Yacht from the Wolf of Wall Street." *Insider*,
September 2, 2022. https://www.businessinsider.com/the-insane-life-of
-john-mcafee-2015-7.

Jeff Parsons. "John McAfee: Wild Life of the Gun-Toting, Drug-
Munching Tech Mogul." *Metro*, June 24, 2021. https://metro.co.uk/2021
/06/24/john-mcafee-wild-life-of-the-gun-toting-drug-munching-tech
-mogul-14821866/.

"Drug Fact Sheet: Bath Salts." DEA.gov. https://www.dea.gov/sites
/default/files/2020-06/Bath%20Salts-2020.pdf.

**Chapter 40: Steve Jobs Loved LSD and Soaking His Feet
in the Toilet**

Walter Isaacson. *Steve Jobs*. Simon & Schuster, 2011.

Malcolm Gladwell. "The Tweaker." *New Yorker*, November 6, 2011.
https://www.newyorker.com/magazine/2011/11/14/the-tweaker.

John Markoff. "Apple's Visionary Redefined Digital Age." *New York
Times*, October 5, 2011. https://www.nytimes.com/2011/10/06/business
/steve-jobs-of-apple-dies-at-56.html.

Phil Patton. "Steve Jobs: Out for Revenge." *New York Times*, August 6,
1989. https://www.nytimes.com/1989/08/06/magazine/steve-jobs-out-for
-revenge.html.

Martin Lindstrom. "You Love Your iPhone. Literally." *New York Times*,
September 30, 2011. https://www.nytimes.com/2011/10/01/opinion/you
-love-your-iphone-literally.html.

Maia Szalavitz. "Steve Jobs Had LSD. We Have the iPhone." *Time*,
October 6, 2011. https://healthland.time.com/2011/10/06/jobs-had-lsd-we
-have-the-iphone/.

Rebecca Greenfield. "Steve Jobs FBI File Confirms He Was a Jerk, Drug
User, and Poor Student." *Atlantic*, February 9, 2012. https://www.theatlantic

.com/technology/archive/2012/02/steve-jobs-fbi-file-confirms-he-was-jerk
-drug-user-and-poor-student/332018/.

Rebecca Greenfield. "The Inventor of LSD Asked Steve Jobs for PR Help."
*Atlantic*, November 14, 2011. https://www.theatlantic.com/technology
/archive/2011/11/inventor-lsd-asked-steve-jobs-pr-help/335512/.

Hayley Tsukayama. "Steve Jobs' Unflattering FBI File Mentions Drug
Use, 2.65 GPA." *Washington Post*, February 9, 2012. https://www
.washingtonpost.com/business/economy/steve-jobss-unflattering-fbi-file
-mentions-drug-use-265-gpa/2012/02/09/gIQAza8d2Q_story.html.

Ryan Faughnder. "Steve Jobs' Pentagon Papers: Blackmail Fears and
Taking LSD." *Los Angeles Times*, June 11, 2012. https://www.latimes.com
/business/la-xpm-2012-jun-11-la-fi-steve-jobs-pentagon-file-20120611
-story.html.

Kim Zetter. "FBI File on Steve Jobs Notes Use of LSD, Dishonesty."
*Wired*, February 9, 2012. https://www.wired.com/2012/02/steve-jobs-fbi
-file/.

Luis Martinez. "Steve Jobs US Files Provide New Details on Drug Use,
Kidnap Worry." ABC News, June 11, 2012. https://abcnews.go.com/blogs
/politics/2012/06/steve-jobs-us-files-provide-new-details-on-drug-use
-kidnap-worry.

Dan Lyons. "Steve Jobs's FBI File Calls Him Smart, Tough, and Not Very
Honest." *Daily Beast*, July 13, 2017. https://www.thedailybeast.com/steve
-jobss-fbi-file-calls-him-smart-tough-and-not-very-honest.

Larry Greenemeier. "A 'Deceptive Individual': Steve Jobs's FBI File."
*Scientific American*, February 9, 2012. https://blogs.scientificamerican.com
/observations/a-deceptive-individual-steve-jobss-fbi-file/.

Erica Fink and Laurie Segall. "I Did LSD with Steve Jobs." CNN,
December 18, 2015. https://money.cnn.com/2015/01/25/technology
/kottke-lsd-steve-jobs/#:~:text=Jobs%20has%20been%20quoted
%20as,another%20fellow%20tripper%20from%20Reed.

Wendy M. Grossman. "Did the Use of Psychedelics Lead to a Computer
Revolution?" *Guardian*, September 6, 2011. https://www.theguardian.com
/commentisfree/2011/sep/06/psychedelics-computer-revolution-lsd.

Emma Brockes. "The Daughter Steve Jobs Denied: 'Clearly I Was Not
Compelling Enough for My Father.'" *Guardian*, September 1, 2018. https://
www.theguardian.com/global/2018/sep/01/daughter-steve-jobs-denied-lisa
-brennan-jobs.

Brian Palmer. "Did Dropping Acid Make Steve Jobs More Creative?" *Slate*,
October 6, 2011. https://slate.com/news-and-politics/2011/10/steve-jobs
-implied-that-taking-lsd-made-him-more-creative-does-that-work-for
-everyone.html.

Matthew Yglesias. "Steve Jobs Told the Pentagon LSD Was 'a Positive
Life-Changing Experience for Me.'" *Slate*, June 11, 2012. https://slate.com

/business/2012/06/steve-jobs-on-lsd-a-positive-life-changing-experience
-for-me.html.

Sharan Shetty. "How Accurate Is *Jobs*?" *Slate*, August 16, 2013. https://
slate.com/culture/2013/08/jobs-movie-true-story-fact-and-fiction-in-mostly
-accurate-steve-jobs-movie-with-ashton-kutcher.html.

Seth Fiegerman. "Steve Jobs Did Acid 10–15 Times and Smoked Pot
Every Week for 5 Years." *Insider*, June 11, 2012. https://www.businessinsider
.com/the-most-shocking-revelations-from-steve-jobs-pentagon-file-2012-6.

Drake Baer. "How Steve Jobs' Acid-Fueled Quest for Enlightenment
Made Him the Greatest Product Visionary in History." *Insider*, January 29,
2015. https://www.businessinsider.com/steve-jobs-lsd-meditation-zen-quest
-2015-1.

Adam Fisher. "Silicon Valley Figures Remember Steve Jobs' Death—and
Debate the Rumor That He Was 'Tripping' When He Died." *Insider*,
September 25, 2018. https://www.businessinsider.com/steve-jobs-death
-silicon-valley-figures-share-experiences-on-lsd-and-funeral-2018-9.

Freek Vermeulen. "Steve Jobs: The Man Was Fallible." *Forbes*, October
17, 2011. https://www.forbes.com/sites/freekvermeulen/2011/10/17/steve
-jobs-the-man-was-fallible/?sh=3299b8285ee1.

Jonathan Ore. "How Lunch with Bono Led Steve Jobs to Reveal He
Named a Computer After His Daughter." CBC Radio, September 20, 2018.
https://www.cbc.ca/radio/thecurrent/the-current-for-september-20
-2018-1.4830050/how-lunch-with-bono-led-steve-jobs-to-reveal-he-named
-a-computer-after-his-daughter-1.4830529.

Yoni Heisler. "Steve Jobs' LSD Habit, Why He Indulged in Marijuana,
and His 1975 Arrest." *Network World*, June 12, 2012. https://www
.networkworld.com/article/2222575/data-center-steve-jobs-lsd-habit-why
-he-indulged-in-marijuana-and-his-1975-arrest.html.

Louis Anslow. "When the Mac Was Introduced 33 Years Ago, People
Thought Graphical User Interfaces Were a Real Problem." *Medium*, January
24, 2017. https://medium.com/timeline/mac-graphical-user-inteterface
-960d5f548d08.

# INDEX

# ABOUT THE AUTHOR

**Sam Kelly**, a history grad from Stanford University, is on the autism spectrum, and his interest in and passion for history have become an almost physical compulsion. He loves to dig up forgotten weird historical stories and spends hours uncovering every last stubborn detail. As a deep believer that history can be as exciting as any Marvel movie, Sam aims to make history both engaging and accessible to all. *Human History on Drugs* is his first book.